The Fairy Way of Writing

The Fairy Way of Writing

SHAKESPEARE TO TOLKIEN

Kevin Pask

The Johns Hopkins University Press
Baltimore

© 2013 The Johns Hopkins University Press
All rights reserved. Published 2013
Printed in the United States of America on acid-free paper
2 4 6 8 9 7 5 3 1

The Johns Hopkins University Press
2715 North Charles Street
Baltimore, Maryland 21218-4363
www.press.jhu.edu

Library of Congress Cataloging-in-Publication Data
Pask, Kevin.
The fairy way of writing : Shakespeare to Tolkien / by Kevin Pask.
pages   cm
Includes bibliographical references and index.
ISBN 978-1-4214-0982-5 (hardcover : acid-free paper) — ISBN 978-1-4214-1074-6
(electronic) — ISBN 1-4214-0982-8 (hardcover : acid-free paper) —
ISBN 1-4214-1074-5 (electronic)
1. Fantasy literature, English—History and criticism. 2. Supernatural in literature.
3. National characteristics, English, in literature. 4. Imagination in literature.
5. Supernatural in art. I. Title.
PR149.F35P37 2013
820.9'15—dc23   2012047016

A catalog record for this book is available from the British Library.

Special discounts are available for bulk purchases of this book. For more information,
please contact Special Sales at 410-516-6936 or specialsales@press.jhu.edu.

The Johns Hopkins University Press uses environmentally friendly book materials,
including recycled text paper that is composed of at least 30 percent post-consumer waste,
whenever possible.

CONTENTS

This book had a long gestation. I originally thought that I would like to work on the emergence of key critical concepts that define modern literature, including the imagination and originality, as well as the modern sense of literature as essentially national in its sources and orientation. The "fairy way of writing" only gradually began to appear as an adequate means of addressing some of these interests, and that was partly because, as a Renaissance scholar, I found myself immersed in the history of Shakespeare criticism as a point of departure for my project.

The eventual scope of this project would have been impossible without the constant encouragement, and generative criticism, of my wife, Marcie Frank. I have consistently relied on her expertise in the literature and criticism of the eighteenth century, which is at the heart of this book, as the derivation of the phrase "the fairy way of writing," from a combination of Dryden and Addison, makes clear. There is no part of this book that has not been improved by her critical attention.

The book benefited immensely along the way from the readings and suggestions of friends and colleagues, including Danielle Bobker, Mike Bristol, Jason Camlot, Mark Dow, Meredith Evans, Adam Frank, Noelle Gallagher, Jonathan Goldberg, Judith Herz, Jonathan Kramnick, Michael McKeon, Michael Moon, John Miller, Nicola Nixon, Ed Pechter, Manish Sharma, and Aurélie Zygel-Basso. I was, moreover, lucky enough to have several astute and committed research assistants work on parts of this book with me: John Berto, Viviane Boileau, Jason Katz, Nate Szymanski, and Elizabeth Walker.

Throughout my years at Concordia University, participation in the Shakespeare and Performance Research Team, based at McGill University and funded by the Fonds de recherche du Québec—Société et culture, has been a stimulus for my Shakespeare research. Mike Bristol originally asked me to join the team, and Paul Yachnin and Wes Folkerth have sustained and energized it in recent years. Much of the research and writing of the book occurred, moreover, while I was a member of a collaborative research project initiated by Paul Yachnin and funded by the Social Sciences and Humanities Research Council of Canada: "Making Publics: Media, Markets & Association in Early Modern Europe, 1500–1700." Although this book is somewhat "off topic" for my work more directly connected to the "Making Publics" project, the two could not help but inform each other. I am grateful to Paul and to my many colleagues on the project for the opportunity to participate in the intellectually stimulating work of "Making Publics."

In addition to its funding of the "Making Publics" project, the Social Sciences and Humanities Research Council of Canada also provided me with an individual research grant during the time I was researching and writing this book. Earlier, I received research funding from the Fonds de recherche du Québec—Société et culture and from the Faculty Research Development Program at Concordia University, both of which made it possible to begin my research. Sabbatical leaves, as well as sabbatical research funding from the Faculty of Arts and Science at Concordia, made the writing of this book possible. Funding from the Concordia English Department, the Faculty of Arts and Science, and the Office of the Vice-President, Research and Graduate Studies, helped me acquire the illustrations for the book.

An earlier version of chapter 2 originally appeared as "Caliban's Masque" in *ELH* 70 (2003): 739–56. Some parts of the first chapter draw on an essay, "Engrossing Imagination: *A Midsummer Night's Dream*," that first appeared in the *Shakespearean International Yearbook* no. 3 (2003), and I wish to thank Graham Bradshaw for his encouragement with that essay. Some of the material in chapter 3 was first vetted in a study day devoted to Michael McKeon's book, *The Secret History of Domesticity*, at McGill University in 2007, and I wish to thank Brian Cowan and Leigh Yetter for organizing that event as well as for the special issue of *History Compass* (vol. 10, issue 9, September 2012) that developed out of the study day. I presented some of the material in chapter 4 at two conferences: the American Society of Eighteenth-Century Studies (2010) and the Shakespeare Association of America (2012). My thanks to Charlotte Trinquet and Kaara Peterson for organizing the sessions in which I presented those papers.

When I began to think about fairy writing as a potential means of organizing my research interests, my two daughters, Emma and Violet Pask, were still young enough to be readers of fairy writing, even if of a different sort than the kind generally discussed in the book. Although they have long since graduated to other interests, it was a great pleasure for me to have a research project that sometimes engaged them. This book, then, is for them.

The Fairy Way of Writing

Introduction

"The fairy way of writing" is a phrase ultimately derived from John Dryden but more generally associated, to the extent that it is still recognized, with Joseph Addison's *Spectator* essays, "The Pleasures of the Imagination." In Addison's essays, the phrase names a mode of writing he considers the most purely imaginative:

> There is a kind of Writing, wherein the Poet quite loses sight of Nature, and entertains his Reader's Imagination with the Characters and Actions of such Persons as have many of them no Existence, but what he bestows on them. Such are Fairies, Witches, Magicians, Demons, and departed Spirits. This Mr. *Dryden* calls *the Fairie way of Writing*, which is, indeed, more difficult than any other that depends on the Poet's Fancy, because he has no Pattern to follow in it, and must work altogether out of his own Invention.[1]

For Addison, what we might call "fantasy" is bound up with the status of the creative imagination, but this also identifies the potentially vertiginous quality of such writing: lacking any "Pattern" in nature, it turns the poet back onto "his own Invention." Conjoined notions of creative imagination and creative originality underlie Addison's formulation, although neither concept was at all common in the previous century. Addison is reaching toward a conjunction of ideas—imagination and originality—which characterizes the modern conception of literature after the middle of the eighteenth century. ("Literature" itself replaced "poetry" as the general name for creative writing only over the course of the late eighteenth and early nineteenth centuries.) Addison, then, sketches out the future of the literary system, but the association of the ascendant concepts of that system—imagination and originality—with fairy writing is somewhat jarring for the modern reader. Supernatural motifs of the sort enumerated by Addison still possess for us the alibi of their use in Shakespearean drama, which are the instances Addison has in mind, but our sense of the canon of literature tends to marginalize works felt to rely too much on such motifs.

The aim of this book is to restore the centrality that Addison assigned to the fairy way of writing in the English construction of a national literary canon. This entails the interrogation of the strict distinction between mainstream literature and fantasy that has defined the literary field since the early twentieth century. Although the book is interested in the prehistory of modern fantasy fiction, as the final chapter on Tolkien testifies, its primary work is uncovering the significance of the fairy way of writing for the early articulation of English national literature. The bulk of the book addresses an eminently canonical list of English writers, if from a new perspective: Shakespeare, Jonson, Dryden, Addison, Pope, Collins, Coleridge, and Keats.

Despite the centrality of the English literary canon in the book, it also contains a chapter on the British tradition of fairy painting, largely Shakespearean in inspiration, which discloses the erotic nature of the tradition of fairy "writing" in English culture. I remain, however, less interested in fairies per se than in the literary tradition they represent, and for this reason I also follow the interest, implicit in Shakespeare and explicit in Addison's critical essays, in a wide variety of popular forms, both oral and written, that engaged popular superstitions and old wives' tales. The literary mobilization of such forms was foundational for a national literature that self-consciously attempted to blend elite and popular cultural formations.

Theater and Secular Magic

Because the key early figure in my account is Shakespeare, a dramatist whose theater is superbly self-referential, the fairy way of writing in the English tradition is closer to the stage performance of magic than the fantasy traditions of other European literatures, especially the French and German, both of which developed the fairy tale as a literary form. Instead of the popular or literary fairy tale, Shakespeare's theater occupied the place partly abandoned by old folk beliefs and recently discredited Catholic rituals, replacing older forms of magic with theatrical magic. *As You Like It*, for example, is not a Shakespearean play usually associated with the supernatural, but Rosalind, speaking as Ganymede, promises Orlando that she will deliver Rosalind to him through the magic learned from her longstanding conversation with "a magician, most profound in his art, and yet not damnable." The magic turns out, in an offhand moment of great power, to be that staple of theatrical experience: the simple offstage costume change. Ganymede leaves the stage and returns as Rosalind. Rosalind is apparently uninterested in elaborating the distinctions between damnable magic and its innocent cousin, and we might even say that hers is a form of magic that has almost dropped below the radar of religion altogether. It is another cultural version of what Simon During has recently called the "secular magic" of the world of the performance magician and which, in *Modern Enchantments: The Cultural Power of Secular Magic*, he has traced from the Renaissance to film.

As the example of Rosalind suggests, the magic explored in this book is generally comic and pastoral, and thus, in Shakespeare, inevitably connected to questions of marriage and sexuality. The tragic power of the Weird Sisters, to name an important example of popular magic associated with tragedy, is discussed only in passing. Puck, the common village hobgoblin, transformed into Oberon's courtier in *A Midsummer Night's Dream*, represents Shakespeare's first attempt to synthesize popular and elite magic. He is the factotum for the aristocratic Oberon, but the excessive and topsy-turvy nature of his application of Oberon's magic suggests an affiliation with Shakespeare's own theatrical practices. Like Shakespeare himself, Puck has a rural and village background but finds himself with new courtly connections. The theatrical synthesis of the high and the low, partly in the relationship of Puck to the fairies of the play, is an important part of the play's impact from Shakespeare's time onward, which repeatedly associated Shakespeare, and the *Dream* in particular, with a popular, and ultimately national, sensibility. *The Winter's Tale*, on the other hand, rationalizes its use of magic—Paulina does not actually bring a dead Hermione back to life, as it at first appears—but it also creates affiliations between theatrical magic and the world of old wives' tales strongly associated with Paulina and set in opposition to the patriarchal authority of Leontes. Prospero's elite and patriarchal magic in *The Tempest*, by contrast, is severely put into question.

A specifically theatrical magic occupies much of the first two chapters of the book, but loses its prominence thereafter. This is partly due to the transformation of Shakespeare's theater into the cornerstone of an emergent English national literature in the seventeenth and especially the eighteenth centuries, a period when theater itself slowly loses its claim to cultural innovation. Dryden, for example, is more attentive to the specifically theatrical nature of Shakespeare's achievement than is Addison. Although this is partly due to Dryden's own theatrical practice, it reveals the growing tendency to locate Shakespeare's achievements as generally imaginative and readerly rather than theatrical. Even the English visual arts of the eighteenth century staked their claim to Shakespearean fantasy, partly in tacit competition with theatrical representation, as chapter 4 demonstrates. By the time the book reaches the twentieth century and the fantasy of J. R. R. Tolkien, the hostility to theater as a specific medium for the representation of fantastic beings is much greater. This is partly because Tolkien himself is very clear-sighted about the theatrical nature of Shakespeare's achievement—which is the aspect of that achievement he most wishes to distance from fairy stories, properly understood.

Disenchantment and Creative Imagination

The fairy way of writing is not to be conceived as the attempt to extend a traditional superstitious culture into modernity but rather as the complex result of demystification itself. Shakespeare, I argue in chapter 1, seizes the opportunity provided by Protestant skepticism about the world of popular and Catholic superstitions—Protestantism tended to lump the two together—including beliefs about witches and fairies. This historical process of disenchantment represented an opportunity for the theater, which could present "falsehoods" on the stage, at least in the form of fictions, with relative impunity. If popular magic no longer carried the ability to charm and to harm, it might still carry the potential to entertain. The fairy way of writing thus also belonged to the age of the new science, despite the nostalgia sometimes evinced, after Shakespeare, for the "old England" of "rewards and fairies."

In the two centuries after Shakespeare, the old superstitious magic (along with, in a higher register, divine inspiration) was replaced by a new and internalized power, the creative imagination. Tolkien's essentially religious insistence on "sub-creation"—God as the primal creator—as the faculty engaged in literary creation indicates the extent to which creativity was originally an audacious imaginative claim. Chapters 2 and 3, which track the move from Shakespeare's theatrical appropriation of superstition and magic to the development of a critical and poetic tradition that engages with Shakespeare's theatrical magic, are particularly attentive to the history of the creative imagination as an outgrowth of Shakespearean fantasy. These chapters chart the generalization of a specifically theatrical practice into a mode of creativity understood to support a national literature.

In the long tradition of faculty psychology, going back to its sources in Plato and Aristotle, imagination mediated between judgment and sensation. When loosed from its dependence on judgment and reason, however, the imagination became the agent of misperceptions, dreams, daydreams, and other forms of mental delinquency. Its gradual elevation to an independent and positive power of the mind largely took place during the seventeenth and eighteenth centuries.[2] During this period, the creative imagination was consistently conjoined to the fairy way of writing, which, because it explored the obviously unreal and the supernatural without a foundation in observed nature, was considered a particularly imaginative form of writing, a kind of updating of the older association of imagination with dreams. The fantastic nature of Shakespeare's character Caliban is one example of this elevation of the creative imagination. Although Caliban is also an outlier to the domain of popular fairies, chapter 2 argues for his creation out of a complex theatrical rivalry with Ben Jonson that also saw Shakespeare revisit and revise the fairy writing of *A*

Midsummer Night's Dream, a process that, I suggest, entailed the demonization of Caliban. His distance from popular or literary legend only highlighted the complex relationship of the period to the idea of literary originality. The early critical reception of Caliban was at best ambivalent regarding Shakespeare's "creation"—a term previously reserved for divine creation—of a character with no source in nature or classical myth, but the eighteenth century and the Romantics celebrated Caliban as the signal instance of Shakespeare's "originality."

Dryden's initial formulation of the fairy way of writing is explicitly derived from the imagination: "that Fairy kind of writing, which depends only upon the Force of Imagination."[3] Addison, as we have already seen, made this into a critical principle of literary creativity. Coleridge's retrospective formulation of his own contributions to the *Lyrical Ballads* retains the same association between the supernatural and the creative imagination:

> It was agreed that my endeavours should be directed to persons and characters supernatural, or at least romantic; yet so as to transfer from our inward nature a human interest and a semblance of truth sufficient to procure for these shadows of imagination that willing suspension of disbelief for the moment, which constitutes poetic faith.[4]

Between Dryden's "Force of Imagination" and Coleridge's "shadows of imagination" lies more than a hundred years. Although much separates their evaluation of the imagination as a creative force, Dryden and Coleridge both casually equate marvelous and "romantic" incident with the creative imagination. The "poetic faith" constituted by this suspension of disbelief suggests something beyond the domain of shadows: a literary system that has internalized some of the powers once associated with religious belief but within a general context that assumes disbelief and disenchantment. In this respect, literature is increasingly disentangled from questions of belief, and the fairy way of writing can emerge as a particularly heightened expression of the aesthetic partly *because* of its lack of credibility. By this point, however, the fairy way of writing appears to have completed its service to the history of the creative imagination. Although Coleridge here seems to rely on a version of the special association of the creative imagination with supernatural incident, his larger theory of the creative imagination expanded it well beyond its base in the fairy way of writing or the supernatural. Indeed, from the Victorian period onward, and with the development of the children's fairy tale, the fairy way of writing could be associated with the concept of fancy, which Coleridge had sharply distinguished from the imagination and demoted to a lesser creative power. And there it has largely remained. Fancy has to some extent informed the concept of fantasy and the fantastic (the latter heavier on horror and science fiction effects), as fantasy has increasingly become identified with the fiction of J. R. R. Tolkien.[5]

The Mediation of Nation

The fairy way of writing was never a pure product of an individuated and internalized imagination; it relied on popular tales and beliefs, or at least the aura of that popular world. This allowed fairy writing to be simultaneously social, hearkening to the idea of popular beliefs and communal experience, and individuated, located in the unique creative imagination of the artist (an early version of Ezra Pound's sense of artists as the "antennae of the race"). For this reason, the fairy way of writing was central to the early articulation of an English national literature. (Other European national literatures would make similar use of folk tradition in the form of the fairy tale.) The "discovery of the people," as Peter Burke has termed this historical process, produces a pastoral of (national) literature: the sense that the literary author will derive material from "the people."[6] Lady Macbeth scathingly dismisses her lord's anxieties as nothing more than an old wives' tale, "a woman's story at a fire / Authoriz'd by her grandam" (III.iv.64–65), but domesticity, including the domestic hearth and the old wives' tale as well as the more abstract political sense of the "domestic" as the internal domain of a state, began to emerge as a positive value out of the slow devolution of the older absolutist and "patriarchalist" unity of the private and the public.[7] Addison is the first English critic to produce a positive evaluation of the writing thought to express the domestic world of "the people": old tales, fables, ballads, and so forth. The national author is probably not of the people, but he will henceforth be *with* the people.

Although the poet was celebrated from the eighteenth century onward as the exemplar of a vernacular literary language that was national in scope, the fairy way of writing as a specific form of the medium of *writing* underlines some of the distance between the national author and his popular subject matter. The fairy way of writing belongs to a print-based high literary culture, but it "remediates," or transforms for another media environment, oral culture, borrowing plot motifs and formal characteristics from old tales that circulated orally or were associated with oral culture. It thus reflected the growing interest of European intellectuals in oral culture.[8] "Remediation makes the medium as such *visible*," writes John Guillory in his discussion of the historical emergence of the concept of media. As Guillory adds, however, there was little discussion of the transformation of writing into print. "It was as though print were there, already, in the medium of writing."[9] Print, however, made oral culture very visible to intellectuals. Medieval intellectuals, the clergy, jealously guarded a near monopoly on literacy in the "truth language," Latin. They were, as Benedict Anderson has nicely put it, "tiny literate reefs on top of vast illiterate oceans."[10] The basic assumptions connected with literacy were cosmological and hierarchical, and the vernacular dialects were largely left to their own devices. By contrast, print capitalism's desire to conquer potential markets, Anderson argues, entailed the creation of standardized print languages that aggressively reorganized European dialects.[11] Unlike the earlier role of Latin, or even the older administrative vernaculars, the authority of the print languages relied on the claim to potential universality (within certain linguistic and, eventually, political boundaries). As a result, the intellectuals of print culture, unlike their predecessors, increasingly claimed to represent the traditional oral cultures they were in the process of displacing.

Scholarship is now, with some justice, highly suspicious of such claims, which it tends to look on as "invented traditions." Extensively developed during the eighteenth and nineteenth centuries and surrounded with the glamour of the nationalist mystique, the concept of an oral culture now looks to be easy pickings for demystification, from both poststructuralist theory, with its insistence on the primacy of textuality, and the more recent claims to the excavation of material and media cultures, which look skeptically at the necessarily patchy remnants of earlier oral cultures. The result has been the critical tendency to discredit claims to oral culture as the source of literary forms such as the fairy tale and the ballad, which were admittedly overstated or distorted by generations of scholars and collectors from the mid-eighteenth century onward. Susan Stewart's designation of the fairy tale and the ballad as "distressed" genres, whose prestige came to rely on the creation of an aura of timeless popular antiquity, has come to dominate scholarly work in this area.[12] One recent attempt to rewrite the history of the fairy tale, for instance, is most concerned to eliminate oral tales as a major source for the European fairy tale tradition.[13] The recent study of the ballad, likewise, has disenchanted the longstanding sense of the purity of the popular voice in the "Child ballads," the ballads that Francis James Child, in his immense collation of ballad scholarship in the late nineteenth century, claimed to belong to an unbroken oral tradition stretching back to medieval Europe, quite distinct from the broadside ballads, which belonged to a later world of popular print and entertainment. The current scholarly tendency is directly opposed to the idea governing that of the "Child ballad," emphasizing instead the variety of mediations coming between a contemporary "audience" for a ballad and anything that might, or might not, reflect oral tradition.[14]

Such work has been salutary in many respects, overturning, for example, academic fussiness about the "appropriation" of supposedly authentic cultural and social identities or, revealingly, "voices."[15] It is also a symptom of our postnationalist age. The rejection of claims to the authenticity of representations of oral culture has made something like Addison's fairy way of writing, in all of its nationalist glamour, look like a decidedly rickety structure. (Addison himself did not strongly distinguish print culture from oral culture in his seminal discussions of the ballad.) The interest of the fairy way of writing as an aspect of English literary history, however, does not rely on the transmission of an authentic oral culture; it was always *writing*, even canonical writing, first and foremost. Only when we arrive at Keats and Romanticism, for example, do we find any sustained poetic effort to represent the speech markers of the old tales. Never itself a "folk" culture, the fairy way of writing nevertheless participated in the long-term reconfiguration of the relations between "high" and "low" cultures in Europe, including the incorporation of old superstitions and tales as literary motifs for vernacular high culture.

The announcements of the end of an oral folk culture, meanwhile, were regularly updated throughout the early modern period and continued through the nineteenth century. "The popular culture of the years around 1800," writes Peter Burke, "was found just in time, or so the discoverers thought. The theme of a vanishing culture which must be recorded before it is too late recurs in their writings."[16] Before the end of the seventeenth century, however, John Aubrey had already assumed the disappearance of popular rural beliefs, which he associated with the spread of literacy since the Civil Wars. The arrival of printing had put "all the old Fables out of dores."[17] But literacy, in the form of standardized schooling, had not finished conquering oral culture two centuries later, as Thomas Hardy's *Tess of the D'Urbervilles* (1891) attests:

> Between the mother, with her fast-perishing lumber of superstitions, folk-lore, dialect, and orally transmitted ballads, and the daughter, with her trained National teachings, and Standard knowledge under an infinitely Revised Code, there was a gap of two hundred years as ordinarily understood. When they were together the Jacobean and the Victorian ages were juxtaposed.[18]

Burke argues that the "discovery of the people" was a reaction to the progressive estrangement of the intellectuals from the mass of the people. "In 1500, they despised the common people, but shared their culture. By 1800 their descendants had ceased to participate spontaneously in popular culture, but they were in the process of rediscovering it as something exotic and therefore interesting."[19] There is much to be said for this formulation, and it does capture the general trajectory of the intellectual relationship to popular culture. With regard to the fairy way of writing, however, the elite discovery of an evanescent "oral culture" stretches back to the sixteenth century, if not earlier, as Burke's own examples often testify. Although the standardization of print vernaculars only unevenly extended literacy, it relied on an idea of horizontal community, whose boundaries roughly corresponded to those of the new print languages: nations.

One significant means of imagining this new form of community was the re-mediation of an oral culture, increasingly assumed to belong to "the people," by a high literary culture. Thus, returning for a moment to the bellwether genre of the ballad, I would emphasize something rather different from Maureen McLane in her analysis of the mediations of a ballad generally known as "The Bonny Hynd." In the first edition of Sir Walter Scott's *Minstrelsy of the Scottish Border* (1802–1803), the ballad appears with the note, "Copied from the mouth of a milkmaid, 1771, by W. L." The process of authentication through the milkmaid's *mouth* is McLane's primary concern. But the orality assigned to the milkmaid cannot be separated from the nationalist desire to bring together the educated ballad collector, the editor (Scott himself), and the lowly milkmaid.[20] As with Addison' fairy way of writing, we have what is effectively a nationalist pastoral: the collector among the shepherds and shepherdesses. The long eighteenth century joins this nationalist pastoral to the imaginative power that is consistently associated with the fairy way of writing. The result is a concept of literature that largely remains recognizable to us: socially bounded by national languages or traditions and psychologically grounded in the creative imagination.

Fairy Eroticism

Fantasy, unlike imagination, retains significant traces of its longstanding association with the erotic, in, for example, the colloquial verbal use of "fancy" in contemporary British English as a synonym of desire. "Fantasy" itself possesses a psychoanalytic pedigree in the analysis of desire. *The Fairy Way of Writing* explores this aspect of fantasy, which has been downgraded partly as a result of Coleridge's strong distinc-tion between imagination and fancy. The fairy seductress of medieval romance is generally somewhere in the background of the fairy way of writing—at least until the time of Keats. Shakespeare can still take the sexuality of the fairy enchantress for granted even while the action of *A Midsummer Night's Dream* diminishes the power of its fairy queen, Titania, in its battle of the sexes. More generally, the sexuality of the fairy way of writing is a consistent refrain throughout the chapters of this book, ranging from the light touch of *A Midsummer Night's Dream* to an increasingly internalized, and sometimes demonized, mystery. Caliban, in chapter 2, represents the latter and also anticipates the increasing emphasis on the grotesque and fantastic eroticism that becomes particularly apparent in the visual arts of the late eighteenth century and the literary texts of Romanticism, ultimately informing the psycho-analytic sense of the uncanny (a concept introduced by Freud through a reading of E. T. A. Hoffman's fantastic story, *The Sandman*).

Keats, it seems to me, is the culmination of this movement in the fairy way of writing. Although versions of fairy sexuality do not simply disappear after Keats, they are increasingly pressed by the rise of the children's fairy tale. Partly because of this association with fairy sexuality, Lionel Trilling once argued, Keats is among the last of the canonical writers we associate with the celebration of pleasure. Trilling, however, also allowed Keats his ambivalence about pleasure:

> Keats, then, may be thought of as the poet who made the boldest affirmation of the principle of pleasure, and also as the poet who brought the principle of pleasure into the greatest and *sincerest* doubt. He therefore has for us a peculiar cultural interest, for it would seem to be true that at some point in modern history the principle of pleasure came to be regarded with just such ambivalence.[21]

Trilling goes on to illustrate Keats's ambivalence with *Lamia* and "La Belle Dame Sans Merci," poems that feature supernatural seductresses.

The literary and artistic representation of fairies discussed in this book seldom forget, even if they suppress, the erotic content of fairyland, which seems to be associated with the earliest instances of fairies in medieval European literature.[22] The fairy queen is a figure of female sexual predation that haunts European literature generally committed to social models of patriarchal marriage. The eroticism of fairyland reaches a crescendo in the British visual arts of the late eighteenth century and the poetic Romanticism of the early nineteenth century, sometimes simultaneously engaging forms of erotic and political rebellion. The visual representations discussed in chapter 4 reveal with almost startling frankness the sexual content of the Shakespearean fairyland of *A Midsummer Night's Dream*. Keats's version of fairy writing is the most arresting synthesis of erotic and political rebellion. By the early twentieth century, however, fairy writing was caught between the pincers of the Victorian children's fairy tale and the modern, perhaps especially Modernist, suspicion of "mere" pleasure. Keats's insistence on both the pleasures and the perils of fairy seduction thus appears, as Trilling intuited, as one of the last Bowers of Bliss in the English literary tradition.

In the latter part of the twentieth century, however, fairy writing—tale and fantasy—returned to prominence along two rather different tracks: the adventure romance of Tolkien's *Lord of the Rings* (1954) and psychoanalytic/feminist revisions and interpretations of the fairy way of writing. The latter begin to come to the fore in the 1970s, with Maureen Duffy's under-recognized study, *The Erotic World of Faery* (1972), and Bruno Bettelheim's much more regarded psychoanalytic recuperation of the fairy tale tradition, *The Uses of Enchantment* (1976). Angela Carter's signal revision of the old fairy tales, *The Bloody Chamber* (1979) extended the feminist/ erotic and the penumbra of psychoanalysis into a creative synthesis that intersected with the contemporary interest in various forms of magic realism. More recently, the extensive and generative scholarship of Marina Warner has significantly expanded the terrain in which a feminist interest in myth and tale might operate.[23] The success of the Tolkien franchise means that adventure fantasy now has a strong foothold in popular fiction, but there also appears to be room enough for the erotic possibilities of a fairy world so often ruled by a fairy queen who is also a domineering seductress. The sexual undercurrent—sometimes a flood—of fairyland is almost as important to the structure of the book as its interest in the history of the imagination and national culture.

Ways and Means

Something perhaps remains to be said about the long historical scope of the book, which is unusual in current literary scholarship. The bulk of the book offers a literary history of the fairy way of writing in the context of an emergent English national literature. This represents a break with period boundaries commonly used for the study of English literature, which, while possessing a rough and ready utility, too often determine the limits of research projects. The fairy way of writing is a coherent tradition within English literature, but this is precisely the area least developed in recent critical work on questions related to fantasy, imagination, and popular literature. Work on the role of the fairy tale in Victorian culture, for example, proceeds with little reference to Addison; eighteenth-century and Romantic scholars largely ignore the Shakespearean and sixteenth-century background of the interest in oral, popular cultural forms; Shakespeare scholars have paid little attention to the long-term literary consequences of the Shakespearean appropriation of fairy materials. The fairy way of writing, as a subject, *might* exist as a topic completely inside Renaissance studies or eighteenth-century criticism, but I think that the book demonstrates that it is better understood as a coherent literary-historical development across the period from the sixteenth century to Romanticism, including significant consequences for the post-Romantic period. Since Romanticism, those developments have increasingly been in marginalized areas of literature, especially fantasy and children's literature. This latter-day association with genre fiction and children's literature has also meant that the fairy way of writing has received a kind of embarrassed half-attention in literary criticism. This trajectory of the fairy way of writing, however, also presents an opportunity to take the measure of the conceptual boundaries of literature as it has developed over the centuries, particularly now that literature itself can no longer plausibly claim to occupy the center of our culture. In our own period, "after" literature, most particularly after the rigorous definition of literature inherited from Modernism, the boundaries between "high" and "low" literary forms have been reopened to examination. Peter Burke has recently commented that the age of television has allowed for a "a kind of return to the situation in 1500, the revival of a common culture based on the small screen, allowing the many interactions between higher and lower forms that some critics like to call 'postmodern.' "[24] Now ensconced in print, television, movies, and gaming, fantasy has benefitted from the cultural constellation that Burke associates with the small screen. This is also in part the occasion for a study such as this one, which takes the current era of multiple forms of cultural mass mediation as an opportunity to examine the historical boundaries of literature in its longer-term interactions with popular culture.

CHAPTER ONE

The Fairies' Farewell

Shakespeare's Old Wives' Tales

Witness those rings and roundelays
Of theirs, which yet remain,
Were footed in Queen Mary's days
On many a grassy plain;
But since of late Elizabeth,
And later James came in,
They never dance on any heath
As when the time had been.

By which we note the fairies
Were of the old profession,
Their songs were *Ave Maries*,
Their dances were procession;
But now, alas, they all are dead,
Or gone beyond the seas,
Or further from religion fled,
Or else they take their ease.

—*Richard Corbet (1582–1635), "A Proper New Ballad, Entitled the
Fairies' Farewell, or God-a Mercy Will"*

In English literary history, Shakespeare mediates between the "rings and rounde-lays" of "old England" and the relatively disenchanted age of national literatures, the two constitutive historical poles of the fairy way of writing. He both assumes and transforms the relationship of the high and low cultures of late medieval and Renaissance Europe. The "topsy-turvydom" of Shakespearean drama is a belated response to traditional medieval culture, particularly the cultural proximity of the feudal aristocracy to the common people, a relationship on the wane in Shakespeare's time when new circumstances forced the feudal aristocracy to accommodate itself to "the new avocations of a disciplined officer, a literate functionary, a polished courtier, and a more or less prudent estate-owner."[1] Sir John Falstaff is Shakespeare's retrospective emblem of the older cultural dispensation: the bluff medieval knight practically indistinguishable from the lowlife tavern world of London. Shakespeare, as C. L. Barber persuasively argued in *Shakespeare's Festive Comedy* (1959), captures forms of festivity threatened by the new culture of post-Reformation England, but he is equally attracted to the theatrical possibilities of the old magic associated with Catholicism and popular superstition. This chapter examines the background, both medieval and Elizabethan, to Shakespeare's experimentation with popular superstitions and forms of magic, and it concludes with an extended discussion of his use of such materials in the new space of the public theater. Shakespeare makes an effectively aesthetic claim on what we call folktale and fantasy, including the fairies and spirits of both popular belief and romance tradition, as the ingredients of theatrical magic. This synthesis of a new form of entertainment with older popular forms and beliefs marks the instauration of the fairy way of writing as a distinctive form of English writing: looking back to medieval forms and forward to an emergent formulation of national literature.

Medieval Origins

In the course of Erich Auerbach's great survey of the late classical and medieval creation of a European literary public, he discusses one of the giants of medieval theological literature, Pope Gregory the Great (540–604). What particularly attracts Auerbach's attention, however, is not theological debate but the book of miracles, the *Dialogues*,

> in which the supernatural continually, even on seemingly trivial occasions, takes a hand in everyday life. Of course it was not unusual to believe in miracles; a belief in certain supernatural events is an essential component of the Christian faith. What is striking is the scope and character of this belief in miracles in a man of Gregory's stamp. The dialogues disclose an almost childlike, fairy-tale world.[2]

Auerbach goes on to provide several examples, including one in which a nun accidentally ingests a devil along with a head of lettuce that she forgets to bless with the sign of the cross. In another, a priest returns home one day and orders his servant, "Come, you devil, take off my shoes":

No sooner had he said this than the straps of the shoes began to unfasten themselves with the utmost speed. Obviously the devil he had invoked was obeying his order to take off his shoes. As soon as the priest saw what was happening, he was overcome by terror and began to cry loudly: "Go away, you wretch, go away." . . . One can hardly fail to note the grotesque humor: the little devil, whimpering in self-justification like a little boy after he has been bitten with the lettuce, the shoe straps that untie themselves with the speed of lightning. These devils are comical goblins.[3]

Before the advent of "history from below," Auerbach is sensitive to the indirect forms of popular pressure exerting themselves on the high cultural texts of medieval period. Despite the strong distinction between the Latin culture of the clergy and the vernacular popular culture shared by the rest of the population, the boundaries were permeable at certain key junctures: miracles, spirits, and carnivalesque celebrations.[4] The fairy tale, understood since Romanticism as the foundation of a popular and vernacular—thus implicitly national—culture, was also transmitted in the language of the official culture of medieval Europe, Latin.[5]

The case of the medieval aristocracy is even more telling for the longer history of the relationship between high and popular cultures in Europe. The aristocracy of the early Middle Ages was culturally little different from the peasantry. Small and medium lords of early European feudalism, Marc Bloch tells us, "were illiterates in the full sense of the word."[6] When the aristocracy of the High Middle Ages came to assert an independent cultural identity in the vernacular, the aristocratic genre of romance made use of "that popular, folk culture from which the nobility had never distinguished itself."[7] This popular culture appears in what Auerbach calls the "fairyland" aura of Chrétien de Troyes's *Yvain*, written in the late eleventh century, several centuries after Gregory's dialogues:

> The landscape is the enchanted landscape of the fairy tale; we are surrounded by mystery, by secret murmurings and whispers. All the numerous castles and palaces, the battles and adventures, of the courtly romances—especially of the Breton cycle—are things of fairyland: each time they appear before us as though sprung from the ground; their geographical relation to the known world, their sociological and economic foundations, remain unexplained."[8]

This "fairyland," derived, according to Auerbach, from Breton folklore, is a fusion of folk and heroic materials at the center of the aristocratic romance. When the monstrous *vilain* of *Yvain* tells the knight Calogrenant of the magic spring, which is the narrative center of the romance, it serves as a narrative emblem of the relationship between folktale and aristocratic narrative. Calogrenant recalls him as "a peasant who resembled a Moor, ugly and hideous in the extreme—such an ugly creature that he cannot be described in words," before going on to describe his beastly features at great length.⁹ Calogrenant asks the peasant where he might find "any adventure or marvelous thing." "I know nothing of adventure, nor have I heard any talk of it," responds the peasant, who is a complete outsider to chivalric society. "But should you wish to go to a spring near here, you will not return untested if you abide by the custom of the place."¹⁰ In other words, the popular origin of a key aspect of romance, its aura of mystery, is simply hidden in plain sight. The *vilain* has not been discarded from the story; he remains at its symbolic center, even if transformed and debased.

As the aristocratic romance entered into greater popular circulation over the course of the later Middle Ages, its aristocratic assumptions were increasingly opened to critique. By the time of Chaucer's Wife of Bath, fairies already belonged to the glow of an imagined socially harmonious past: "Al was this land fulfild of fairye. / The elf-queene with her joly compaignye / Daunced ful ofte in many a grene mede."¹¹ This older, implicitly feminine, world, however, has been displaced—and replaced—by the mendicant orders:

> But now kan no man se none elves mo,
> For now the grete charitee and prayeres
> Of lymytours and othere hooly freres,
> That serchen every lond and every streem
> As thikke as motes in the sonne-beem,
> Blessyinge halles, chambres, kichenes, boures,
> Citees, burghes, castels, hye toures,
> Thropes, bernes, shipnes, dayeryes—
> This maketh that ther been no fairyes.
> For ther as wont to walken was an elf
> Ther walketh now the lymytour hymself,
> In undermeles and in morwenynges,
> And seyth his matyns and his hooly thynges
> As he gooth in his lymytacioun.
> Wommen may go now saufly up and doun;
> In every bussh or under every tree
> There is noon oother incubus but he,
> And he ne wol doon hem but dishonour.¹²

As Peter Burke has remarked, "the friars were amphibious or bi-cultural, men of the university as well as men of the market-place."[13] In the Wife's tale, they can be found just about everywhere, from castles to dairies, staking their claims to the domain once associated with fairy sexual predations. The Wife herself, however, is not so entirely unlike the friars she attacks: a mobile and domineering figure of the marketplace. Like the aristocratic romance before her, the Wife wishes to challenge the perceived domination of the clergy over literate culture, but she also claims the fairies for ends that certainly exceed the scope of aristocratic dissemination of a high culture. The young nobleman of the story must overcome his disdain for the Loathly Lady's appearance, which, according to romance conventions, entailed her lack of gentle status. This, rather than her lesson about accepting the "maistrie" of women, was probably the aspect of her tale most challenging to the world of the aristocratic romance. The Wife of Bath represents a new public, neither clergy nor aristocracy, which emulated the culture of aristocratic romance for its own ends. Partly as a result of this new pressure, the romance began its long and uneven "downmarket" journey, which made it one of the genres of modern writing that migrated from elite to popular culture, where it remains today, firmly separated from "literature."[14]

Protestant Fancies

If the Wife of Bath made the friars into the historical opponents of the fairies, the Protestant Reformation tended to heap together the old religion and the old popular beliefs. The Catholic Church in its heyday was, as Keith Thomas has nicely put it, "a vast reservoir of magical power, capable of being deployed for a variety of secular purposes."[15] Although the official church was hostile to alternative sources of magic, including witchcraft and fairies, the popular appropriation of church magic often did not clearly discriminate between the Christian and the pagan. Medieval Catholicism as a total system was capacious and syncretic enough to absorb such potential contradictions.

The Protestant discrediting of church magic furthered the association of popular superstition and Catholic magic. The result, according to Thomas, was the "Protestant myth that fairy-beliefs were an invention of the Catholic Middle Ages."[16] Thus, in Shakespeare's early *Comedy of Errors*, the slave Dromio of Syracuse responds to the uncanny events in Ephesus in terms that blend his implicit Catholicism with popular superstition:

> O for my beads! I cross me for a sinner.
> This is the fairy land. O spite of spites!

We talk with goblins, owls, and sprites;

If we obey them not, this will ensue:

They'll suck our breath, or pinch us black and blue.   (II.ii.188–92)

In Shakespeare's own lifetime, and perhaps in response to Shakespeare's popular-
ization of the figure of Puck, William Warner's *A Continuance of Albion's England*
(1606) associated Robin Goodfellow himself with the old religion: "When Nunnes,
Monks, Friers, and Votaries were here of every sort, / We were accustomed, ye wot,
to this and merrier sport," declares Robin to his fellow fairy revelers.[17]

Protestants, however, were not immune to the association of fairy beliefs with
devil worship and witchcraft. The juridical pressure on witchcraft only increased in
some areas, particularly Scotland, after the Reformation. In his essay "On the Fairies
of Popular Superstition," included in *Minstrelsy of the Scottish Border* (1802–1803),
Sir Walter Scott intriguingly proposed that this was the result of a concentration
of magical beliefs in the world of popular superstition after the Reformation's banishment of Catholic magic. "The trials of sorcerers and witches, which disgrace
our criminal records, become even more frequent after the Reformation of the
Church; as if human credulity, no longer amused by the miracles of Rome, had
sought for food in the traditional records of popular superstition."[18] J. A. Mac-
Culloch long ago demonstrated the juridical association between fairies and demons
in early modern Scotland, and Scott's essay provides instances of witchcraft trials in
which concourse with the "Queen of Faëry" was taken to indicate association with a
devil.[19] Even in the presumably more sophisticated world of London theater, Simon
Forman's diary entry about a performance of *Macbeth* simply calls the Weird Sisters
"three women fairies or nymphs."[20] Although we associate *A Midsummer Night's
Dream* with comic lightness of touch concerning the supernatural world of fairies,
Shakespeare is also careful to have Oberon distinguish his fairies from black magic
(III.ii.378–95).

Despite the strong links between Protestant state building and witchcraft trials
in the sixteenth and seventeenth centuries, the ultimately stronger Protestant skepticism about superstition and demons made possible the literary and theatrical appropriation of such beliefs as ingredients of literary and theatrical fantasy. Protestant
theologians, as Stuart Clark has shown, attempted "to correct popular misapprehen-
sions about the basic causation of unpleasant events. . . . It was constantly urged
that to blame these afflictions only on witches was at least a kind of hypocrisy, and
probably outright atheism."[21] Protestant skeptics such as Reginald Scot attacked the
belief in witchcraft's efficacy, which he clearly felt to be a continuation of Catholic
magical beliefs: "Amongst us there be manie women, and effeminat men (marie pa-

pists alwaies, as by their superstition may appeere) that make great divinations upon the shedding of salt, wine, &c: and for the observation of daies, and houres use as great withcraft [*sic*] as in anie thing."[22] Francis Bacon's *The Advancement of Learning* (1605) later argued for the necessity of clearing away "old wives' fables, impostures of the clergy, illusions of spirits, and badges of antichrist" in order to produce a sound basis for knowledge.[23] Tellingly, Bacon, like Scot before him, associates clerical chicanery with old wives' tales, effectively merging the Catholic magic of a masculine clergy with popular superstitions associated with women.

Protestant skepticism did not simply and immediately clear away enfeebled old beliefs. James I had copies of Scot's *Discoverie* burned at his accession in 1603 and invigorated the prosecution of witchcraft in England. Still, it began the destruction of an entire structure of belief that underlay both Catholic and pagan magic: the belief that words could "work upon the world."[24] Language began to lose its incantatory power: the Eucharist's "hoc est corpus meum" became mere "Hocus Pocus." The old magic of the Catholic Church and popular belief were either discredited or under tremendous pressure, but the attachments to such magic did not disappear so quickly.

A Midsummer Night's Dream (ca. 1595) makes self-conscious use of popular and Catholic magic for theatrical ends. At the end of that play, Oberon, who is leading a dance of the assembled fairies, blesses, in incantatory couplets, the bridal beds of the newlywed couples:

> Now until the break of day
> Through this house each fairy stray.
> To the best bride bed will we,
> Which by us shall blessèd be,
> And the issue there create
> Ever shall be fortunate.
> So shall all the couples three
> Ever true in loving be,
> And the blots of nature's hand
> Shall not in their issue stand.
> Never mole, hare-lip, nor scar,
> Nor mark prodigious such as are
> Despisèd in nativity
> Shall upon their children be.
> With this field-dew consecrate
> Every fairy take his gait

And each several chamber bless
Through this palace with sweet peace;
And the owner of it blessed
Ever shall in safety rest.   V.i.392–411

The blessing of the bridal bed with holy water—here associated with the prevention of birth defects—was a Catholic practice, largely discontinued by the time of Elizabeth, and associated (by Protestants) with the false magic of Catholic ritual.[25] It was, however, entirely appropriate to comedy's concern with marriage, and Shakespeare shows little apparent hesitation in blending the magic of Catholic "superstition" with popular superstition and aristocratic romance respectively embodied by Puck and Oberon. Holy water becomes Oberon's "field-dew consecrate," and the fairies replace the Catholic clergy in applying it. The blessing of the bridal bed with field-dew replaces the inept theater of the mechanicals, which has occupied the stage for most of act 5, with the magic of the fairies. Shakespeare here appropriates both folk belief and Catholic "magic" in order to produce a secular magic that is fully identified with neither folklore nor the church.[26] In the place of old belief is something altogether novel: the claim to magic by the public theater.

Scot claimed that it was partly "the want of Robin goodfellowe and the fairies, which were woont to maintain chat" that explained the belief of common people in the powers of witches.[27] One senses for a moment Scot's sympathy for a waning popular culture, perhaps anticipating Shakespeare's use of Robin Goodfellow. Indeed, as Nathalie Zemon Davis has argued, the sixteenth century saw widespread elite interest in collecting and disseminating aspects of traditional oral culture. "Learned interest in proverbs intensified in a way that would not be seen again in Europe until the romantic national movements of the late eighteenth and nineteenth centuries; and the collectors were not just modest clerics but often important humanists."[28] English poets and dramatists began to make new incursions into popular superstition and older forms of magic, and the reduction of fairies in particular to false, but largely unthreatening, superstition enabled them to assert their own equivalence to the mythologies of the ancients. In *The Terrors of the Night* (1594), Thomas Nashe expressed the growing sense of the similarity between the fairies of the native tradition and the classical machinery of the learned culture of the Renaissance: the "Robbin-good-fellowes, Elfes, Fairies, Hobgoblins of our latter age" were those "which idolatrous former daies and the fantasticall world of Greece ycleaped *Fawnes, Satyres, Dryades, & Hamadryades*."[29]

Late Elizabethan culture thus had ready access to a vernacular mythology that could compare to that of the ancients. When, almost at the conclusion of *The Faerie Queene* (1590 and 1596), the courtly Sir Calidore stumbles upon the scene of poetic inspiration at Mount Acidale, he first discovers "Nymphes and Faeries," classical and local spirits, sitting together at the banks of the mount's spring. "At last the aboriginals of the heavily colonized faery land make their debut," exclaims his recent editor, A. C. Hamilton.[30] Hamilton's response measures the modern expectation, partly a result of Shakespeare's influence, that fairyland is, or should be, essentially popular. Spenser does not generally meet this expectation although the introduction of Spenser's lowly alter ego Colin Clout at Mount Acidale is a clear signal that Spenser identifies the deepest sources of his own poetry with a popular world that can only be disrupted by the courtly presence of Calidore. This aspect of Spenser, however, has been relatively neglected because of his largely submerged use of popular sources of fairy mythology, compared to his use of Italian romances or the famous Elizabethan entertainments directed specifically to the queen.[31] "The Fairyland and Fairies of Spenser, have no connection with popular superstition, being only words used to denote a Utopian scene of action, and imaginary and allegorical characters," wrote Scott in *The Minstrelsy of the Scottish Border.* "The stealing of the Red Cross Knight, while a child, is the only incident in the poem which approaches to the popular character of the Fairy."[32] The twentieth-century folklorist, Katharine Briggs, like Scott before her, found little to say about Spenser in her extensive work on the subject of literary uses of folk fairies in English literature: "Spenser used the fays of romance for his allegory, but they had already become a little bookish and faded."[33] In his 1580 public letter exchange with Spenser, Gabriel Harvey worried that the proposed use of fairy mythology would have *"Hobgoblin* runne away with the Garland from Apollo."[34] If Spenser avoided that fate, Shakespeare appears to have embraced it.

Shakespeare's Fairy Court

Shakespeare, rather than Spenser, captured the popular materials of English superstition as his own, but he was not the first English dramatist to recognize the potential of such materials for the new world of the London popular stage. George Peel's *The Old Wives' Tale* (printed 1595) creates a frame device of an "old wife," Madge, who introduces the popular romance tales that intersect in the drama.[35] John Lyly's *Endymion* (ca. 1590) apparently used younger boy actors as fairies (the fairies are referred to as "babies") and made them guardian spirits for Cynthia, who now appears as a classically inflected fairy queen. They pinch one of the male characters as he stumbles upon Endymion, her would-be lover:

Pinch him, pinch him, black and blue.
Saucy mortals must not view
What the Queen of Stars is doing,
Nor pry into our fairy wooing.[36]

They kiss Endymion and depart, having previously announced a "midnight hay-de-guise," a country dance appropriate to the popular character of Lyly's fairies.[37] But they are also good Elizabethan courtiers, primarily devoted to guarding the virginal Cynthia from prying eyes.

Lyly's version of the classical tale of Endymion multiplies romantic love around the character of Endymion while retaining the virginal character of Cynthia her-self—appropriately enough, given the obvious connection to Elizabeth. Shake-speare dramatically reverses the erotic trajectory of this story in *A Midsummer Night's Dream*, having the fairy queen, Titania, pursue the love of a mortal, who has been (partly) transformed into an ass. In doing so, Shakespeare signals a fundamental re-versal of the regal chastity governing the fairy worlds of Spenser and Lyly: the "top" of the fairy world, Titania, humiliatingly in love with the Bottom of the human.

This amorous conjunction of high and low recalls Apuleius' *The Golden Ass,* in which a member of the Roman imperial elite experiences, in the form of an ass, the treatment of slaves. The Roman association of the ass with Saturnalian rever-sal continued until the Renaissance (the Christmas Fool with his ass-eared cap).[38] Shakespeare probably knew Apuleius from William Adlington's translation of 1566, which domesticated the story as a "pleasant old wives' tale," based on Apuleius' own description of his tale as a "Milesian discourse," full, that is, of popular stories adapted for an educated audience.[39] Female magicians and storytellers populate his narrative, culminating with the divinized version of such magic in the goddess Isis. Shakespeare's Bottom, unlike Lucius, the well-born central character of *The Golden Ass*, is upwardly mobile in his relationship to Titania, but he is, partly for this reason, cast aside at the end of the play.

Titania herself is a fairy queen filtered through Saturnalian reversal. In the course of Lucius' adventures as an ass, a wealthy noblewoman falls in love with him, and bribes his trainer for a night alone with him. Apuleius treats the woman's passion with sympathy, which might have influenced Shakespeare's treatment of Titania, but Titania winds up as a tamed version of the powerful enchantress of medieval narrative. The humiliation of Titania shadows every other romantic entanglement in the play: Hippolyta, the Amazon queen, subjugated in marriage to Theseus; Hermia and Helena winning their apparently appropriate lovers, but only after experiencing a disenchanting vision of male infidelity. Titania's fate is simply the most evidently demeaning of the female characters in the play, but this is significant in itself, since Titania belongs not only to the line of Cynthia/Diana, as in Lyly, but to the world of fairy queens from medieval romance who enchant and commandeer their mortal lovers.[40] Titania is neither chastely powerful, like Lyly's Cynthia, nor sexually powerful, like a medieval fairy queen or indeed the female magicians of *The Golden Ass*. The apparently more agreeable fates of Hermia and Helena are arranged by Oberon while he simultaneously tames Titania. As Oberon regains control of fairyland, Puck provides the more general formula of male domination in marriage:

> Jack shall have Jill,
> Nought shall go ill,
> The man shall have his mare again,
> And all shall be well. (III.ii.461–64)

Oberon himself comes from the thirteenth-century *chanson de geste*, *Huon de Bordeaux*, translated by Lord Berners in the early sixteenth century. Oberon's literary genealogy is firmly aristocratic and dynastic; his name ultimately derives from Alberich, the sorcerer brother of Merovech, legendary founder of the Merovingian dynasty. In *Huon of Bordeaux*, Oberon is a dwarf, having been enchanted at birth by an offended fairy, and the son of Julius Caesar and the Lady of the Secret Isle, whose secreted identity suggests fairy origins. Oberon, like Titania, claims both classical and vernacular origins, just as the play itself takes place in what appears to be a very English wood outside of the classical and heroic Athens governed by Theseus.

By the Renaissance, a fairy court could hardly be said to exist without a fulsome array of courtiers and entertainers. Titania has a range of courtiers, whose names first locate them in the kitchens and gardens of English villages: Mustardseed, Peaseblossom, and so forth. Bottom first encounters them in the typically English form of address between nonaristocratic equals: Master Cobweb, Master Mustardseed (III.i.175–86). By the time of his second and final scene among the fairies, Bottom appears to have learned enough of Titania's court to have elevated them—and presumably himself as well, if with comic results—to continental courtiers: Masters Mustardseed and Cobweb have become Mounsieur Mustardseed and Cavalery Cobweb, and Bottom has learned that their function is to provide for his personal comfort (IV.i.1–38). Shakespeare has reversed the social trajectory of *The Golden Ass*. The man transformed into an ass is now of common origin, and his transformation opens up the world of the aristocratic court; the comedy of the scene derives from the spectacle of someone like Bottom in a courtly setting. At the same time, though, the court is gently mocked as well. The popular and domestic world of the English fairy has entered the world of continental sophistication, which is both feminized and reduced, even in terms of size, in the case of Titania's court.[41]

Although Oberon is also a fairy prince, the masculinity of his retinue never appears to lend itself to quite the same degree of comic reduction as Titania's feminine court. The struggle between the two is one that informs the entire play: a mythopoesis of masculine domination. This is made clear around the issue that divides them: the possession of the Indian changeling:

> And jealous Oberon would have the child
> Knight of his train, to trace the forests wild:
> But she perforce withholds the lovèd boy,
> Crowns him with flowers, and makes him all her joy.   (II.i.24–27)

Titania's possession of the boy feminizes him, and Oberon wishes to induct him into the masculine domain of the hunt. Even the identification of the boy's lineage indicates the implicit mobilization of conflict around gender. Puck simply identifies him as "a lovely boy stol'n from an Indian king" (II.i.22). Titania later offers the other side of the story: "His mother was a vot'ress of my order" (II.i.123). Neither acknowledges the role of the other sex.

The play knows that the masculine will triumph in this battle of the sexes, and sometimes appears to give this inevitable victory the taste of tragedy, in the form of rape. Hippolyta, the Amazon bride-to-be of Theseus, is war booty, "wooed" with his sword (I.i.16). The "office" of Titania's fairies is to protect their fairy queen, but the chorus of their lullaby to her seems to acknowledge the inevitability of female defeat and rape. The fairies invoke Philomela, the classical victim of Ovidian rape and transformation, in order to aid them in their task, but her symbolic presence also colors Oberon's intrusion into Titania's bower at the conclusion of the song: "Philomel with melody, / Sing in our sweet lullaby" (II.ii.13–14). Oberon is, at least for a moment, another version of Tereus, Philomela's rapist (although here the "rape" is one that also transforms him into a cuckold).

In a play symbolically governed by the feminine moon from its very first lines, the weight of masculine domination is felt as a particularly heavy one. Mary Ellen Lamb suggests that the play dramatizes another version of the dilemma of schoolboys as they confronted a childhood spent among women giving way to the rigors of education and the masculine world of Latin.[42] Lamb proposes Bottom as a kind of negative example for the schoolboy, lost to the world of female domination. Schoolboys, however, were an unlikely market niche for the Lord Chamberlain's Men, and pedagogical admonition is not usually Shakespeare's mode. Even the sententious

Theseus prefers the lowbrow spectacle of the mechanicals' version of *Pyramus and Thisbe* to the humanist Spenserian complaint of "The thrice-three Muses mourning for the death / Of learning, late deceased in beggary" (V.i.52–53). In fact, there is no reason why Shakespeare's first audiences could not have derived great pleasure in Bottom's abandonment to the feminine domain of the play, as audiences continue to do to this day. The imagined alliance of the queen and the plebeian was only a "dream" for the audience, but not necessarily one to be condemned.

Puck and "Strong Imagination"

If the alliance of Titania and Bottom is necessarily temporary, Puck offers another model for the relationship of high and low: a synthesis of rural and courtly entertainments in the new space of the public theater. He is first introduced to us as the well-known figure of country pranks, most of them directed at women:

> Are not you he
> That frights the maidens of the villag'ry,
> Skim milk, and sometimes labour in the quern,
> And bootless make the breathless housewife churn,
> And sometime make the drink to bear no barm,
> Mislead night wanderers, laughing at their harm?   (II.i.34–39)

If Puck is the very recognizable spirit of village mischief, he also acquires, like Titania's attendants, courtly functions as well. He is Oberon's entertainer:

> I am that merry wanderer of the night.
> I jest to Oberon, and make him smile
> When I a fat and bean-fed horse beguile,
> Neighing in likeness of a filly foal. . . .   (II.i.43–46)

Puck arranges pantomimes for Oberon, of the sort that exploit the Elizabethan theater's potential for comic eroticism built on cross-dressing and gender confusion: a very Shakespearean model for theatrical comedy. His is also consistently the voice in the play that names the confusions of the younger lovers, their "fond pageant" (III.ii.114), as the experience of specifically theatrical pleasure:

> Then will two at once woo one:
> That must needs be sport alone;
> And those things do best please me
> That befall prepost'rously.   (III.ii.118–21)

Puck's pleasure is the Shakespearean one of topsy-turvydom, events that "befall prepost'rously," and he has come very close to identifying himself with the spirit of Shakespearean comedy, or even with Shakespeare himself: another figure from the country who was partly occupied with courtly entertainments.

It is, then, entirely appropriate that Puck should speak the epilogue to the play, characteristically offering a veiled threat to his audience of "gentles":

> If we shadows have offended,
> Think but this, and all is mended,
> That you have but slumbered here
> While these visions did appear;
> And this weak and idle theme,
> No more yielding but a dream,
> Gentles, do not reprehend.
> If you pardon, we will mend.
> And as I am an honest puck,
> If we have unearnèd luck
> Now to 'scape the serpent's tongue,
> We will make amends ere long,
> Else the puck a liar call.
> So, goodnight unto you all.
> Give me your hands, if we be friends,
> And Robin shall restore amends.   (V.i.414–29)

Puck's apparent desire to please is not completely ingenuous; we can assume that Shakespeare's audience would know that calling a puck a liar is probably not a good idea. Better to applaud ("give me your hands").

Puck's apparent willingness to have a displeased audience write off the play as a dream contains an implicit challenge: to dismiss the play as a dream is to be in the same position as the four young lovers when they awaken with the memory of the previous evening's events transformed into dreamlike memories. Demetrius, who has been left in a state of enchantment by the love magic, is also the one most convinced of the complete clarity of his new vision: "My love to Hermia, / Melted as the snow, seems to me now / As the remembrance of an idle gaud / Which in my childhood I did dote upon" (IV.i.164–67). Hermia and Helena, on the other hand, appear to have some greater intuitive grasp of the night's events:

> HER. Methinks I see these things with parted eye,
>   When everything seems double.

HEL.   So methinks,

    And I have found Demetrius like a jewel,

    Mine own and not mine own.

DEM.   It seems to me

    That yet we sleep, we dream.   (IV.i.188–92)

The "double vision" of the two women, Helena in particular, is appropriate to the plot of the four younger lovers, revealing a world in which male love is subject to dramatic and irrational change as well as the extreme homosocial competition that Shakespeare derives from the lovers of Chaucer's *Knight's Tale*. It is perfectly appropriate for Helena to see Demetrius as a "mine own, and not mine own." He is hers only insofar as he remains under Oberon's enchantment, and his own sense of living in a continuing dream is dramatic irony: he *is* in a kind of dream. This doubleness of vision suggests imaginative insight into the events of the previous night, which has become, according to the rules of Oberon's enchantment, nothing more than a dream, the traditional domain of the wayward imagination. The association of imagination with the younger women intersects with the dramatic response to the performance of *Pyramus and Thisbe*; Hermia and Helena do not speak during the performance while their mates add to the courtly ridicule of the mechanicals' performance. They are perhaps less inclined to scoff at theatrical "shadows," even the naïve theatricality of the mechanicals.

    The play's tendency to give women rather than men, with the exception of Bottom, imaginative insight is perhaps compensatory in a play that so firmly presents the apparently inevitable triumph of the masculine in the domain of marriage. ("Buyer's remorse" for an Elizabethan woman in her marriage was likely to be more consequential than for a male, and imaginative insight into the behavior of men, whose world was less than fully open to her, was thus more necessary.) Imagination, in medieval and Renaissance faculty psychology, remained subordinate to the critical and discriminating power of reason. Theseus' stern dismissal of the lovers' tales as "antique fables" and "fairy toys" (V.i.3), and thus the tricks of "strong imagination" (V.i.18), belongs to that tradition, which also aligns his paternalism with his rationalism. Hippolyta's greater willingness to believe the stories of the lovers seems, however, to gender imagination female, which would accord with the hierarchy of Renaissance faculty psychology. Although the play's comic conclusion ratifies traditional masculine domination in marriage, the mythic struggle of the sexes enacted by the play is also a test of the theatrical imagination, and Puck rather than Oberon administers that test in the epilogue. Associated with pranks directed at women, Puck also operates somewhat independently of his master, speaking on behalf of a new form of theatrical engagement—and one that appears to align the all-male theatrical company, for which Puck speaks, with an audience that could and did include women.[43]

Puck's association with the popular world of the English countryside is at the heart of this alliance between the imaginative world of the London theatrical audience and the men who entertained them; the association moves beyond the subservience represented by the amateur theatricals of the mechanicals, linked to ecclesiastical and aristocratic domination of theatrical performance.[44] That London audience, moreover, sees exactly what the courtly audience of *Pyramus and Thisbe* does not: the fairies who ultimately preside over the successful weddings that are celebrated by its performance. Courtly condescension is replaced by a quite different sense of possible theatrical engagement. As Wendy Wall remarks, in response to her own question as to why Puck enters the final scene of the play with a broom (one of his traditional village attributes), "Puck sweeps, it seems, so that the Athenian court can entertain an Englished folk tradition within its bounds, though the court's inability to see its fairy servants suggests a crucial distance between the court's and the play's perspectives."[45] In effect, what Wall calls the "Englished folk tradition" inhabiting the court is available to the London audience rather than to the court itself. Puck's epilogue is from neither the village nor the court; it is from the stage of the public theater, relying upon his previous identification with both village and court (as Oberon's entertainer), but now merged into the incipiently national space of the theater. The bonds established there are simultaneously imaginative—between "shadow" creatures and presumably sophisticated London theatergoers—and the real interactions of actors and audience in the theater. The powerful realization of this aspect of the play was Peter Brook's legendary 1970 production for the Royal Shakespeare Company. In that production, the actors left the stage after Puck's epilogue, shaking hands with members of the audience as they left the theater. Puck's "Give me your hands, if we be friends," suddenly became a more immediate bond than the request for applause that it appears to be.

Fairies to Tale: Natural Magic

If fairies are largely absent from late Shakespeare, the insistence of the marvelous is heightened. The witches of *Macbeth* and Prospero's status as magus in *The Tempest* testify to the continuing use of the supernatural. Other plays, such as *Cymbeline* and *The Winter's Tale*, classicize their use of the supernatural: classical gods and oracles, but no local spirits. Another, more rationalized form of the marvelous, however, is present in the late plays: the aura of the old wives' tale come to life that is built up around even such apparently unlikely plays as *King Lear* and *All's Well That Ends*

Well. This is particularly true of *The Winter's Tale*, whose title signals the centrality of the old tales, and whose plot emphasizes the role of femininity and domesticity in challenging Stuart patriarchalism, which made explicit the traditional analogy between the father's authority in the home and the king's in the state.[46] The magic of the play is explicitly theatrical: Paulina's mise-en-scène of the "resurrection" of Hermione is a form of magic that is fundamentally domestic in nature and scope, explicitly designed to curb the wild excesses of Leontes' patriarchalism, which itself has the force of the powerful magic of paranoid belief.

The jealousy of Leontes does, however, possess its own form of rationality: a competition with his "brother" Polixenes over aristocratic gift exchange: an economy in which prestige depends on the maintenance of expenditure in various forms of largesse and liberality.[47] The play opens with the anxiety of Polixenes's entourage about their inability to repay Leontes for his hospitality, leading to the possibility of serving the court of Leontes "sleepy drinks" (I.i.13), or sedatives that turn anxiety about a proper "counter-gift" into aggression. The aristocratic exchange of gifts is thus collapsing even as the play begins. In the second scene, Leontes comes to be consumed by the delusion that his "gifts" to Polixenes have included his wife, Hermione. The idealized homosocial exchange between the two friends and rulers, mediated by Hermione as go-between, suddenly and violently explodes into a fantasmatic version of homosocial rivalry. The boundaries between the positive and negative versions of aristocratic gift exchange are radically unstable in character from the first lines of the play. The ultimate restoration of dynastic stability in the interlocking domains of family and foreign relations requires the "domestic" intervention of Paulina, who operates in the symbolic register of the old wives' tale. This register of the play completely belongs to Shakespeare. There is no equivalent of Paulina in the primary source for the play, Robert Greene's prose romance *Pandosto* (1588); nor is there any equivalent of Autolycus, the ballad-monger, who handles the retail end of another version of popular marvels.

The winter's tale itself is a form that is simultaneously courtly and domestic, mobilized by the son, Mamillius, whose name, perhaps derived from "mammary," suggests his immersion in the feminine world of the court, along with the old wives' tales that here seem to mark the longstanding participation of the aristocracy in oral popular culture.[48] He is an advanced student of courtly love, flirting with the court ladies, even while he is also the vehicle of the old wives' tale—the prince as storyteller:

Her.   Pray you sit by us,
        And tell's a tale.

MAM.   Merry or sad, shall't be?

HER.   As merry as you will.

MAM.   A sad tale's best for winter; I have one
        Of sprites and goblins.

HER.   Let's have that, good sir.
        Come on, sit down, come on, and do your best
        To fright me with your sprites; you're powerful at it.

MAM.   There was a man—

HER.   Nay, come sit down, then on.

MAM.   Dwelt by a churchyard—I will tell it softly,
        Yond crickets shall not hear it.

HER.   Come on then, and give't me in mine ear.   (II.i.22–32)

Mamillius is almost, but not quite, under his mother's sway. "Come on, sit down," is her refrain to her apparently kinetic son. The tale is interrupted by the arrival of Leontes, now convinced of his wife's infidelity. The mise-en-scène is striking: Mamillius is apparently whispering to his mother while his father storms on about the fantastical example of the spider that can only kill its victims once they are aware that they have taken its poison. "I have drunk, and seen the spider" (II.i.45), Leontes ominously declares. "All's true that is mistrusted" (II.i.48). Leontes is himself consumed by the logic of the old wives' tale as a principle of paranoia, which replaces, for the theatrical audience, the "sad tale" which the audience never hears. He lives "inside," so to speak, his son's tale even while he succeeds in extirpating the legacy, represented by his son, of masculine aristocratic participation in tale-telling.

The end of the play, however, seems to realize the merry tale that Mamillius found to be inappropriate for winter. This is the Christian (and, as we shall see, classical) mythos of rebirth, organized as a form of magic by Paulina, whose name evokes a feminized version of Pauline theology, but who seems to represent the absorption of Christian truths into the world of the old tales. By the end of the play, she has taken over the "tale-telling" aspect of the drama from the dead Mamillius: "That she is living, / Were it but told you, should be hooted at / Like an old tale" (V.iii.115–17). When Paulina first confronts Leontes over his accusation of Hermione, he charges her with "witchcraft"; she refuses the charge—a potentially very dangerous one for her, if the example of James I is kept in mind—with the countercharge that Leontes verges on tyranny, also of course dangerous to her:

LEO.   I'll ha' thee burnt.

PAULINA.   I care not:

It is a heretic that makes the fire,
Not she which burns in't. I'll not call you a tyrant;
But this most cruel usage of your Queen,
Nor able to produce more accusation
Than your own weak-hing'd fancy, something savours
Of tyranny, and will ignoble make you,
Yea, scandalous to the world.   (II.iii.113–20)

Their dispute is, among other things, a political one and partly about the difference between what are coded as feminine and masculine forms of authority. Absolutist patriarchalism is the play's model of masculine power, and it is implicitly Stuart in character. Paulina's authority comes from a source that Leontes can only understand as witchcraft. Act 5 gives us several examples of his submission to her feminine authority. Even at the climactic moment of the play, she asks for yet another reassurance of his transformation: "[Y]ou'll think, / Which I protest against, I am assisted / By wicked powers" (V.iii.89–91). Leontes is of course now receptive to the lesson: "O, she's warm! / If this be magic, let it be an art / Lawful as eating" (V.iii.109–11). The "art," of course, is also nature, as, in a different context, Leontes's brother king, Polixenes, had explained to Perdita earlier in the play. Paulina's natural magic, now fully distinguished from witchcraft, is also, as in *A Midsummer Night's Dream*, theater.[49] This apparently domestic magic that seems to arise from the world of old wives' tales is now a form of court theater recognized by Leontes:

Good Paulina,
Lead us from hence, where we may leisurely
Each one demand, and answer to his part
Perform'd in this wide gap of time, since first
We were dissevered. Hastily lead away.   (V.iii.151–55)

Leontes possesses the last words of the play, and recent criticism has tended to emphasize his continuing control of the play at its conclusion, right down to the surprise announcement (to Paulina, at least) of her engagement to Camillo. "What is restored, finally, in this quintessentially Jacobean drama, is royal authority," Stephen Orgel announces in his superb introduction to the play.[50] At the risk of appearing to fall back into an idealizing reading of the play, I would emphasize the implied stage direction of "Good Paulina, / Lead us from hence." Paulina continues to lead Leontes, at his own command. However much the royal authority of Leontes is restored at the end of this play, theater belongs to Paulina. The lineage that it finally celebrates is a feminine one: that of Hermione to Perdita; the masculine line, Leontes to Mamillius, is tragically extinguished, and we cannot be confident that Hermione will produce another male heir. Although we are assured that Hermione embraces Leontes in the final scene, the only words she speaks are addressed to her daughter, and they are a maternal blessing: "You gods, look down / And from your sacred vials pour your graces / Upon my daughter's head!" (V.iii.121–23). If mothers are more often than not absent from Shakespeare's drama, the maternal returns here in a particularly powerful form.

Nature's Bastards

Around this feminine mystery swirls the primary social fact of the play: the social mobility that courses through its final half. This includes the fairy-tale, if also comic, rise in social status of the two "clowns," father and son. (Their new wealth is not the mundane result of being improving farmers, as might have been suggested by historical context, but rather their discovery of the "fairy gold" that comes along with the lost Perdita.) Autolycus, by contrast, appears at first to map a fall in social status: he is a former courtier to Prince Florizel, fallen into peddling and theft. By the end of the play, though, he has recovered courtier's attire. The equation of the rogue and courtier is a Shakespearean joke, one to be widely shared in the seventeenth century.

The myth of Perdita herself, however, is apparently one of aristocratic restoration, clearly marked as another version of the old tales that structure this play. "Like an old tale still, which will have matter to rehearse though credit be asleep and not an ear open" (V.ii.60–62), says one of the gentlemen reporting the (undramatized) scene of the revelation of Perdita as the long-lost daughter of Leontes. The play is generous—and critical—enough to include Autolycus in this general pattern of restoration, and this seems to be part of its understanding that the court cannot refuse its own affiliations with the entirety of the social world it governs. Perhaps most surprisingly, in a play that is scrupulous to defend the sexual honor of Hermione, her daughter's burgeoning sexuality is a key link between court and country.

Not that she herself fully realizes the nature of the association. In fact, Shakespeare goes out of his way to establish a kind of unconscious aristocratic supremacy in her own garden: her refusal to plant hybrid flowers, "nature's bastards" (IV.iv.83). Even Polixenes, who will soon dash plans for a "mixed" wedding of prince and peasant, finds a soft spot in his heart for the garden version of the same thing:

> You see, sweet maid, we marry
> A gentler scion to the wildest stock,
> And make conceive a bark of baser kind

By bud of nobler race. This is an art
Which does mend nature—change it rather—but
The art itself is nature.   (IV.iv.92–97)

The problem here is that what goes in nature contradicts aristocratic imperatives, which the play both upholds (Perdita is herself a princess, and, ironically, even more attuned to an aristocratic sense of bloodline than her future father-in-law) and critiques (sexual mixing is natural anyway). This is clear enough in the case of Polixenes, but it also goes for Perdita, if in a form less immediately discernible.

At her most mythic, Perdita rummages through a classicized inventory of flowers that she associates with Proserpina without recognizing herself as another version of Proserpina—the same classical deity who was sometimes identified as the "fairy queen" in medieval texts, including Chaucer's *Merchant's Tale*, which, like *A Midsummer Night's Dream*, has "fairy" kings and queens invest their own prestige in a symbolic struggle between the masculine and the feminine. She is, however, decked out as Flora for the sheep-shearing feast, a goddess the Romans associated with Proserpina. (Shakespeare was no doubt familiar with the old tradition, first reported by Ovid, that Flora was originally a Roman prostitute who had left a legacy to Rome in exchange for her celebration in the Floralia.) Shakespeare has heaped up the floral connections of the scene: Florizel, Flora, Proserpina. We are not allowed to forget that Perdita and Florizel are in the full bloom of their sexual development, even if this is a source of embarrassment to Perdita herself:

PER.   O Proserpina,
       For the flowers now that frighted thou letst fall
       From Dis's wagon! Daffodils,
       That come before the swallow dares, and take
       The winds of March with beauty; violets, dim,
       But sweeter than the lids of Juno's eyes,
       Or Cytherea's breath; pale primroses,
       That die unmarried, ere they can behold
       Bright Phoebus in his strength—a malady
       Most incident to maids; bold oxlips, and
       The crown imperial; lilies of all kinds,
       The flower-de-luce being one—O, these I lack,
       To make you garlands of, and my sweet friend,
       To strew him o'er and o'er.
FLORIZEL.   What, like a corpse?

PER.   No, like a bank for love to lie and play on,
        Not like a corpse; or if, not to be buried,
        But quick and in my arms. Come, take your flowers;
        Methinks I play as I have seen them do
        In Whitsun pastorals—sure this robe of mine
        Does change my disposition.   (IV.iv.116–35)

Here, in response to Florizel's suggestion that she would treat him like a corpse, the raising of the dead takes on a ribald meaning that appears to shock Perdita herself: "Not like a corpse; or if—not to be buried, / But quick and in my arms." The absent flowers, first associated with maidenly purity, become both "bold" and increasingly monarchical as the list proceeds: crown imperial, fleur-de-lis. This is yet another moment, clearly played up by Shakespeare, in which Perdita's natural condition—the princess of Sicily—necessarily reveals itself despite her lowly upbringing. This is of course pure aristocratic ideology: blood will out.

Why, then, does Shakespeare choose to set the scene in summer, when those flowers are missing, rather than spring, which is so strongly suggested by Perdita's own status as a virginal model of youthful aristocratic purity?[51] The flowers themselves are so convincingly imagined that, as Jonathan Bate has commented, it comes as a surprise to discover that they are not in fact present in the scene.[52] Autolycus, after all, has already entered the play, singing a song that also associates him, like Perdita, with both spring, when the daffodils bloom, and a summertime roll in the hay (IV.iii.1–12). Perdita seems to build up her own catalogue of (missing) flowers in association with youthful purity, but its immediate effect on her is in fact much closer to the casual eroticism of Autolycus: her sexual invitation to Florizel to "bury" himself in her arms. She is poised, then, between spring and summer, between the innocence of the young Proserpina and the ribald Autolycus. Perdita herself, in her embarrassment, cannot be entirely sure whether her own erotic "play" is influenced by the "Whitsun pastorals" that she has seen in the countryside—the popular festivities of May games and Robin Hood plays, which seem to align her temporarily with the sexual free-for-all of *A Midsummer Night's Dream*—or by "this robe of mine," which is the robe of Flora, Roman goddess appropriate to a masque of aristocrats but not to a shepherdess. She had earlier objected to being "most goddess-like pranked up" (IV.iv.10). Her confusion is social: Does her sexual boldness derive from her "temporary" aristocratic status associated with her robe, or from the folk culture in which she has been raised? At this particular moment, peasant and aristocratic sexuality cannot be fully distinguished.

Despite her own best efforts, then, Perdita slips into the symbolic place of sexual leveling also (unjustly) occupied by her mother when Leontes says that Hermione is like "any flax-wench that puts to / Before her troth-plight" (I.ii.274–75). It is her theatrical/mythical unconscious—and Shakespeare reminds us that the theatricality of her *role* as Flora is crucial here—that bespeaks an eroticism belonging to both court and country. Eroticism, moreover, is really of her essence, as much as she seems to want to deny it. As a kind of Protestant fertility goddess and a rustic aristocrat, she is understandably conflicted about her symbolic function in the world, and she elicits equally contradictory responses in others. Uncovering the clandestine engagement of Florizel and Perdita, Polixenes transforms her erotic power into black magic, addressing her as "thou fresh piece / Of excellent witchcraft" and "enchantment" (IV. iv.419–20, 431). Leontes, however, welcomes her as the principle of natural renewal when Perdita and Florizel unknowingly return to her home: "Welcome hither, / As is the spring to th'earth" (V.i.150–51).

Leontes himself, however, proceeds to drift into a reverie that suggests another flirtation with tragedy, this time in the form of incest:

> FLORIZEL.   at your request
>   My father will grant precious things as trifles.
> LEO.   Would he do so, I'ld beg your precious mistress,
>   Which he counts as a trifle.
> PAULINA.   Sir, my liege,
>   Your eye hath too much youth in't. Not a month
>   Fore your queen died, she was more worth such gazes
>   Than what you look on now.
> LEONTES.   I thought of her,
>   Even in these looks I made.   (V.i.220–27)

In this richly mythic world, Leontes is the avatar, even at this late moment in the play, of the classical world of unbridled passions and their tragic conclusions—the world of Ovid fastened to the world of the Renaissance court. His courtiers are at this point encouraging him to remarry, over Paulina's strong objections. Their motivations are explicitly political: the production of a (male) heir. For Perdita to arrive at just this moment, and first as an object of desire, is symbolically to align incestuous desire with dynastic realpolitik. She just might be his last chance to produce another male heir, but this only heightens the critique of dynastic desire in the play. Paulina wants to redirect his attention to his lost wife, but Leontes' incestuous desire conflates mother and daughter. The play perhaps highlights dynastic desire as both politically and morally unhealthy: the logical extension of dynastic endogamy as incest. This is certainly the direction taken by the primary source for the play, Greene's

Pandosto (1588), in which an equivalent incestuous desire is central to a plot that leaves both Pandosto and Bellaria (Leontes and Hermione) dead. In Shakespeare's version, Paulina's correction enables Leontes to sublimate incestuous desire into paternal domesticity, and the scene ends with his willingness to support the marriage of the young couple against the fury of Polixenes, who now occupies the position of the patriarchal tyrant. Shakespeare's comic ending, which this scene inaugurates, is a remarkable synthesis of classical sexuality and a Protestant and domestic ethos.

National Theater?

If the sexual carnival of *A Midsummer Night's Dream* is somewhat muted by the time of *The Winter's Tale*, the latter play is simultaneously more clearly engaged in the contestation of patriarchalist prerogatives. In the meantime, Shakespeare had molded the world of the old tales to his own purposes, which included the attempt to associate their power with the enchantments of the new public theater. The supernatural appears to be more contained in *The Winter's Tale* than in *A Midsummer Night's Dream*, but perhaps it would be more accurate to say that in the latter part of his theatrical career, Shakespeare both diffuses and naturalizes the effects of the "old tales" throughout a variety of his plots. This can appear to us as a process of "domestication" in the negative sense of co-optation and enclosure. For Shakespeare, however, the claims of the domestic are bound up with the claims of both femininity and the popular, and sexuality is often, as with Titania and Perdita, a powerful leveler.

This leveling, in tandem with Shakespeare's mobilization of old tales and popular superstitions, looks retrospectively like the emergence of a national theater. National culture, as both Ernest Gellner and Benedict Anderson have argued, is founded on what is essentially a horizontal model of identification across status, religious, and regional boundaries.[53] A character such as Shakespeare's Puck perhaps hearkens back to an idea about "old England," but he also represents a glimpse of the future, in which some of the older boundaries are, at least temporarily, suspended.[54] There are of course very strong limitations to the extent and force of national feeling in the sixteenth century, and Krishan Kumar has patiently elaborated the limits to the claim, advanced by Liah Greenfield, for a precocious Tudor nationalism.[55] Perry Anderson's older formulation of the limits of protonationalism in the period remains the most compelling: "It was always manipulated by grandees or sovereigns more than it governed them."[56]

Shakespeare himself produces an early and very powerful image of protonational "fraternal" bonds—and their limits—in *The Comedy of Errors*. At the conclusion of the play, after a scene of familial recognition among the well-born characters that is remarkable primarily for its lack of much evidence of family feeling between the twin brothers Antipholus, their two slaves, also twins, negotiate the problem of age hierarchy: which of the two is older and thus entitled to precedence? Dromio of Ephesus finally rejects the idea of a hierarchy between them, replacing it with fraternal warmth: "We came into the world like brother and brother, / And now let's go hand in hand, not one before another" (V.i.425–26). Egalité and fraternité, but not, it appears, liberté. They remain slaves to the very end, and their continuing bondage to the brothers Antipholus underlines the essentially subordinated character of fraternal popular bonds.[57]

We cannot, then, simply claim nationalism for (or against) Shakespeare, but the age of nations, and of national literatures, was on the horizon, and Shakespeare's theater would eventually become the centerpiece of an English national literature. That theater, rather than poetry, occupied this position in England is not simply the accident of Shakespeare's particular genius for theater. Shakespeare's theater was produced in conditions that necessitated a broader range of appeal than, for example, Spenser's fairy epic. Shakespeare, moreover, self-consciously exaggerated that appeal by bringing elements of a rural "old England" into the largely urban phenomenon of the London theater. By highlighting its own connections to festivity, Shakespearean theater remained very close to the Elizabethan and Stuart transformation of the old medieval and Catholic calendar of feasts and holidays into the Protestant and national calendar.[58]

Shakespeare's theater was thus particularly well suited to the role of an emergent national theater, emblematized in the figure of Puck. Puck's engagement with the audience establishes one form of horizontal identification—that between a sophisticated urban audience and the embodiment of rural superstition—that gains some of its power from the transformation of rural into urban and the rough equivalence between elite and popular cultures. Puck's ability to circumnavigate the globe reveals the transformed power of this once localized spirit, perhaps also linking him to the expanding world of English trade, glimpsed briefly in "th'embarkèd traders on the flood" (II.i.127). In Shakespeare's hands, he is both rural and global. Shakespeare's folk fairies and his old wives' tales adumbrate a version of pastoral for the age of nations. As we shall see, this version of pastoral, which gathers together the old tales, fairies, spirits, and beliefs of the common people, became, by the eighteenth century, the pastoral of national identity: the imagined bond between an elite culture and the simplicity of rural life and its beliefs. Even three hundred years after Shakespeare, when the imperial "creole," Rudyard Kipling, returned "home" and settled in England, Puck remained closely associated with idea of a national pastoral. Kipling's *Puck of Pook's Hill* (1906), and later *Rewards and Fairies* (1910), established

Puck as the figure of "Old England," intimate both with old Hobden, the emblem of the English common man as well as with the heroic figures from the English past that he presents to the children of Pook's Hill. (Kipling's publication of *A History of England* in 1911 suggests how much England and Englishness was on Kipling's mind in the years that he turned out his Puck books.) For Kipling, Puck still identified a spirit of leveling embedded in the national culture.

CHAPTER TWO

Caliban's Masque

Drollery, Concupiscence, Creativity

Ben Jonson, presumably like many viewers and readers of *The Tempest* throughout
the seventeenth century, found Caliban disturbing. The source of the disturbance
was not, as criticism from the Romantics onward would suggest, Caliban's colonial
or racial otherness; Caliban's fault, rather, lay in his lack of verisimilitude:

> If there bee neuer a *Seruant-monster* i'the *Fayre*; who can helpe it? he sayes; nor nest
> of *Antiques*? Hee is loth to make Nature afraid in his *Playes*, like those that beget
> *Tales, Tempests*, and such like *Drolleries*, to mixe his head with other mens heeles,
> let the concupiscence of *Iigges* and *Dances* raigne as strong as it will amongst you;
> yet if the *Puppets* will please any body, they shall be entreated to come in.[1]

"Servant-monster" is the term applied to Caliban by Stephano: "servant-monster,
drink to me" (III.ii.3). Caliban's unnaturalness in the "Induction" to *Bartholomew
Fair* (1614) is the central example of Jonson's own distinction from Shakespeare, who
represents a generalized monstrosity of improbable and crowd-pleasing theatrical
practices without the warrant of verisimilitude or classical myth. As a character,
Caliban seems to embody the entire domain of improbable "tales" and "drolleries"
Jonson associates with late Shakespearean entertainments.

More than sixty years later, in his Preface to his adaptation of *Troilus and Cressida*
(1679), Dryden remained apprehensive about the relation of Caliban to nature:

> To return once more to *Shakespear*; no man ever drew so many characters, or
> generally distinguished 'em better from one another, excepting only *Johnson*. I will
> instance but in one, to show the copiousness of his Invention; it is that of *Caliban*,
> or the Monster, in the *Tempest*. He seems there to have created a person which
> was not in Nature, a boldness which, at first sight, would appear intolerable: for
> he makes him a Species of himself, begotten by an Incubus on a Witch; but this

as I have elsewhere prov'd, is not wholly beyond the bounds of credibility, at least the vulgar still believe it.[2]

Shakespeare, moreover, has naturalized Caliban's monstrosity. He

> has most judiciously furnish'd him with a person, a Language, and a character, which will suit him, both by Fathers and Mothers side: he has all the discontents, and malice of a Witch, and of a Devil; besides a convenient proportion of the deadly sins. . . . His person is monstrous, as he is the product of unnatural Lust; and his language is as hobgoblin as his person: in all things he is distinguish'd from other mortals.[3]

Jonson's accusation of pandering concupiscence becomes fertile copiousness, but not without some critical anxiety: Dryden's use of the verb "create," applied to a literary production for perhaps the first time in the history of the English language, measures what is for him Shakespearean audacity.[4]

If Dryden remains ambivalent about this aspect of Shakespeare's artistry, we can recognize it retrospectively as a key conceptual turning point in the transformation of Shakespeare into the central example of imaginative genius in the English language. For Addison in *The Spectator*, "It shews a greater Genius in *Shakespear* to have drawn his *Calyban*, than his *Hotspur* or *Julius Caesar*. The one was to be supplied out of his own Imagination, whereas the other might have been formed upon Tradition, History, and Observation."[5] Despite the very different value they assign to the creation of Caliban, Jonson and Addison share a sense of the close association between Caliban and the distinctiveness of Shakespeare's art, whether that art is mere drollery or a work of imaginative genius. For Addison, artistic creation implies imaginative control in terms that we largely retain: the more fully fictive the character the greater the originality. Prospero's control of Caliban in the play can thus easily come to represent the controlling genius of Shakespeare outside the play.

Joseph Warton elaborated Addison's "Genius" as "creative power," the precursor of the modern "creativity," in his essay on *The Tempest* for *The Adventurer* (1753):

> Of all the plays of Shakespeare, *The Tempest* is the most striking instance of his creative power. He has there given the reins to his boundless imagination, and has carried the romantic, the wonderful, and the wild, to the most pleasing extravagance. The scene is a desolate island; and the characters the most new and singular that can well be conceived: a prince who practices magic, an attendant spirit, a monster the son of a witch, and a young lady who had been brought to this solitude in her infancy, and had never beheld a man except her father.[6]

Finally, William Hazlitt's *Characters of Shakespear's Plays* (1817) also took Caliban to be proof of Shakespeare's imaginative genius, but he also associates Caliban with natural sexuality, through a comparison to the god Pan:

> The character of Caliban is generally thought (and justly so) to be one of the author's masterpieces. It is not indeed pleasant to see this character on the stage any more than it is to see the god Pan personated there. But in itself it is one of the wildest and most abstracted of all Shakespear's characters, whose deformity whether of body or mind is redeemed by the power and truth of the imagination displayed in it.[7]

Hazlitt, moreover, proceeds to draw out the poetic and imaginative side of Caliban himself. Character and creator now seem to some extent bound together in a shared imaginative disposition.

Caliban seemed to many early commentators to lie outside the domain of poetic inspiration: ancient myth, romance, or popular belief. In this respect, he was even less recognizable than characters such as Oberon, Puck, and Titania, all of whom have familiar literary and popular sources. Logan Pearsall Smith long ago argued that originality came to include "not only the direct observation of Nature, but also the invention or creation of things (for the most part supernatural beings) which did not exist in Nature."[8] As originality increasingly became a positive virtue, so also the creativity in the production of Caliban was correspondingly highlighted as particularly original.

Caliban, unlike Ariel, is not a Shakespearean fairy, but Caliban, as we have already seen, is the more consequential figure for the history of the creative imagination. Jonson's remarks suggest some of the connections between Caliban and what came to be called the fairy way of writing, which, when first articulated by Dryden, implied any form of writing that relied on the "Force of the Imagination" rather than the representation of fairies in particular.[9] When Dryden calls Caliban's language "hobgoblin," Caliban momentarily enters the orbit of Puck. Criticism of the eighteenth century and Romanticism, moreover, frequently coupled *A Midsummer Night's Dream* and *The Tempest* as Shakespeare's most imaginative dramas. I wish to renew this association of the two plays in order to elicit some important connections between fantasy, sexuality, originality, and imagination in the longer story of Shakespearean fantasy and its legacy in the modern literary system.

Jonson and Shakespeare

Jonson, as we have already seen, read Caliban as the mark of a larger artistic weakness, a pandering to the theatrical public reflected in Jonson's recollection of Caliban as the "servant-monster." (His "Induction" attempts to avoid such servitude in its elaborate contract with the audience.) Audiences, then, presumably enjoyed the spectacle of Caliban, and Jonson took the opportunity to reduce late Shakespearean theater to a grab bag of comic illusions and tricks: "drolleries." It seems to me, however, that Hugh Craig asks exactly the right question about Jonson's invocation of Caliban in his Induction: "Why does Caliban awaken such scorn in Jonson, given his penchant for deformed quasi-human characters?"[10] Caliban bears some relationship to the Jonsonian antimasque, as Ernest R. Gilman has argued. Gilman takes this resemblance to mean that Shakespeare inverts the Jonsonian masque, placing the antimasque, the arrival of Caliban and his cohorts, significantly after the masque itself.[11] Certainly, Prospero undergoes a quite noticeable change in disposition after the sudden dissolution of the masque, experiencing himself for the first time as old and weak: "Bear with my weakness, my old brain is troubled" (IV.i.159). David Bevington and Stephen Orgel, in recent essays sensitive to the history of the Jacobean masque, have extended the detachment of Prospero's masque from the question of Shakespearean authority. Bevington understands Shakespeare's masque as the diminishment of the masque as a form rather than its enhancement in the hands of the magus-author Shakespeare. Shakespeare stages the masque for a paying audience only in order to finally return to the collaborative space of the public theatre, with Prospero asking for the applause of the audience in the epilogue. Orgel notices, almost in passing, the Jonsonian quality of Prospero's renunciation of magic, itself readily adapted from Ovid's Medea: "This is a Jonsonian moment in Shakespeare, the invocation of a classic text to establish the authority of the fiction, to strike the audience with a shock of recognition, to place the drama in the context not of ephemeral performance, but of the history of poetry."[12]

If Prospero carries the ambience of Jonsonian authority, are we then to assume that Caliban's "antimasque" figures the somewhat more chaotic conditions of Shakespeare's own public theater? Although at first glance this seems implausible, given the elaboration of Caliban's character throughout the play, it is somewhat more in line with Jonson's later response to *The Tempest*. At about the time of *The Tempest*, moreover, Jonson was using the both the masque and the public theater as forms of commentary on Shakespearean fairy theater, making it more likely that Shakespeare was responding on the public stage. Jonson's *Oberon, The Fairy Prince* was performed at court on January 1, 1611, ten months before the first recorded performance of *The Tempest*, also at court, November 1, 1611. Robin Goodfellow, Shakespeare's Puck, played the central role in Jonson's masque, *Love Restored*, on Twelfth Night, January 6, 1612.[13] Jonson's 1611 entry for the public theater, *The*

Alchemist, meanwhile, revolves around the scam of presenting the "Queen of Fairy," played by the prostitute Doll Common, to credulous Londoners.

The name "Oberon" itself locates the first of these productions in the moonlit world of *A Midsummer Night's Dream*. *Oberon* is set at night, and the rising moon with which the masque begins invokes the world of Shakespeare's *Dream*, where it is as omnipresent as it is in Jonson's masque. Apart from the political context for the moon—where it stands for the powerful and radiant but still secondary (with regard to his father) qualities of Prince Henry—the moon is also Shakespearean "fancy," where it is also radiant, if still subordinate to the (Jonsonian) sun. "In *Oberon*," Orgel remarks, "Jonson first fully conceives of the transition from anti-masque to revels as the ordering and redirecting of a vital energy that is both essential and good."[14] This might have also suited Jonson's relationship to a Shakespearean "energy" about which the masque appears to have considerable ambivalence, associating the moonlit erotic topsy-turvydom of *A Midsummer Night's Dream* with the same "concupiscence" for which he later scolds *The Tempest* and other Shakespearean tragi-comedies.

The satyrs of Jonson's masque, like Comus in Milton's later confrontation with Shakespearean influence, seem to have absorbed *A Midsummer Night's Dream* as the dream of erotic license, which they insistently project onto the moon herself. In Milton's masque (performed 1634), the "light fantastic round" of Comus' followers appears to be sponsored by a Shakespearean moon that unites the world of *Dream* and *The Tempest*:

> The Sounds and Seas with all their finny drove
> Now to the Moon in wavering Morris move,
> And on the Tawny Sands and Shelves
> Trip the pert Fairies and the dapper Elves;
> By dimpled Brook and Fountain brim,
> The Wood-Nymphs deckt with Daisies trim,
> The merry wakes and pastimes keep
> What hath night to do with sleep?[15]

In Jonson's masque, Silenus rebukes the satyrs for their inability to associate the moon and its annunciation of Oberon as anything more than further occasion for licentiousness:

> Chaster language! These are nights
> Solemn to the shining rites

Of the fairy prince and knights,
While the moon their orgies lights.   (37–40)

Jonson's note to "orgies" in the earlier *Hymenaei* insists on differentiating the term from its "abusive" association with the rites of Bacchus (516). The satyrs, however, are apparently happy to follow the "abusive" reading of the moon's role, considering the moon little more than the erotic opportunity presented by a maid and her "green sickness" (to be cured with the loss of virginity):

Now, my cunning lady, moon,
Can you leave the side so soon
    Of the boy [Endymion] you keep so hid?
Midwife June sure will say
This is not the proper way,
    Of your paleness to be rid.
But perhaps it is your grace
To wear sickness i' your face,
    That there might be wagers laid
    Still, by fools, you are a maid.   (186–95)

In the eyes of the satyrs, the moon feigns innocence—not an entirely unreasonable reading of the role of the moon in Shakespeare's *Dream*, which sponsors both romantic love and the vows of virginity.

Oberon (played by Prince Henry) and his "nation of fays" arrive at the end of this song and immediately assume their distance from its association of the moon with female sexuality. Still, in one of the songs, a fay warns the masquers to keep dancing. Failure to do so will show

    that you have no more worth
Than the coarse and country fairy
That doth haunt the hearth or dairy.   (333–35)

This appears to be Robin Goodfellow, the Puck and village hobgoblin, relegated to the outskirts of Jonson's masque. The more complicated formal relationship between masque and antimasque noted by Orgel also appears to bear on the relationship to Shakespearean theater enacted in the course of the masque. Its positive avatars—Oberon, the nation of fays—displace, but never in a complete fashion, the rougher magic of Shakespeare's night world.

Robin Goodfellow appears yet again in *Love Restored*, this time as a country character who attempts to crash the scene of a masque. He also, however, facilitates the central action of the masque: the revelation of Plutus (Mammon) who has disguised himself as Cupid. As a protest against the Puritan pressure that had forced James to limit expenditures on masques, Jonson appears more willing to enter into alliance with Robin's "rude good fellowship" (63) against the common enemy of the antitheatrical "hoarding" of resources and energies. Shakespeare's Puck stands as the principle of theatrical "expenditure," both financial and erotic. The masque remains careful to distinguish between its own "court sports" and Robin's "gambols o' the country" (48, 49), and the masque proper does not include Robin.

In the period around the appearance of *The Tempest*, Jonson used *A Midsummer Night's Dream* to position his own theatrical practice with regard to Shakespeare's "festive comedy," filtered particularly through the figure of Puck. The result is no simple dismissal of Shakespearean theater, but an attempt to incorporate it as a kind of junior partner into the norms of his own theater. If *The Tempest* is a response to Jonson, it is as nuanced as Jonson's appropriation of *A Midsummer Night's Dream*.[16] Indeed, it seems to have digested Jonsonian theater. *The Tempest*, unlike most Shakespearean plays, is classically correct in its observance of the unities, and Prospero's masque is Jonsonian.[17] The magisterial Prospero is, as Orgel suggests, in many ways more Jonsonian than Shakespearean. The hierarchal relationship between Prospero and Caliban, not to mention the equally hierarchical one of father and daughter, Prospero and Miranda, is bound up with the success of the masque. The masque stages the two forms of Prospero's authority as one: the properly constituted marriage of Miranda depends on the exclusion of Caliban's threatening sexuality. Prospero expresses a good deal more anxiety about this aspect of his authority—including the abrupt command, "Be more abstemious / Or else good night your vow" (IV.i.53–54), to the dalliance of Ferdinand and Miranda—than seems warranted by any apparent threat to his triumphant march to restoration.

Prospero's masque promises the restitution of pastoral golden time through the triumph over Venus and Cupid. Iris reports that their attempted "wanton charm" on the couple (perhaps the dalliance of a few lines previous) has been foiled, and both have retired from the field. Cupid in fact "has broke his arrows, / Swears he will shoot no more, but play with sparrows, / And be a boy right out" (IV.i.99–100). Marriage and fertility, Juno and Ceres, have effectively driven sexuality from the field, a curious event for a marriage masque. This hollowness at the core of the masque highlights the even more disconcerting situation of Miranda throughout the play. She effectively represents the evacuation of the independence of Shakespeare's earlier comic heroines, including that of Hermia and Helena in the *Dream*. Even her moments of apparent rebellion against her father are effectively part of Prospero's script. He is there unseen to oversee Miranda's daring proposal of marriage to Ferdinand: "Hence, bashful cunning, / And prompt me, plain and holy innocence! / I am your wife if you will marry me" (III.i.81–83). The frank desire of Miranda, who is no older than fifteen, here recalls that of the even younger Juliet. If, as we shall see, later versions of *The Tempest* amplified the play's invocation of a natural feminine sexuality, the masque seems to be designed to quash it.

Prospero's sudden recollection of Caliban's conspiracy and his immediate dissolution of his masque is the play's climacteric. "The threat . . . is less in the conspiracy itself," Orgel observes, "than in Prospero's forgetfulness of it: this is the first moment when the magician loses his awareness of the play's continuing action, and is in danger thereby of losing his control over it."[18] This relocates the interest of the moment to Prospero and to the toll exacted by his paternalistic control that is celebrated in the masque itself. The return of Caliban at this particular moment seems to exist primarily *for* Prospero: it is, as Richard P. Wheeler argues, a return of the repressed.[19]

Caliban is a plausible Early Modern precursor of the Freudian id—as the science fiction film, *Forbidden Planet* (1956), nicely intuited when it replaced Caliban with a "monster from the id"—and his return in the midst of Prospero's masque is nothing if not timely. Caliban represents at least partly what the masque temporarily succeeded in eliding; he is aligned with the masque's evocation of "dusky Dis" (Pluto) who has carried Proserpine away with the connivance of Venus and Cupid (IV.i.88–91).[20] *The Tempest* effectively stages the return of Caliban in terms not simply of sexuality but of Shakespearean theater itself: Caliban's co-conspirator, the seedy Trinculo, is a withered reminder of the great Shakespearean clowns. Never more than a shadow of the threat represented by Antonio and Sebastian, the conspirators nevertheless seem to have a considerably greater effect on Prospero himself. Their own instincts are the theatrical ones of the huckster, those which Jonson's Induction associates with Shakespeare himself. Trinculo's initial impulse is to put the Caliban on display in England (II.ii.27–30); Stephano imagines soon afterward making him a courtly present in Naples (II.ii.66–68).

Although Stephano and Trinculo are sidetracked by the effects of the masque—they come across the sumptuous apparel from the masque and fall into a reverie of courtly splendor—Prospero has already used the intimations of Caliban's arrival to announce his abandonment of theater. The language in which he ends his "revels" (court entertainments) evokes particularly masque-like effects as well as the famous allusion to The Globe: "The cloud-capped towers, the gorgeous palaces, / The solemn temples, the great globe itself" (IV.i.152–53). The abandonment of the masque is precipitous; it obviously continues to enchant, and the spirits who chase the conspirators away are also masque-like. What impels Prospero here is a return of the repressed material of Shakespearean theater in almost unrecognizable form.

This material, both erotic and dramatic, coalesces around a Caliban who can now appear as the return of an alienated version of festive comedy, including both Puck (as Dryden seems to have noticed in calling his language "hobgoblin") and Bottom of *A Midsummer Night's Dream*. Both Caliban and Bottom are highly imaginative characters associated with illicit desire. (Hazlitt celebrates the imaginative powers of both characters.) Caliban is partly a bestialized rendering of Bottom. As the name Bottom itself suggests, moreover, one form of that exaggeration would parallel the Renaissance discourse of sodomy: charming "bully Bottom" transformed into Caliban's more threatening "bully-monster" (V.i.258).[21] Repeatedly addressed by Stephano and Trinculo as "moon-calf," Caliban is likewise absorbed by them into English popular beliefs, which associated an aborted fetus with the sinister influence of the moon. In this also, Caliban seems to suggest a kind of monstrous version of Bottom, the Shakespearean mortal most completely under the influence of the moonlit world of the *Dream*.

Like Bottom before him, Caliban seems to threaten the collapse of the hierarchies regulated by aristocratic marriage. Caliban possesses a plausible claim to aristocratic status: possession of the island by inheritance from his mother Sycorax. (Prospero never really disputes this claim, and only denounces the character of Sycorax.) The play consciously juxtaposes Caliban's attempted rape of Miranda with the forced marriage of Claribel to the African "King" of Tunis. The audience learns of Claribel's marriage in the scene immediately after the revelation of Caliban's attempted rape; the extended first encounter between Miranda and Ferdinand provides the only real intervening material, as if to highlight the importance of the match in attempting to distance Miranda from Claribel. Generally associated with "earthy" sexuality, Caliban also resembles a noble blackguard like Cloten of *Cymbeline* and is thus closer to the system of aristocratic marriage than anyone in the play cares to admit.[22] Milton's Comus, with his "rout of monsters," is a perhaps surprising descendant of Caliban's condensation of decayed aristocracy, sexual license, and plebeian revolt.

Prospero's masque attempts to convert Shakespearean topsy-turvydom into a contradiction: antimasque, masque. The internal logic of the form requires the taming of festive release and its transformation into the grotesque: the effective containment of the Shakespearean by the Jonsonian. Prospero himself has the strongest experience of the uncanniness of Caliban's reappearance, producing his most vehement statement of Caliban's monstrosity:

A devil, a born devil, on whose nature
Nurture can never stick; on whom my pains,

Humanely taken, all, all lost, quite lost;
And as with his age his body uglier grows,
So his mind cankers.   (IV.i.188–92)

"The charge," Orgel points out in his gloss of the passage, "may be less straight-
forward than it appears: Prospero has just become conscious of his own advancing
age, and has expressed fears for his own mind." There remains, however, a remarkable—and largely undramatized—distance to travel between this demonization of
Caliban and the sudden recognition at the end of the play: "this thing of darkness
I / Acknowledge mine" (V.i.275–76).

The recognition is indirect, mediated by the renunciation of what is now ac-
knowledged as a form of "rough" or black magic in Prospero's valediction to magic:
"But this rough magic / I here abjure" (V.i.50–51). That speech begins with the invocation of Prospero's spirits:

Ye elves of hills, brooks, standing lakes, and groves,
And ye that on sands with printless foot
Do chase the ebbing Neptune, and do fly him
When he comes back; you demi-puppets that
By moonshine do the green sour ringlets make,
Whereof the ewe not bites; and you whose pastime
Is to make midnight mushrooms, that rejoice
To hear the solemn curfew. . . .   (V.i.33–40)

Although adapted from Medea's speech in Ovid's Metamorphoses, the spirits invoked here are recognizably the fairies of *A Midsummer Night's Dream*. They are, he
adds, "weak masters" (V.i.40)—"masters" in the sense of artisanal master-workers—
who have effectively been the lowly instruments of a regal magus. It is not, needless to say, a union shop, and the impish Puck of the earlier play is replaced by the
chastened Ariel of this play. It has, of course, been easy to identify this magus with
Shakespeare himself, and every aspect of Prospero's description of his "rough magic"
evokes Shakespearean theater: fairies, storms, ghosts. Prospero's authority, however,
is different in kind from Shakespeare's, as Orgel's comment on its "Jonsonian" quality has already reminded us.

G. Wilson Knight helps to identify this difference by placing Prospero, whom he
strongly identifies with Shakespeare and with the British character more generally,
in the context of the history of the British empire:

Great Britain has laboured at ocean-mastery; the "ocean" being both the actual
ocean and those oceanic instincts, or forces, within man which it so consistently

throughout the ages symbolizes. British colonization from the start went hand in hand with Puritanism; the early colonizers, not unlike Prospero, being impelled by political or religious tyrannies to follow their soul-cravings across the sea and there work out the controlled magic of personal integration.[23]

Knight provides insight into a Prospero who after all seems to anticipate so much of the character of British colonialism. Although Knight does not hesitate to associate this Prospero with Shakespeare, the "controlled magic of personal integration" is a radical—that is, singular—exercise of authority, Jonsonian rather than Shakespearean. It is strikingly different from the Prospero who appears in the epilogue to speak on behalf of the King's Men: a Prospero whose project "was to please" and who must ask the audience to "release me from my bands / With the help of your good hands" (V.i.327–28). Prospero's appearance in figurative bonds reverses his relationship with Caliban and Ariel (the latter set free as Prospero's last act in the play), not to mention just about everyone else in the play. In returning Prospero from the masque to the public theater, the play also releases those "weak masters" of Shakespearean theater. These include the Shakespearean Puck, who, as we have seen in the previous chapter, concludes the *Dream* on a considerably less chastened note than Prospero: "Give me your hands, if we be friends, / And Robin shall restore amends" (V.i.423–24). Puck impudently assumes the possible friendship of the "gentles" in his audience. Prospero, however, extraordinarily powerful throughout much of the play, emerges as a prisoner. The magus, it seems, is not Shakespeare's preferred form of theatrical magic. *The Tempest*, read through and against Jonson, represents a theatrical leveling of Jonsonian classical authority.

Natural Sexuality

Caliban's affiliation with Shakespearean "concupiscence" perhaps set the tone for some of the early revisions of *The Tempest*, which multiplied marriageable couples even as they consistently downplayed the relationship between Prospero and Caliban. "In Shakespeare's romances," remarks Walter Cohen, "the core family relationships are vertical" in distinction from the "horizontal" (fraternal) emphasis of other tragi-comedies from the period.[24] Revisions of the play could then be said to have "corrected" this Shakespearean anomaly.

John Fletcher and Philip Massinger appear to have effectively divided up the subplots of *The Tempest* in the early 1620s. David Norbrook notices that *The Double Marriage* (ca. 1621) evokes *The Tempest's* exiled duke and his daughter as central characters, and glorifies the tyrannicide of the King of Naples.[25] *The Sea Voyage* (ca. 1622), however, evinces no real dramatic interest in Sebastian, the paternal figure of the play—an echo of Prospero, but one who has nothing to rely on but the pity of the shipwrecked party of men—and instead elaborates the encounter between the shipwrecked party, largely male, and the previously shipwrecked women. The women have formed an Amazonian "commonwealth."[26] The younger women have begun to resent the chaste terms of this commonwealth, and much of the play is given over to an exploration of a natural female sexuality hinted at in *The Tempest*: the sexual desires of a woman, Clarinda, who has never seen a man. The rebellion of the other women against the authority of the matriarch, Rosella, splits the commonwealth around the question of Rosella's "liberty" (from men) against Hippolita and Crocale's insistence on the primacy of sexual desire:

> HIPPOLITA.   We must and will have men.
>
> CROCALE.   I or wee'l shake off all obedience.[27]

The terms of the female commonwealth, however, seem less harsh when we discover that on the adjacent island the larger part of the shipwrecked men propose to eat the "noble French virgin," Aminta: cannibalism as the trope of natural male sexuality.[28] The revelation that Sebastian is the long-lost husband of Rosella hastily resolves the largely female conflicts dramatized in the play. Those conflicts, however, are the only aspect of the play with dramatic resonance; the elimination of a central patriarchal figure allows for the exploration of alternatives to sexual subjection even if those alternatives are finally rejected as unworkable. Between *The Sea Voyage* and *The Double Marriage*, Fletcher and Massinger explore the contradictory possibilities inherent in Shakespeare's treatment of Prospero: opponent of a corrupt Italian (and indirectly Spanish) aristocratic rule and patriarchal absolutist on his own island. In this retrospective light, *The Tempest* emerges as an exotic test case for patriarchalism, the analogy between the authority of the monarch and that of the father, rather than its simple reaffirmation.

The Restoration stage characteristically diminished the political utopianism associated with *The Tempest*, but it simultaneously seems to have rejoiced in dismantling the authority of the father. The major adaptation of *The Tempest* in the seventeenth century was Dryden and William Davenant's *The Tempest, or the Enchanted Island* (1667). This production was successful enough to spawn a parodic version set in Bridewell, the workhouse prison for prostitutes, Thomas Duffett's *The Mock-Tempest; or, The Enchanted Castle* (1675), as well as Thomas Shadwell's operatic adaptation (1674). Dryden and Davenant's adaptation held the stage throughout the eighteenth century, only to be finally displaced by William Macready's reversion to the Shakespearean text in 1838. Dryden's preface to the printed edition of the play

(1670) points out the importance of *The Sea Voyage* in what he considered the essential nature of the emendation of Shakespeare:

> Those who have seen [Fletcher's] Sea-Voyage, may easily discern that it was a Copy of Shakespear's Tempest: the Storm, the desart Island, and the Woman who had never seen a Man, are all sufficient testimonies of it. . . . But Sir William D'avenant, as he was a man of quick and piercing imagination, soon found that somewhat might be added to the Design of Shakespear, of which neither Fletcher nor Suckling had ever thought: and therefore to put the last hand to it, he design'd the Counterpart to Shakespear's Plot, namely that of a Man who had never seen a Woman; that by this means those two Characters of Innocence and Love might the more illustrate and commend each other.[29]

Dryden considers the invention of Hippolito, foster-child of Prospero, to be the defining characteristic of his adaptation of *The Tempest*, allowing for an extended exploration of natural sexuality and the addition of a libertine masculine sexuality to complement Fletcher's emphasis on female sexuality. It is, as Michael Dobson has argued, an account of sexuality suited to the age of Baconian science, "its love scenes resembling a hybrid between a court masque and a carefully rigged Royal Society experiment."[30] Having discovered that one woman is good, as Katharine Maus nicely puts it, Hippolito "inductively reasons that if one is good, more are better."[31]

Dryden has little to say about the revisions to the characters of Prospero and Caliban, but it is fair to say that both poles of Shakespeare's hierarchical axis are effectively demoted in the adaptation. In the Davenant-Dryden adaptation, Prospero loses a good deal of his anxious irritability, quickly announcing his forgiveness of Antonio and Alonzo, themselves wracked with guilt. This evacuates Shakespeare's main plot of much of its interest, and Prospero is reduced to what Maus terms "the neurotic and domineering father of a farce."[32] His substantial action in the play switches to the love plot, where he plans to execute Ferdinand for the apparent death of Hippolito (when battling over the possession of Miranda) until Hippolito's miraculous recovery. In general, the play takes Prospero severely to task for his failure to provide his children and wards with a proper introduction to the ways of the world. Hippolito is almost killed because of his lack of training in swordplay; Dorinda, Miranda's more daring sister, wants to see a man precisely "because my Father has forbidden me" (II.iv.133).

If Prospero is an almost comically overweening father, Caliban dwindles to the status of pimp. Dryden and Davenant retain Prospero's denunciation of him for the attempted violation of Miranda, even heightening it by using the word "children" to imply assaults against both Miranda and Dorinda (I.ii.263–66). Caliban's criminality, however, is quickly drained of dramatic interest. He organizes no conspiracy against Prospero, does not even tell Stephano and Trinculo about the presence of Prospero on the island. The transformation, meanwhile, of Sycorax, the (dead) mother of Caliban in Shakespeare's *Tempest*, into Caliban's sister and sometime lover, makes Caliban a grotesque and even comic foil to the sexual pairings elsewhere emphasized in the play rather than a genuine challenge to Prospero. (Dynastic incest is, however, continuous with Caliban's debased aristocratic status in *The Tempest*.)

The Restoration *Tempest* subtly but firmly marginalizes both Caliban and Prospero; the vertical relationship that provides so much of the bristling energy in Shakespeare's *Tempest* is effectively cleared from the boards. Davenant and Dryden diminish the two characters representing the greatest threats to the "innocence" of the play's exploration of sexuality: Prospero's patriarchal control over the domain of sexuality and Caliban's sexual threat from below. Prospero's wedding masque, which in Shakespeare represents his attempt to regulate his daughter's sexuality, disappears altogether. In effect, the monstrous sexuality of Shakespeare's Caliban is regularized and generalized as the natural sexuality Prospero struggles vainly to control, to the point that Miranda's and Dorinda's initial speculations about men are based on a naïve incestuous desire not so distinct from Caliban's relationship to Sycorax. Prospero is cautious to raise Hippolito and his daughters with a sense of the dangerous monstrosity of the other sex. This borrows a motif from *The Sea Voyage*, where Rossella insists on men as "monsters" (II.ii.189). Hippolito, on the verge of meeting Dorinda for the first time, reflects that

> *Prospero* has often said that Nature makes
> Nothing in vain: why then are women made?
> Are they to suck the poison of the Earth,
> As gaudy colour'd Serpents are? I'le ask that
> Question, when next I see him.   (II.v.1–5)

These are lessons, the play insists, necessarily overcome along with both Prospero and Caliban. In the place of Jonson's "concupiscence," Shakespeare's authority now appears to sanction the discourse of a natural sexuality.

Maus observes that for Dryden "Shakespeare, not Prospero, is the ultimate patriarchalist authority figure, embodying the monarch, the father, the artist, and the magician all at once."[33] The prologue is the first instance in the critical tradition in which Prospero is conflated with his creator:

But *Shakespear*'s Magick could not copy'd be,
Within that Circle none durst walk but he.
I must confess 'twas bold, nor would you now,
That liberty to vulgar Wits allow,
Which works by Magick supernatural things:
But *Shakespear*'s pow'r is sacred as a King's.
Those Legends from old Priest-hood were receiv'd,
And he then writ, as people then believ'd.   (19–26)

Shakespeare's magic is regal, but it takes its power from Catholic belief, which the "people," if not Shakespeare himself, then believed. In place of Shakespearean magic, however, Dryden proposes a kind of experimental libertinism outside the playhouse. Hippolito was a "breeches" part—a male part played by an actress—and Dryden's prologue heavily promotes this as a source of erotic discovery:

And that's a transformation you will say
Exceeding all the Magick in the Play.
Let none expect in the last Act to find,
Her Sex transform'd from man to Woman-kind.
What e're she was before the Play began,
All you shall see of her is perfect man.
Or if your fancy will be farther led,
To find her Woman, it must be abed.   (31–38)

Sexual "experiment," might trump the old Catholic magic appropriated by Shakespeare. Duffet's parodic association of the play with the world of London's brothels in his *Mock-Tempest* is thus an astute reading of Dryden and Davenant's play. Samuel Pepys, however, insisted on the "innocence" of the play: "The house mighty full; the King and Court there: and the most innocent play that ever I saw." The sexual innocence of the younger characters, however, only enhances the sexual prurience of the play, something that Pepys surely would have relished.[34]

Dryden also uses the prologue to discuss the two playwrights, Jonson and Fletcher, he considers followers of Shakespeare. Fletcher, we have already seen, was for Dryden an important link to Shakespeare's *Tempest*, but Jonson's presence in the prologue is less immediately justified and more a matter of general theatrical criticism. The figurative terms of this criticism, however, are based on Dryden's work with the material in *The Tempest* and perhaps even Jonson's Induction to *Bartholomew Fair*:

Shakespeare, who (taught by none) did first impart
To *Fletcher* Wit, to labouring *Johnson* Art.
He Monarch-like gave those his subjects law,
And is that Nature which they paint and draw.
Fletcher reach'd that which on his heights did grow,
Whilst *Johnson* crept and gather'd all below.   (5–10)

If Jonson's Induction seems to identify Shakespeare's theater with Caliban, Dryden dramatically reverses the judgment: the "labouring" Jonson is himself *Shakespeare's* Caliban, condemned to collecting Shakespearean windfall.

Shakespeare and Jonson are the central figures of Dryden's theatrical criticism; it is hardly unusual for Dryden to evoke Jonson alongside Shakespeare. Still, it seems quite possible that the criticism of Jonson is particularly barbed here, a consciously belated salvo in the Elizabethan "poet's war" that included Jonson and Shakespeare. Dryden's own commentary on his adaptation of Shakespeare emphasizes the absolutism of imaginative genius, its magic clearly associated with Prospero, but his adaptation reduces the authority of Prospero himself. The misreading is a crucial and enormously productive one in the history of the reception of Shakespeare: Shakespeare becomes a *Jonsonian* author whose "concupiscence" is to some extent naturalized and absorbed into an account of sexuality.

Caliban, however, retained his association with a monstrous, antisocial sexuality even after the Dryden-Davenant *Tempest* had diminished his threatening power. More than sixty years after Dryden and Davenant's adaptation of the play, William Hogarth's early painting "A Scene from *The Tempest*" (ca. 1730–1735) is the first major painting of a Shakespearean scene (fig. 2.1). It inaugurates a tradition of the representation of the monstrous and supernatural, particularly with regard to Shakespearean drama, which, as we shall see in another chapter, British painting felt to be an appropriate site for staking its own claim to imaginative power. Hogarth clearly went back to the Shakespearean text, rather than the Dryden and Davenant adaptation, since his scene portrays the first encounter of Miranda and Ferdinand, which is not represented in the adaptation. Unlike the other figures in the painting, which, according to David Dabydeen, clearly harken back to the chestnuts of the Old Masters, Caliban "bears on him the stamp of Hogarth's originality, which is his mastery of the degraded form. . . . The dribble escaping Caliban's mouth is Hogarth's own relishing of his self-made creature. 'This thing of darkness I acknowledge mine,' he is saying with open fervour."[35] The strongest intuition in Dabydeen's reading of the painting is its suggestion of the mirroring in the desires of Miranda and Caliban. Both are shown spilling something: Miranda spilling the bowl of milk that

Fig. 2.1. William Hogarth, *A Scene from The Tempest (act I, scene II)*, ca. 1730–1735. Nostell Priory, The St Oswald Collection (acquired by the National Trust in 2002, with the help of the National Art-Collections Fund), © NTPL / John Hammond

she had been feeding a pet lamb (and thus abandoning a saintlike virginity devoted to the Lamb of God?) and Caliban drooling spittle from his mouth, which is shaped into a lascivious grin. In effect, then, Caliban becomes the spirit who presides over Miranda's sexual awakening, even as he also represents the monstrous possibilities of that awakening.

In the reception of *The Tempest*, the notion of an innocent sexuality, which is embedded in a new discourse of nature and the natural developing across the early modern period, is never fully distinguished from a monstrous sexuality. This conjunction lends itself to the development of an idea of human sexuality escaping from social determinations. (The conjunction of political, religious, and sexual freedoms in the libertine literature of the seventeenth century is another example of this phenomenon.) Ultimately, this becomes part of a modern sense of selfhood in which sexuality is no longer simply a behavior but a fundamental *identity*, the truth of which requires its own discourse.[36] The discourse of sexuality is ultimately conjoined to that of fantasy and the creative imagination, both of which are also thought to speak the truths of the self. We might, then, extend Hans Ulrich Gumbrecht's insight about love in the Early Modern literary system to the wilder terrain of sexuality. Love after courtly love, writes Gumbrecht, becomes "a general metaphor for any kind of attempt to evade social determination." With Corneille, Gumbrecht later adds, "the semantics of the literary system nourishes itself in the first instance on the semantics of love."[37] Sexuality is the intensified and sometimes threatening elaboration of love, just as fantasy, by the end of the eighteenth century, comes to be the intensified version of the creative imagination. In this respect, the early elaboration of the character Caliban, both as Shakespeare's fantastic creation and avatar of antisocial sexuality, is a kind of preparatory study for the fuller integration of fantasy and sexuality that will characterize the Romantic period examined in the fourth and fifth chapters.

CHAPTER THREE

The Fairy Way of Writing

John Dryden has given us the phrase "that Fairy kind of writing," which, after it was taken up as "the fairy way of writing" by Joseph Addison in his essays "The Pleasures of the Imagination," became a familiar part of English literary criticism for more than two hundred years. In effect, the phrase served to name not a new form of writing but a new conceptual basis for what we might call fantasy fictions. This kind of writing was no longer to be classified solely along with what Michael McKeon has called the "ancient and equivocal whole of 'fiction.'"[1] Instead, probable fictions were separated from the old, "false" fictions, randomly scattered through both the vernacular texts and even the myths and legends of the ancient classics (although the latter were sanctioned by the authority of the classical literatures). This was a crucial and consequential division for the modern concept of literature. If this division produced the terms in which the novel would eventually thrive, it also charged the fairy way of writing with the conceptualization of the power of the creative imagination bound within a literary system organized as national literatures.

The "ancient and equivocal whole of 'fiction'" increasingly troubled seventeenth-century thinking about literature, particularly in the moments when poetic fictions intersected with religious truths. This is clear enough in Andrew Marvell's initial anxiety, recorded in his commendatory poem to the 1674 edition of *Paradise Lost*, that Milton's poem might "ruin (for I saw him strong) / The sacred truths to fable and old song."[2] Milton's particular religious beliefs were indeed controversial, but Marvell would have been reasonably sympathetic to them. Somewhere in the background, however, lies another concern: the gnawing suspicion that sacred truths were already too much like the old fables. This heightened the need to quarantine religious truth from fiction, especially supernatural fiction, and that separation, explicitly designed to protect religion, contributed to the "secularization" of inspiration as a poetic quality. Even before the publication of *Paradise Lost*, Thomas Hobbes' "Answer to Davenant's Preface to *Gondibert*" (1650) connected

poetic claims to inspiration with the religious controversies of the Civil War and In-
terregnum, a period dominated by "unskillful Divines" who promoted "*Controversie*
instead of *Religion*." Divine machinery, meanwhile, whether classical or Christian,
had increasingly become an embarrassment:

> But why a Christian should think it an ornament to his Poem, either to profane
> the true God or invoke a false one, I can imagin no cause but a reasonless imita-
> tion of Custom, of a foolish custome, by which a man, enabled to speak wisely
> from the principles of nature and his own meditation, loves rather to be thought
> to speak by inspiration, like a Bagpipe.[3]

Hobbes associates inspiration with "enthusiasm," the claim to divine inspiration
on the part of Protestant sectarians, which continued to be associated with late
Stuart dissenting religious culture into the eighteenth century. In the same period,
however, circumscribed poetic enthusiasm emerged as a secularized form of the creative imagination. Dryden's essay, "Of Heroique Playes," appended to *The Conquest
of Granada* (1672), insisted that the canonical writers, including Spenser, could not
"have form'd their Poems half so beautiful, without those Gods and Spirits, and
those Enthusiastic parts of Poetry, which compose the most noble parts of all their
writings." The "Heroick Poet," continues Dryden, "is not ty'd to a bare representation of what is true, or exceeding probable: but that he may let himself loose to visionary objects, and to the representation of such things, as depending not on sence,
and therefore not to be comprehended by knowledge, may give him a freer scope for
the imagination."[4] Anthony Ashley Cooper, Third Earl of Shaftesbury, confirmed
Dryden's appropriation of enthusiasm for poetry in "A Letter Concerning Enthusiasm" (1707), which is sympathetic to "visionary fancy" and "the innocent kind of
fanaticism" that is the province of poets, both of which are properly reticent about
their truth claims.[5] The epistemological uncertainty of inspiration did not render
it unproductive; instead enthusiasm, insofar as it was understood as a poetic rather
than religious spirit, was increasingly embraced by the criticism of the period.

The devolution of vatic inspiration into poetic enthusiasm allowed the emergent discourse of aesthetics to claim poetic fictions and fancies as objects of secular
knowledge. The claim to inspiration, and the elevated truth claims that went along
with it, were never entirely abandoned by modern aesthetics; they of course remain
part of our own discourse about literature. On the other hand, inspiration no longer
needed to come from heaven. Indeed, part of the sea change that followed from
the emergent discourse of the New Science and Locke's epistemology was the very
strong sense that poetry no longer needed to look above itself for inspiration, but
rather, *around* itself, in the empirical domain of observation and experience.

The convergence of these two factors was the crucial background to the eighteenth-century formulation of the fairy way of writing as a form of writing with its own aesthetic rules. By the time of the Romantics, this aesthetic domain was increasingly tempted to distinguish itself from scientific knowledge.[6] As we shall see, however, the fairy way of writing was in other respects strongly suited to empiricism, at least in the form of the empirical observation of the superstitions of the common people. In William Collins' poem, *An Ode on the Popular Superstitions of the Highlands Considered as the Subject of Poetry* (ca. 1749–1750), the fairy way of writing had effectively become a form of poetic ethnography rather than a species of pure fantasy, now grounded in the observation of the "popular" and ultimately the "national spirit."

Poetic License

From an early stage in Dryden's career, Shakespeare was the occasion for significant revisions of developing Neoclassical critical precepts, complicating the reception of French Neoclassicism in England. In the *Essay of Dramatick Poesy* (1668), Neander admits Shakespeare's irregularity, but also commends his "comprehensive soul."[7] Dryden was already experimenting with a model of criticism located in the person of the writer (his soul) rather than textual adherence to external rules or examples. In the previous year, Dryden's praise of Shakespeare in the prologue to his own adaptation of *The Tempest*, linked Shakespeare's *personal* power, as poetic monarch, to a supernatural subject matter that now apparently requires some kind of defense:

I must confess 'twas bold, nor would you now,

That liberty to vulgar Wits allow,

Which works by Magick supernatural things:

But *Shakespear*'s pow'r is sacred as a King's.

Those Legends from old Priest-hood were receiv'd,

And he then writ, as people then believ'd.[8]

If Shakespeare is a monarch, his subject matter remains associated with Catholicism (the "old Priest-hood") and history: "he then writ, as people then believ'd." Historical consciousness, as well as poetic power, complicates the application of strict decorum to Shakespeare's subject matter.

By the time of his publication of "The Author's Apology for Heroic Poetry and Poetic Licence," which he appended to his unstaged version of Milton's *Paradise Lost, The State of Innocence* (1677), Dryden had read Nicolas Boileau's translation of Longinus, and this no doubt inflected his understanding of the time-honored concept of *licentia poetica*, the poetic practice of giving new twists to old plots and narrative motifs. The task of adapting *Paradise Lost* for the stage could now have appeared to Dryden as a problem of adapting a sublime text for a context, the theater, which did not seem a ready vehicle for the sublime—or indeed for sacred truth. Later critics, in fact, have consistently condemned *The State of Innocence* for its banalization of Milton, but the theatrical "de-sublimation" of the master text perhaps usefully intersected with a new understanding of the possibilities of poetic license: the replacement of Milton's own claims to inspiration with something more proximate to what we would call literary imagination.[9] In this later emendation of poetic license, Dryden maintains the standard of imitation, but now applied to something as ephemeral as "other mens fancies" and modified by the appeal to poetic "liberty":

> Poets may be allow'd the . . . liberty, for describing things which really exist not,
> if they are founded on popular belief: of this nature are Fairies, Pigmies, and the
> extraordinary effects of Magick: for 'tis still an imitation, though of other mens
> fancies: and thus are *Shakespeare's Tempest*, his *Midsummer Night's Dream*, and
> *Ben. Johnson's Masque of Witches* to be defended.[10]

That mental state that Dryden proposes for imitation appears to be simply superstitious and "popular," unmoored from the faculty of judgment or the direction of true religion. In theatrical terms, it takes Dryden away from epic and toward the theater of Shakespeare and Jonson. Unlike Milton, who had famously claimed the blank verse of his epic as "ancient liberty recover'd to heroic Poem from the troublesome and modern bondage of Riming," Dryden gives poetic license an aristocratic birthright rather than republican virtue.[11] Poetic license is "that Birthright which is deriv'd to us from our great Forefathers, even from *Homer* down to *Ben.* and they who would deny it to us, have, in plain terms, the Foxes quarrel to the Grapes; they cannot reach it."[12] Dryden has significantly reformulated poetic license as a domain simultaneously aristocratic (the poet-monarch) and popular (subject matter).

"Force of Imagination"

By the time of Dryden's semiopera, *King Arthur* (1691), with the gorgeous music of Henry Purcell, imagination had begun to displace poetic license in Dryden's critical vocabulary. His dedicatory letter, to George Savile, Marquis of Halifax, offered a tribute to his "first and best Patroness the Dutchess of *Monmouth*," who Dryden names as one of the first readers of the text (begun as early as 1684). Dryden speculates that "the parts of the Airy and Earthy Spirits, and that Fairy kind of writing, which depends only upon the Force of Imagination, were the Grounds of her liking the Poem."[13] Dryden's association of the project with a female reader is perhaps an important one in the context of the pervasive association of tales of spirits with female and oral traditions, even if the Duchess of Monmouth hardly qualified as a woman to be associated with the world of popular superstition. Dryden probably saw the drama in the tradition of both *The Tempest* and *Comus*. His airy and earthy spirits, Philidel and Grimbald, seem to roughly correspond to Ariel and Caliban, and, after the drama's conciliation of the Britons and the Saxons, Comus himself enters the stage along with three peasants in a harvest home that celebrates both Old England and the peasants' ability to cheat the parson out of his tithe (an aspect of the drama that later enraged Jeremy Collier).

Michel de Montaigne's essay, "Of the Force of the Imagination," famously catalogued instances of the marvelous and magical that the imagination has been said to produce. Aphra Behn had written, but not printed, a tale entitled, *The Dumb Virgin, or the Force of the Imagination* in the late 1680s, in which love and fancy had the capacity to make the dumb speak. Philosophers, however, borrowed Montaigne's phrase in the interest of dismantling such tales as the effect of error. Nicolas Malebranche had used Montaigne's phrase to denounce the belief in sorcery in his *De la recherche de la vérité* (1674–1675). In the context of conventional faculty psychology, Malebranche ascribed accounts of sorcery partly to the simple desire to come up with gripping tales. As Jean-Paul Sermain has written of Malebranche's account, "Le plaisir de conter est le père de l'erreur" ("The pleasure of tale-telling is the father of error").[14]

Both Pierre Bayle and Bernard de Fontenelle continued this line of attack in France. In England, the Baconian tradition had long associated discredited or uncertain marvels with the effects of the imagination. Reviewing stories about corpses bleeding anew in the presence of their murderers, his comment seems to dismiss the imagination from its central, if subordinate, status in medieval faculty psychology: "It may be, that this participateth of a miracle, by God's just judgment, who usually bringeth murders to light: but if it be natural, it must be referred to imagination."[15] Baconian science often downgraded imagination to a source of deceit; it is where the old, false miracles go to die. John Spencer's *A Discourse concerning Prodigies* (1665), follows both Bacon and Robert Burton's *Anatomy of Melancholy* (1621) in lumping together imagination with "*Superstition, Melancholy, natural weakness of sight, softness of imagination*" as well as other infirmities.[16] Melancholy and imagination, qualities increasingly associated with the poet and the artist in the Early Modern period, are here simply assigned to the same domain as popular superstition.[17]

John Locke was also concerned with such errors, but less interested in their sources than in their effectiveness once they have been lodged in the mind. The pedagogical program, *Some Thoughts Concerning Education*, first printed in 1693 (and thereafter widely reprinted throughout the eighteenth century), transforms

Locke's more general approach to the problems occasioned by the association of ideas into a general pedagogical principle:

> Always whilst he is Young, be sure to preserve his tender Mind from all Impressions and Notions of *Spirits* and *Goblings*, or any fearful Apprehensions in the dark. This he will be in danger of from the indiscretion of Servants, whose usual Method is to awe Children, and keep them in subjection, by telling them of *Raw-Head* and *Bloody Bones*, and such other Names, as carry with them the Ideas of some thing terrible and hurtful, which they have reason to be afraid of, when alone, especially in the dark. . . . And there is stamped upon their Imaginations Ideas, that follow them with Terror and Affrightment: Such *Bug-bear* Thoughts once got into the tender Minds of Children, and being set on with a strong impression, from the Dread that accompanies such Apprehensions, sink deep, and fasten themselves so as not easily, if ever, to be got out again. . . . [18]

Locke has no sense here of a fairy way of writing operating at one remove from popular world. The stories that concern him are effectively old wives' tales in oral circulation, and, for precisely that reason, readily available to children. The link between imagination and superstition remains a powerful one. Locke identifies the power of such stories in their perdurability: they are not to be readily dislodged by reasoning. For this very reason, however, they are all the more dangerous to his pedagogical system. In this, however, Locke was not entirely breaking new ground. Adam Fox has demonstrated the extent to which Locke's hostility to superstitious influence from servants, as well as his fear of its long-lasting effects on children, was in fact widely shared in the educational theories of the sixteenth and seventeenth centuries. [19]

The problem of folk superstition in Locke also suggests something of the imaginative power of the mind in Locke's epistemology. The discovery of the untruth of an old wives' tale does not simply eliminate it from the mind. Locke's work on the association of ideas is partly about errors, but it shows just how powerful the imaginative force of error can be. Since, moreover, Locke's epistemology allowed for a greater role of the imagination in the formation of complex ideas, whether true or false, imagination was no longer understood as completely subordinate to judgment. [20] Ultimately, Locke would provide the basis for a positive revaluation of the role of the imagination, one which perhaps began as early as Gottfried Wilhelm Leibniz's *Nouveaux essays*, an early attack on Locke (withdrawn from publication upon Locke's death in 1704, and first published in 1765). Leibniz proposes a more active model of the mind to counter what he took to be Locke's tabula rasa: "*la puis-sance active*" is the central force of the mind, which is "the one creative, building, and productive power of the mind—the imagination."[21]

There was, moreover, another aspect of Locke's educational program that worked against the explicit denigration of popular tales. Like other educational reformers— including Milton, John Evelyn, and John Aubrey—Locke also de-emphasized Latin as the linguistic barrier between the "mother tongue" and the language of learning. Although Locke separated knowledge from folk superstition, a door had been par-tially opened, and the eighteenth century saw the massive influx of children's tales that, following Lockean principles, provided moral instruction rather than mere terror.[22] Since Locke's own philosophy emphasized the power of first impressions on the mind, it was considered no doubt better to replace sprites and goblins with positive moral examples.

Fables "out of Dores"

If Leibniz and others, including Addison, began to qualify Lockean epistemol-ogy with a fuller account of the imagination, Locke's contemporary, John Aubrey (1626–1697) was one of the first to dissent from the complete dismissal of popular superstition as without value. Although Aubrey himself long suffered from a post-humous reputation for "credulity," his researches into the occult were at least partly anthropological, and conceived as topics opened up by the Royal Society's interest in empirical phenomenon.[23] Aubrey was an early member, and remained consistently committed to its projects throughout his life.[24] *Remaines of Gentilisme and Judaisme*, which was not published until 1881, attempts to link English popular customs with those of Roman antiquity. Aubrey is among the first observers to account for such practices without attacking them.[25] The headnote to *Remaines* is thus remarkable in the history of scholarship for its early openness to the interest of superstitious beliefs:

> Old customes, and old wives-fables are grosse things: but yet ought not to be quite rejected: there may some truth and usefulnesse be elicited out of them: besides 'tis a pleasure to consider the Errours that enveloped former ages: as also the present.[26]

The rubric of the "remains" of gentilism allows Aubrey wide latitude in his treat-ment of English fairies and hobgoblins. Robin Goodfellow becomes, as Thomas Nashe had anticipated, a descendant of the fauns and satyrs. "From him [Faunus] ('tis likely) comes our Robin-goodfellow."[27] Reputable men are consulted about possible incidents involving fairies and Robin Goodfellow, and classical precedent is folded into such testimony:

> *Ho, ho, ho,* of Robin Goodfellow. Memorandum: Vergil speakes somewhere (I thinke in the *Georgiques*) of Voyces heard louder than a Man's. Mr. Lancelot Morehouse did averre to me, *super verbum sacerdotis,* that he did once heare such a lowd Laugh on the other side of a hedge, and was sure that no Human voice could afford such Laugh.[28]

Speculation about Robin Goodfellow and his Roman ancestry turns dangerously to the relationship of the goatish satyrs and the Christian representation of Satan in goatlike form. Aubrey appears to accept Sir Thomas Browne's account of the connection between Satan and satyrs, but offers no comment on how this potential common ancestry of Satan and Robin Goodfellow might inflect one's assessment of Robin. No denunciation of a satanic Robin ensues.

Aubrey is perhaps the first thinker explicitly to connect the disappearance of the superstitious world of popular culture with the advent of print, putting him at the head of the line of scholars and collectors from the eighteenth century onward who considered themselves to be rescuing an oral culture on the verge of disappearance:

> Before Printing, Old-wives Tales were ingeniose: and since Printing came in fashion, till a little before the Civil-warres, the ordinary sort of People were not taught to reade: now-a-days Books are common, and most of the poor people understand letters: and the many good Bookes, and variety of Turnes of Affairs, have put all the old Fables out of dores: and the divine art of Printing and Gunpowder have frighted away Robin-good-fellow and the Fayries.[29]

"The popular culture of the years around 1800," writes Peter Burke, "was found just in time, or so the discoverers thought. The theme of a vanishing culture which must be recorded before it is too late recurs in their writings, making them reminiscent of the concern with disappearing tribal societies today."[30] Aubrey is a precocious example, by about a century, of this new attitude toward popular culture. Locke's stricture against the exposure of children to old wives' tales, meanwhile, was an important example of what Burke calls the "withdrawal of the upper classes" from a popular culture that had once been widely shared by both the illiterate and the elite.[31] The ironic result of this withdrawal, as Burke notes, was the "rediscovery" of the people "as something exotic and therefore interesting."[32] Every aspect of this process was played out rapidly in England, as Burke notes, and Aubrey thus emerges as one of the first European intellectuals to engage in the recovery of a popular world thought to be waning. This popular world would, in the eighteenth century, increasingly be conflated with national value. Before literacy, according to Aubrey, the old tales were "ingeniose" (native) to the common people. With the radical transformation of the word "genius" from an external spirit (of a place or person) to an internalized power, the old fables would come to represent the "genius" of the people, sometimes working in tandem with a particular individual "genius" or national author. Aubrey represents the shift from the haphazard recovery of popular beliefs, or their specific use in the fairy way of writing, to the sense of folklore as a positive project in itself. In this respect, ironically, the old fables have also been turned "out of dores": they no longer belong only to the hearths of the simple.

"Nothing but a History of Fiction"

If Locke seems to have inadvertently opened the door to a concept of the creative imagination at the center of empirical epistemology, it remained to Jeremy Collier to force, equally inadvertently, the explicit disentanglement of the literary imagination from the truths of religion. In fact, the phrase, the "fairy way of writing" (altered from Dryden's phrase, "that fairy kind of writing") really enters literary history through Collier's notorious attack on the English stage, *A Short View of the Immorality and Profaneness of the English Stage* (1698), rather than from Dryden himself. (Addison used Collier's phrase rather than Dryden's.) According to Collier, Dryden's *King Arthur* treated matters of sacred truth as no more than fairy belief, and he thus repeatedly lights with outraged fury upon the phrase "the fairy way of writing" as proof:

> And why are Truth and Fiction, Heathenism and Christianity, the most Serious and the most Trifling Things blended together, and thrown into one Form of Diversion? Why is all this done unless it be to ridicule the whole, and make one as incredible as the other? His *Airy* and *Earthy Spirits* discourse of the first state of Devils, of their *Chief* of their Revolt, their Punishment, and Impostures. This Mr. *Dryden* very Religiously calls a *Fairy way of Writing, which depends only on the Force of Imagination.* What then is the Fall of the Angels a Romance? Has it no basis of Truth, nothing to support it, but strength of Fancy and Poetic Invention?[33]

It is difficult for a modern reader to take Collier's attack very seriously, but Collier is perhaps the finest critic, of the very few, that the play has ever produced. *King Arthur* largely continues a secular tradition of magic that can claim Shakespeare, Spenser, and Arthurian romance. However, the spirits, Philidel and Grimbald, also embody elements of Christian theology. They are devils and fallen angels—Philidel with some hope of redemption through his actions—and thus mix elements of Milton's *Paradise Lost* with Shakespeare's *Tempest*.[34]

For Collier, the tincture of Christian truth admitted to the domain of fairy reduces divine truths to the status of mere fiction: "So that notwithstanding the Boldness of this *Opera*, there may be such a Place as Hell; And if so, a Discourse about Devils, will be no *Fairy way of Writing*. For a *Fairy way of Writing*, is nothing but a *History of Fiction*; A subject of Imaginary Beings; such as never had any existence in Time, or Nature."[35] The repetition of the phrase "the Fairy way of Writing" probably cemented the association of this form with fiction in the sense of the merely imaginary, without any foundation in empirical fact or religious truth.

Michael McKeon has recently argued that Collier's attack on the immorality of the actions represented on the English stage produced, in response, the explicit separation of the evaluation of dramatic characters from the evaluation of the author.[36] In a parallel sense, the tacit distinction between falsehood and fiction was already in place by the time of Spenser and Shakespeare, and Dryden simply takes this for granted. Collier, however, obviously felt that Dryden was intolerably cavalier in his careless juxtaposition of false fairies and Christian truths, an equation that, for Collier, simply collapsed religious truth into the domain of superstition. Dryden's recent conversion to Catholicism probably only confirmed Collier's worst fears about the consequences of this potential commensurability of fairy fiction, already closely linked to Catholic superstition, and religious truth. From the vantage of a modern reader, Collier is doing little more than catching Dryden out in a minor inconsistency, but he sees, perhaps more fully than a modern reader, how much Dryden has asserted what McKeon calls "the aesthetic mode of truth" in terms that appear to marginalize, or even to replace, religious truth. What we can only conceive as the obtuseness of Collier is historically part of the construction of the aesthetic from the separation of fiction from falsehood. In this sense, then, the fairy way of writing helped to force the emergence of the aesthetic in England because of its double estrangement from truth claims: aligned with neither empirical actuality nor religious truth, neither modern (novelistic) fiction nor inspiration. "Nothing to support it, but strength of Fancy and Poetic Invention," as Collier plaintively put it in his attack on Dryden. The final effect of this estrangement, however, was to link fantasy firmly to the idea of the creative imagination, which would eventually emerge as central to the modern concept of literature.

The Pleasures of the Imagination: Literature as Pastoral

Collier's attack on Dryden, along with Locke's empirical epistemology, looms in the background of Addison's *Spectator* papers on the "Pleasures of the Imagination," a watershed in the history of aesthetics and literary criticism. Beginning with Lockean premises, Addison overturns the Baconian marginalization of the imagination that Locke had in some respects continued. The imagination possesses, in Addison's account, its own autonomous legitimacy beyond any reference to sacred truth or empirical actuality. The largely negative account of the imagination in early modern science thus made possible the "aestheticization" of the imagination in the eighteenth century. In this process, the fairy way of writing looms large as a crucial test case of the imagination's autonomy:

> There is a kind of Writing, wherein the Poet quite loses sight of Nature, and entertains his Reader's Imagination with the Characters and Actions of such Persons as have many of them no Existence, but what he bestows on them. Such are Fairies, Witches, Magicians, Demons, and departed Spirits. This Mr. *Dryden* calls *the Fairie way of Writing*, which is, indeed, more difficult than any other that depends on the Poet's Fancy, because he has no Pattern to follow in it, and must work altogether out of his own Invention.[37]

Addison's other, unacknowledged, debt here, to Collier, is clear from the use of Collier's "fairy way of writing" instead of Dryden's "fairy kind of writing." The emphasis on nature at the beginning of the paper suggests the ongoing interest in the relationship between aesthetic and scientific viewing that marks "The Pleasures of the Imagination." Here, it serves as the occasion for Addison to blend Locke's empirical psychology with Dryden's poetic license. The earlier essays in the series locate sight as the source of the primary imagination: "My Design [is] first of all to Discourse of those Primary Pleasures of the Imagination, which entirely proceed from such Objects as are before our Eyes; and in the next place to speak of those Secondary Pleasures of the Imagination which flow from the Ideas of visible Objects, when the Objects are not actually before the Eye" (no. 411, 3:537). Explicitly following the example of Locke, Addison builds his account of the imagination from the ground of perceptual experience, as later Alexander Baumgarten did in borrowing the word "aesthetic" for the Greek verb *aisthanomai*, to feel/perceive. Despite the empirical foundation, the creative imagination appears most clearly when it is least bound to the evidence of the senses. The Baconian suspicion of the imagination partially dislodged the faculty from judgment and reason, but at the same time gave it potential autonomy, which Addison is the first to explore.

Addison's version of the "fairy way of writing" is directly connected to popular superstition while also insisting on a strikingly national formulation of imaginative writing. Superstition is, more firmly than in Dryden's formulation, located in England: "There was not a Village in *England* that had not a Ghost in it, the Church-yards were all haunted, every large Common had a Circle of Fairies belonging to it, and there was scarce a Shepherd to be met with who had not seen a Spirit" (no. 419, 3:572). In effect, Addison synthesizes Dryden's "force of imagination" with the growing interest, evident in a figure like Aubrey, in popular beliefs and folkways. English superstition, moreover, produces English character, no longer strictly limited to popular belief, but effectively nationalized as the source of English literary preeminence:

> Among all the Poets of this Kind our *English* are much the best, by what I have yet seen, whether it be that we abound with more Stories of this Nature, or that the Genius of our Country is fitter for this sort of Poetry. For the *English* are naturally Fanciful, and very often disposed by that Gloominess and Mellancholly of Temper, which is so frequent in our Nation, to many wild Notions and Visions, to which others are not so liable. Among the *English*, *Shakespear* has incomparably excelled all the others. That noble Extravagance of Fancy, which he had in so great Perfection, throughly qualified him to touch this weak superstitious Part of his Reader's Imagination; and made him capable of succeeding, where he had nothing to support him besides the Strength of his own Genius.   (no. 419, 3:572–73)

Shakespeare's genius for imaginative invention is, according to Addison, a sign of his personal poetic strength, now derived from imaginative extravagance that has no immediate empirical model. The context, however, qualifies this somewhat. It is also Shakespeare's ability to embody the English national spirit that enables this level of creative imagination.

English popular superstition, combined with an English melancholy of more elite provenance, becomes a key ingredient of the English national culture. For Addison, the fairy way of writing had essentially merged with the ballads that he had earlier celebrated in his essays on "Chevy Chase" and "The Two Children in the Wood."[38] In the first essay, "Chevy Chase," Addison elaborates not simply a popular subject, but an idea of popular literature more generally:

> Human Nature is the same in all reasonable Creatures; and whatever falls in with it, will meet with Admirers amongst Readers of all Qualities and Conditions. *Moliere*, as we are told by Monsieur *Boileau*, used to read all his Comedies to an

old Woman who was his House-keeper, as she sat with him at her Work by the Chimney-Corner; and could foretell the Success of his Play in the Theatre, from the Reception it met at his Fireside: For he tells us the Audience always followed the old Woman, and never failed to laugh in the same Place. (no. 70, 1:297)

The essay on the old broadside ballad, "Two Children in the Wood" (first published in 1595), begins in a humorous vein, with Addison recounting his various discoveries of theological and aristocratic genres in forms that highlight the historicity and ephemerality of print itself: lighting his pipe "with the Writings of a Prelate," seeing "a Poem of an Eminent Author on a Victory day" used to light squibs and firecrackers, and meeting "with a Page of Mr. *Baxter* [Richard Baxter, nonconformist writer, who in Addison's time would have called to mind the religious conflicts of the Civil Wars] under a *Christmas* Pye" (no. 85, 1:361). In a very different vein, however, Addison recounts his own pleasure in collecting broadsides as an activity for his countryside expeditions, visiting "any House in the Country": "For I can't, for my Heart, leave a Room before I have thoroughly studied the Walls of it, and examined the several printed Papers which are usually pasted upon them" (no. 85, 1:361). Addison's earlier insistence on the transience of the high genres of print culture levels the playing field of high and low cultures and prepares the reader for the pleasures of the lowly broadside ballad and its role in defining a common national culture. Although the broadside pasted onto a (presumably humble) country dwelling is no less ephemeral than any other genre Addison had already met with—certainly even more ephemeral, as our own thin archive of such materials indicates—this form carries a special claim as "one of the Darling Songs of the Common People" and "the Delight of most *Englishmen* in some part of their Age" (no. 85, 1:362). The broadside is canonized by the nation although Addison must add the disclaimer indicating that elite Englishmen have presumably taken pleasure from such texts only in their nonage.

Reading the old tales and ballads thus becomes a pastoral of reading. For an elite reader, this pastoral is tinged with the reminder of childhood reading, and might even distantly anticipate the full flourishing of childhood as pastoral in the nineteenth century.[39] Addison himself is more attuned to the idea that national culture, specifically the recovery of popular culture by an educated elite, is a new version of the older, essentially aristocratic model of pastoral. Ernest Gellner has characterized nationalism as the product of a sophisticated urban culture that masks itself as the recovery of a putative folk culture, a national project that finds one of its first proponents in Addison. Culture, according to Gellner, becomes central in an industrial society that privileges literate communication. Gellner calls this "high culture," but it is also a culture that must be universally accessible, unlike the rigid stratification of literacy in premodern societies:

> Culture is no longer merely the adornment, confirmation and legitimation of a social order which was also sustained by harsher and coercive constraints; culture is now the necessary shared medium, the life-blood or perhaps rather the minimal shared atmosphere, within which alone the members of the society can breathe and survive and produce. For a given society, it must be one in which they can *all* breathe and speak and produce; so it must be the *same* culture. Moreover, it must now be a great or high (literate, training-sustained) culture, and it can no longer be a diversified, locality-tied, illiterate little culture or tradition.[40]

Gellner describes the era of fully formed nationalism in the nineteenth century, but Addison's version of the fairy way of writing, and popular literature more generally, anticipates such cultural nationalism. As the local, "little culture" recedes, it can be absorbed into a national culture, often misrecognizing the result as a simple recovery of a popular culture, which Gellner acerbically describes in pastoral terms: "The nationalist intellectuals were full of warm and generous ardour on behalf of the co-nationals. When they donned folk costume and trekked over the hills, composing poems in the forest clearings, they did not also dream of one day becoming powerful bureaucrats, ambassadors and ministers."[41] This nationalist pastoral, however, is significantly different in at least one respect from Renaissance pastoral. National culture, to extend Gellner's argument, needs to merge elements of the "high" and the "low," literacy and popular culture, in order to command general allegiance. The pastoral is no longer simply the aristocrat's holiday; it is the intellectual's vocation.

If Addison's essays on ballads most explicitly explored the possibility of a popular national literature, his version of the fairy way of writing confirmed the separation of poetic enthusiasm from religious enthusiasm and located the foundation of enthusiasm in something that would come to be called "the popular spirit." Hildebrand Jacob's essay, "How the Mind Is Rais'd to the Sublime" (1735), made this clear a generation after Addison. Jacob is primarily concerned with the sublimity of Milton, but he pauses to consider Shakespeare, a writer that no one would consider a religious enthusiast, before moving on to "the Easterns":

> *Shakespear* was no less susceptible of this *Poetic Enthusiasm*, as his *Enchantments*, *Fairy* Way of Writing, *Spirits*, and *Creatures* of his own *Formation* may testify. The *Easterns* swore by the *coming on* of *Night*; by the *Whistling* of the *Winds*; by the

Hour of *Evening. &c.* and by their bold *Metaphors*, and figurative *Style*, we find, they were more than any other People addicted to *Sublimity* of *Expression.*[42]

Although the "addiction" of the "Easterns" might be taken as slighting reference to some uncontrolled nature of their poetry, just as striking is the equivalence to the English greats that such poetry obtains. The example of Longinus and his treatment of the Hebrew Bible (although perhaps interpolated by a later hand) remained to sanction new discoveries of sublimity as contributions to the history of aesthetics rather than as sources of religious controversy or cultural disdain. This is not, then, simply a national moment in the history of literature, but an international one as well—moving from the domain of the ancients not only to the modern vernacular literatures, but, in a kind of lateral movement, to an incipient idea of world literature. This was, after all, also the moment of Antoine Galland's translation of *The Thousand and One Nights* into French (1704–1717). Galland's translation began the process through which European readers could begin to retrace the paths through which many of their popular tales, including fairy tale motifs, had arrived from the Middle East and Asia.[43]

The French Fairy Tale: The Ancients and the Moderns

The two national literatures that would dominate European literature for the next two hundred years were both engaged with formations of fantasy and fairy tale as crucial ingredients of the culture of the Moderns. If French culture did less to develop the national contours of the fairy way of writing, it highlighted both the modernity of the fairy tale as well as the significance of its association with female writers, which is less in evidence in English developments of the same period. Most prominently, of course, France developed the literary fairy tale, which, although popular in translation in England, did not stimulate very many English equivalents. Jean-Paul Sermain has speculated that Shakespeare and the forms of fantasy and the supernatural in his writing effectively provided England with the equivalent of the literary fairy tale.[44] Shakespeare, and to a lesser extent, Spenser, provided a high version of fantasy that seemed to have played the same cultural role in England as the literary fairy tale in France. Shakespeare hereafter remained very much a "Modern" in the European literary consciousness, and his use of supernatural, self-consciously popular, effects in his drama was one significant aspect of that perceived modernity.

The relative strength of Neoclassicism in France, however, effectively made the high literary genres more or less off limits to the fairy way of writing. Instead, a "new" genre needed to be created in order to write in this fashion: the literary fairy tale. The French fairy tale writers were not the first to adapt popular tales to texts aimed at elite audiences; the practice probably goes back to the origins of medieval romance, if not before (Apuleius, for example). Giovanni Francesco Straparola and Giovanni Basile had already published collections of folktales in Italy, Straparola's in the sixteenth century (with Boccaccio's *Decameron* as its clear literary model), and many of the French writers of fairy tales knew and revised the Italian tales.[45] On the other hand, the French tales were novel both in their relationship to absolutist court culture and in the prominence of female writers in their production. Although Charles Perrault remains the best known of the writers of fairy tales in France, he was not the first to produce such tales. The first references to such tales in elite circles come from the letters of Madame de Sévigné (Marie de Rabutin-Chantal). A 1656 letter to the Princess de Montpensier is de Sévigné's sole surviving letter that blends verse and prose in its narrative, and makes a jesting reference to "ma mere l'oie" (Mother Goose). De Sévigné teasingly denies that a verse fable about a woman and her children transformed into a duck and ducklings is "un conte de ma mère l'oie," indicating a genre that seems to exist already.[46] Twenty years later, in a letter to her daughter, de Sévigné described a courtly game of fairy tales in vogue at Versailles, but with the domestic description of "mitonner" ("simmering"), which seemed to involve both the domain of the fairy tale as well as that of contemporary high culture, since the tale ended with everyone singing lines from Luly's contemporary opera, *Atys*.[47] De Sévigné describes a witty game played in the *mondain* salons of *la cour et la ville*, but her letters also appear to suggest a domestic and rural world that was perhaps still within the recollection of the members of her elite circle.

The French literary fairy tale was marked from the first as a female genre. Madame d'Aulnoy (Marie-Catherine Le Jumel de Barneville) is credited with the first published fairy tale in France, which appeared as an inset narrative within her *roman, Hypolite, comte de Duglas*, in 1690. The British provenance of the novel's narrative is perhaps significant. D'Aulnoy had lived in England, primarily in order to escape a bad marriage. Her Parisian salon was known to be, as one contemporary noted, "the clearing house for all persons of quality who came from London to Paris."[48] The English rewarded d'Aulnoy with great publishing success in translation: her "secret histories" overshadowed Madame de Lafayette's *La Princesse de Clèves*, and her later collections of fairy tales outsold Perrault. Joan DeJean has remarked on the challenge this offers to the standard picture of autonomous French literary history in the period, suggesting something of the international milieu in which, perhaps contrary to our expectations of the genre, fairy tales emerged in French literature.[49] To the extent, moreover, that Addison and his generation were beginning to consume literary fairy tales in English, they were more often d'Aulnoy's than Perrault's.[50]

Marie-Jeanne Lhéritier de Villandon, a cousin of Perrault, published the first collection of such stories in French, *Œuvres mêlées,* in 1695 (date given as 1696 on the title page), shortly before Perrault's own *Histoires ou Contes du temps passé* in 1697. (Perrault had already written three tales in verse; a manuscript edition of his prose tale, *Contes de ma mere Loye,* circulated shortly before the printed version.) Perrault's publication surreptitiously continued the *Querelle des anciens et modernes* with Nicolas Boileau, which had also, and not coincidentally, involved a *Querelle des femmes* after Boileau published a satire on women. (The tales, however, were first published under the name of Perrault's son, partly in order to avoid further public controversy surrounding the *Querelle.*) The fairy tale became for Perrault a literary example of the Moderns—and one that, as with Dryden and Addison in England, distinguished the literary Moderns from the philosophical and scientific advocates of modern knowledge who condemned vulgar error.

In her "Lettre à Madame D.G*** (1695)," Lhéritier promoted the fairy tale's lineage from the troubadours of Provence and the chivalric glamour of the medieval romance, and she regretted the "sullying" of the sources of the fairy tale with its subsequent reduction to a mere folktale. Perrault's defense of the modern fairy tale, in his preface to his verse tales, does not rely on its aristocratic lineage. Instead, he distinguishes the modern folktale from somewhat similar ones of antiquity, such as the matron of Ephesus and the fable of Cupid and Psyche. The tales of the ancients, writes Perrault, produce unclear moral lessons, and thus allow Perrault to prefer the modern and "low" form of such tales for their scenes of domestic instruction. As Sermain argues, Perrault produces a new model of imitation, no longer based on the imitation of an established classical text, but rather on the model of an unclearly defined world of traditional domesticity that Perrault assumes his reader to have known from governesses, nurses, and grandmothers.[51] The fairy tale, according to Perrault, ignoring Straparola and Basile, effectively imitates and memorializes a domestic mode of cultural transmission. The stories themselves are simply "des semences qu'on jette qui ne produisent d'abord que des mouvements de joie et de tristesse, mais dont il ne manque guère d'éclore de bonnes inclinations" ("the scattered seeds which produce at first only the movements of joy and sadness, but which scarcely ever fail to bear the fruit of good inclinations").[52] The superior morality of the fairy tale cannot be separated from this novel form of imitation: the elite imitation of the ambience of domesticity.

In fact, Perrault's own moralization of his tales is a complicated affair. They generally seemed aimed at adults, often young women, rather than children. He generally provides two, often subtly modulated, morals at the end of his tales. *Le chat botté* (*Puss in Boots*) celebrates the cat's cunning manipulation of court society, and ends with the exhortation that "industry / Combined with ingenuity" is worth more than the advantages of birth. The second moral, however, reconsiders, asking the reader to notice the external attributes of the miller's son that quickly won over the king's daughter. Both imply critiques of the aristocracy, but the second is considerably more jaundiced. *La barbe bleu* (Bluebeard) concludes with a conventional moral about the dangers of female curiosity (the wife of the tale had discovered her husband to be a serial killer of his previous wives). Is the reader, then, to suppose that some equivalent to such horrors lies secreted in many marriages? A young wife must accept the difficult position that her older husband would generally possess independent contacts and relationships unknown to her. The other moral, however, insists on the obsolescence of such tales—"un conte du temps passé."[53] In fact, it has become difficult, according to Perrault, to determine whether the husband or the wife is the master of a marriage: "Et de quelque couleur que sa barbe puisee être, / On a peine à juger qui des deux est le maître" ("And whatever color his beard may be / It's difficult to tell which of the two the master be.")[54] Perrault's stated elevation of the morality of the modern tale contradicts the considerably more playful morality that his own tales in fact provide their sophisticated readers. The idea of domesticity associated with peasant society is indeed significant for Perrault, but not without the smiling sense that this world is really that of *la cour et la ville*. In other words, the social background of the tales is the newly self-reflective salon culture that, as Erich Auerbach has described it, resulted from the merger of a "nobility [which] had lost its function and ceased to be anything more than the King's entourage" and a *ville* bourgeoisie "alienated from its original function as an economic class."[55] If Lhéritier pushed for a genealogy of the tale that affiliated it more clearly with the court, Perrault, as we have seen, opts for a very different genealogy that moves his tales closer to the apparent simplicity of the countryside—without ever completely leaving the *mondain* world of the Parisian salons.[56]

Perrault and Addison are two of the most significant literary Moderns in France and England in the early years of the eighteenth century. The world of the peasant that both Addison and Perrault invoke was as modern as the childhood of the authors and their readers, and as ancient as peasant society itself, time out of mind.[57] We might here underline the significance of *Contes du temps passé* in Perrault's title. In many respects, the positions on the cultural map of early modernity, Ancient and Modern, might be just as easily reversed for us. Certainly, the great advocates of the Ancients in England, Swift and Pope, look to us to be completely immersed in the developing "modern" culture of their own time; their satirical jabs at their own culture are themselves recognizably modern, and mock-epic is at least as much of a conclusion to classical genres as anything that the Moderns came up with.[58] The combination of the temporal proximity and distance in the literary programs of Addison and Perrault is itself suggestive. The time of the fairy way of writing is that of tradition, both modern and ancient. Its presumptive space is the countryside, inhabited by the peasantry. Its ethos is domestic, including the horizontal relations that were associated with domesticity in the early modern period. In the longer term, this would become the general program of the European national literatures, which as Jonathan Kramnick has argued, dialectically created a national antiquity out of the conflict between the Ancients and the Moderns.[59]

The Rape of the Lock

Alexander Pope's great achievement seems as close to the *mondain* French fairy tale as to the fairy way of writing in England. Despite the work of Pat Rogers, which elaborates the Shakespearean echoes in the poem, there is no strong sense that, instead of in Rosicrucian manuals, Pope found his sylphs and gnomes "in some deep recess of the poetic imagination, among the rural hobgoblins where Shakespeare discovered *his* fairy beings."[60] Rather, Pope discovers them *in* Shakespeare. Pope does not imaginatively venture out among the rural hobgoblins; the precedent of Shakespeare, combined with Rosicrucian spirits, seems to provide him with sufficient knowledge to produce the kinds of "machinery" that are necessary for his poem:

> If e'er one Vision touch'd thy infant Thought,
> Of all the Nurse and all the Priest have taught,
> Of airy Elves by Moonlight Shadows seen,
> The silver Token, and the circled Green,
> Or Virgins visited by Angel-Pow'rs,
> With Golden Crowns and Wreaths of heav'nly Flowers. . . . [61]

"All the Nurse and all the Priest have taught" suggests the longstanding English association of superstition with popular errors aggravated by Catholicism, which, as we saw in the first chapter, was already common by Shakespeare's time. The problem, of course, is that Pope himself was Catholic. Why, then, does Pope introduce his version of the fairy way of writing under the sign of Catholic belief, from which sophisticated readers must then distance themselves, at least insofar as Catholicism is equated with fairy circles?

The poem's editor, Geoffrey Tillotson, notices that Pope's invocation of the nurse and the priest "connects the machinery with the beliefs of his own country, a connection required of an epic poet."[62] However, the Counter-Reformation imagery of the priest's doctrine ("Or Virgins visited by Angel-Pow'rs, / With Golden Crowns and Wreaths of heav'nly Flowers") might suggest that Pope is little concerned to anchor his machinery in the beliefs of his own country. Pope clearly signals through his Baroque imagery that Catholicism is not only a matter of the English past for him, but the European present. However, the now traditional association of fairy beliefs with the nurse and the priest also indicates his playfulness with Catholic dogma. Belinda, after all, is clearly not cut out for some form of virginal martyrdom, and Ariel and the sylphs don't amount to very much in the way of "Angel-Pow'rs."

Pope's domain of fantasy is even more miniaturized than Shakespeare's, partly because that spiritual world is so completely feminized. If *A Midsummer Night's Dream* portrays the immersion of fairyland in the battle of the sexes, Pope's poem certainly also presents us with a more literal battle of the sexes at the end of the poem, but one in which the spiritual domain of the sylphs and the gnomes exists only in order to illustrate Pope's feminine psychology, grounded as it is in various combinations of coquetry and spleen, the air and earth.[63] In this diminished battle of the sexes, Ariel's dire warning about the dangers of men is less consequential than the ministrations of Belinda's lap dog:

> This to disclose is all thy Guardian can.
> Beware of all, but most beware of Man!
> He said; when *Shock*, who thought she slept too long,
> Leapt up, and wak'd his Mistress with his Tongue.   (I.113–16)

There is no equivalent machinery for the masculine. As the name Ariel for the chief sylph suggests, Pope has adapted his psychomachia from the world of *The Tempest*, where the opposition between Ariel and Caliban is of a quite different nature. The missing term of the opposition, Caliban, suggests that Pope has downplayed the more threatening aspects of male sexuality. The central "rape" of the poem is, of course, a humorous one.

The enjoyment of the poem on the part of Pope's Catholic friends depends on their willingness to suspend dogma in favor of the playfulness of the fairy way of writing. Coleridge's "willing suspension of disbelief," presupposes, it would appear, a previous suspension of belief. Shakespeare here seems to mediate between Pope's commitment to Catholicism and the Ancients and the general project of diminishment in the poem: both of the modern and feminized culture of Town and Country (Catholic) gentry, but also of the Ancients themselves. (We generally understand mock-epic to mock the pretensions of modern society, but of course mock-epic necessarily also mocks the conventions of epic itself.) Shakespeare's fairies and spirits were already on their way to becoming the newly classicized machinery of a vernacular—and, perhaps just as importantly for Pope, secular—canon: a national canon that could join Catholic and Protestant writers in a shared aesthetic relationship to Catholic beliefs and popular superstitions.

"Fairy Land of Poetry"

It should at this point come as no surprise that the materials of folk belief and superstition were readily available to the writers of the middle years of the eighteenth century as the royal road to the creative imagination associated with Shakespeare and Spenser. Thus, John Hughes's edition of *The Fairy Queen* (1715) only a few years after Addison's essays on the imagination, included an essay, "On Allegorical Poetry," that made Spenserian allegory into the properly imaginative form of writing by significantly linking it to the domain of fairy. Allegory "has a liberty indulg'd to it, beyond any sort of Writing whatsoever. . . . Allegory is indeed the *Fairy land* of Poetry, peopled by Imagination. . . . "[64] In fact, the ability to go beyond the bounds of observed nature increasingly emerged as the emblem of the poetic power. The mid-century poets, including such figures as Joseph Warton, Mark Akenside, and especially William Collins, self-consciously expanded upon Addisonian aesthetics that enshrined the centrality of the creative imagination. Akenside's vast poem, *The Pleasures of the Imagination* (first published in 1744 and afterward expanded and revised), clearly announced its connections to Addison. Joseph Warton's *The Enthusiast, or, The Lover of Nature* (1744) celebrated what A. S. P. Woodhouse, following A. O. Lovejoy, termed the "soft primitivism" of nature over the achievements of refined civilization.[65] Shakespeare, "fancy's child" since Milton, unsurprisingly manages to enter the poem on the side of nature (in contrast to "the lays of artful Addison").

William Collins is the poet of this generation whose version of the imagination verges on romantic scandal. His *Ode on the Poetical Character* represented what is effectively the marriage of God and Fancy, producing the "rich-haired youth of morn" (Apollo, the sun).[66] Anna Letitia Barbauld commented on this alliance in her edition of Collins's poetry in 1797: "It is difficult to reduce to any thing like a meaning this strange and by no means reverential fiction concerning the Divine Being."[67] Although Earl Wasserman attempted to rescue the propriety and orthodoxy of the poem by insisting that the relationship of Wisdom and God in the Biblical *Proverbs* served as Collins's model, there remains the very strong suspicion that the reverence of the poem is directed elsewhere.[68] In fact, the mythopoesis celebrated by the poem is a secular myth of English literary history itself, which transforms *The Faerie Queene*'s story of the competition for Florimel's girdle into a new "fairy legend" (23): the poetic struggle for the cest, or wedding girdle, of imaginative power. Although the initial terms of the poem are Spenserian, Milton emerges as the clear victor—at a cost. After Milton, Collins laments, Heaven and Fancy "Have now o'erturned the inspiring bowers, / Or curtained close such scene from every future view" (75–76).

If the *Ode on the Poetical Character* signals the perceived inaccessibility of claims to inspiration after Milton, Collins's *An Ode on the Popular Superstitions of the Highlands Considered as the Subject of Poetry* (ca. 1749–1750, unpublished in Collins's lifetime) turns directly to the Shakespearean material of folk belief. There, the "hard primitivism" of Collins, directly connected to the Scots Highlands after the defeat of the Jacobite uprising in 1745 and before the Highland clearances, is also significantly alienated from England itself. If, in Addison, fairy superstition still lingered in the English countryside, Collins displaces it geographically to the remote Highlands. In this setting, Collins seems to portray the possibility of reinaugurating the visionary power of the Miltonic career, but not for Collins himself. Instead this possibility is deflected to John Home, Collins's Scottish friend about to leave England to return to the Highlands:

> There must thou wake perforce thy Doric quill,
>   'Tis Fancy's land to which thou sett'st thy feet;
>   Where still, 'tis said, the fairy people meet
> Beneath each birken shade on mead or hill.   (18–21)

Scotland, not England, is Fancy's land. As a poet, Collins cannot seem to imagine a source of poetic inspiration without simultaneously imagining his own alienation from it. This alienation, moreover, also allows his "hard primitivism" to become something closer to harsh primitivism. He thus celebrates the hard-scrabble lives of the people of the Hebrides island St. Kilda:

> They drain the sainted spring or, hunger-pressed,
> Along the Atlantic rock undreading climb,
>   And of its eggs despoil the solan's nest.
> Thus blest in primal innocence they live,
>   Sufficed and happy with that frugal fare.   (164–68)

The next stanza turns to Shakespeare, but in somewhat mysterious fashion: "Nor need'st thou blush that such false themes engage / Thy gentle mind, of fairer stories possessed" (172–73). Lonsdale remarks that the incongruity of referring to the simplicity of the inhabitants of St. Kilda as a "false theme" is probably to be explained by the late interpolation of the lines on the subject of the island. (The stanza previous to the one about St. Kilda had concerned Highland legends, more appropriate as a "false theme.") Michael McKeon considers the falsity of the supernatural beliefs of the Highlanders to be essential to the aestheticization of tradition in the poem.[69] Such legends "filled in elder time th'historic page" (175), where, it seems, Shakespeare encountered them:

> There Shakespeare's self, with every garland crowned,
> In musing hour his Wayward Sisters found,
>   And with their terrors dressed the magic scene.
> From them he sung, when mid his bold design,
>   Before the Scot afflicted and aghast,
> The shadowy kings of Banquo's fated line,
>   Through the dark cave in gleamy pageant passed. . . .   (176–82)

Shakespeare's reading in Scottish history seems to have occasioned something resembling Macbeth's own direct encounter with the Weird Sisters: "his Wayward Sisters found" and "from them he sung." This, however, appears to remain the privilege of Shakespeare. Other poets need to do their "fieldwork" among the superstitious in order to acquire subjects for poetry.

Collins has taken the Addisonian program of national poetry very far indeed. On the one hand, there is the implied demand for immersion in the world and popular beliefs of the peasantry. On the other, the poetic truth, derived from "Nature," to be discovered in that process is that which is least susceptible to empirical verification: "In scenes like these, which, daring to depart / From sober Truth, are still to Nature true" (188–89). The departure from Neoclassical precepts is no longer here a special instance of the poetic imagination, granting it a temporary visa to the domain of folk beliefs and the supernatural. It is now central to the creative imagination. There was in Neoclassical criticism, A. S. P. Woodhouse argues, "a very marked tendency to accept the reference of art to nature without stopping to define the second term, and consequently a very marked tendency on the part of the term itself to slip. . . into its commonplace meaning of *empirical reality* or, with the slightly more philosophical critic, into the meaning . . . *truth as experience and reason have ascertained it.*"[70] If Collins overturns this central tenet of Neoclassical criticism, he retains one crucial element of empirical reality: the direct experience of a world in which superstitious belief is an everyday reality. Exoticism and empirical realism converge in Scotland. Home must draw upon his Scots nationality and his experience of Scotland in order to access poetic inspiration from false beliefs. This level of experience is unavailable to Collins himself.

Collins thus laments his own "aesthetic" attitude toward both the Shakespearean supernatural and the Highlands folklore. His recognition of the aesthetic power of their tales comes with the price of acknowledging their literal falsehood.[71] That acknowledgment, in turn, seems to him to reduce his own imaginative response—and perhaps as well his own ability to act as a national poet capable of transforming folk belief into powerful poetry. "Proceed, nor quit the tales which, simply told, / Could once so well my answering bosom pierce" (183–84), he commands Home. The lines seem to propose childhood as the time when Collins himself could fully experience the imaginative impact of tales like the Highland beliefs. He cannot seem to imagine producing poetry of imaginative power without at the same time *believing*, or having once believed, in the stories that are thus created. For this reason, he needs to imagine that Tasso "believed the magic wonders which he sung" (199). Tasso, in this poem, is like Milton in the *Ode on the Poetical Character*, the poet who belongs to a kind of Edenic past of poetic inspiration and belief. The modern poet is permanently expelled from that fortunate domain.

Collins represents, then, a particularly fraught version of Addison's fairy way of writing. He wishes to reclaim a "higher," visionary poetry that transcends sober empirical truth, but at the same time he anchors that poetry in a primitive world from which he is himself alienated. Samuel Johnson acutely, but negatively, identified this alienation as his "passive acquiescence in popular traditions."[72] Collins can thus appear as one of the first European writers to mourn his distance from "the people," heralding a particularly modern artistic dilemma. One response that Collins seems to anticipate is the attempt to recapture "primitive" belief. For the fairy way of writing, this came to mean the association of fairy writing with childlike belief, where it intersected both with Locke's ideas about children's susceptibility to old wives' tales and developing idealizations of childhood. Ultimately, this resulted in the banishment of the fairy way of writing to the Victorian fairy tale, but, as we shall see, this was not the only trajectory of the fairy way of writing. Romantic artists and writers mobilized versions of the fairy way of writing to recharge the popular connections of elite culture. In doing so, they reactivated the sexual charge long associated with fairies, but largely dormant in the critical tradition of the eighteenth century, and they sometimes connected that charge to political foment.

CHAPTER FOUR

Painting Shakespearean Fantasy

Collins's poem on the superstitions of the Scottish Highlands mapped out the folk-loric/national research program that would contribute to literary studies for the next century. The cost, at least as Collins seems to experience it in the poem, was a sense of alienation from the wellsprings of fantasy. Fairy beliefs, and the tales and ballads that expressed them, were increasingly seen to belong to the Celtic fringe of Great Britain. Shakespeare, however, remained as an apparently precocious ex-ample of an English imaginative power that also engaged the world of longstanding popular beliefs. In this aspect, the fairy way of writing could seem venerable as well as the source of originality and creativity. Originality as a term of approbation for creative production was widely associated with Edward Young's *Conjectures on Original Composition* (1759), which was especially influential in Germany. It was in German-speaking Europe that an emergent nationalism, different in kind from the relatively settled nature of the British multinational state, theorized the relationship between originality as a representation of origins (national identity, for example) and originality as novelty. In his essay on modern German literature, published in 1766, Johann Gottfried Herder declares, "An original writer in the high sense of the ancients is, with few exceptions, always a national author."[1] This was partly because the truly original writer was also, according to Herder, a practitioner of *Volkspoesie*, or popular poetry, as he explained in his letters on Ossian, and connected to the origins of his own people, a bond that was expressed in the poet's commitment to the *Muttersprache* as well his engagement with national legends and myths. If the classics demanded imitation, the "national spirit" embodied in folk belief seemed to blend imitation with self-expression, nation with imagination.

If such beliefs truly carried a national spirit, then they might also contain other truths about the human spirit. Partly as a result, the fairy way of writing licensed the reshaping of what earlier eighteenth-century writers and critics had described as naive popular superstitions into a point of contact with the inner realities of the human psyche and sexual desire. The female fairy as seductress had already profoundly affected European literature. The increased emphasis on the uncanny experience of fairies as a kind of gateway to the inner depths of sexuality was, however, a novel aspect of the Romantic response to Shakespeare's fairies. This was part of a broader transformation of ideas about the imagination. As Patricia Meyer Spacks has shown, eighteenth-century writers identified, often prophylactically, the link between imagination and the experience of the passions, especially sexual passion:

> What is meant by *imagination*, in Dr. Johnson's usage and Mrs. Thrale's, is more than the image-making faculty which Addison had identified with the term. Among other things, both writers appear to be talking about what we call the unconscious mind, uncontrollable in its very nature, inevitably at war with conscious reason, full of danger because only occasionally and partially knowable. The hidden parts of personality comprise the "self" one must war with; from this hidden area rise the passions which often contradict sense and morality but can only precariously be held in check by such principles. All of us suffer always from "a degree of insanity," a partial dominance of what can't be controlled over what is supposed to control it. Sexual activity may be one specific manifestation of this dominance; literary activity, under some circumstances, is another.[2]

Although still construed negatively by many writers, the association of passion and imagination was, as Spacks indicates, recognizably modern in its sense of an unconscious mental landscape accessible to the imagination. Spacks's analysis usefully brings this quality of the imagination around to the question of literary activity. Because the fairy way of writing was so fully "creative," it was also logically less subject to rational and social limitations. Fantasy unleashed could be readily associated with sexual passion, and the long tradition of fairy sexuality also rendered this association almost inescapable.

Painting, more than the stage, took charge of the imaginative response to Shakespearean fairies over the course of the eighteenth century. The reception of Shakespeare was, at least until the mid-eighteenth century, largely a phenomenon of print and stage, both of which possessed long native pedigrees. Painting, however, remained in some respects a foreign medium in English culture until the time of Hogarth. Even in the late eighteenth century, the Swiss-born Henry Fuseli (Johann Heinrich Füssli, 1741–1825) was probably the first to paint Shakespeare's fairies. Painting's claims to Shakespeare were novel ones, and perhaps accordingly stressed the medium's ability to represent the fantastic and the supernatural.

Painting's apparent title to Shakespeare's fairies was no doubt abetted by the minimal staging of *A Midsummer Night's Dream* in the eighteenth century, which saw no successful full-length production of the play. From Henry Purcell's *The Fairy Queen* (1692) to the beginning of the nineteenth century, the play was the occasion for experiments in musical theater. Purcell's semi-opera transplants Shakespeare's comic world from the court and the woods of Athens to the "town," a barely veiled version of fashionable London, which also affords the opportunity for a "Chinese masque" to be inserted alongside the supernatural world of the fairies and pastoral interludes. Shakespeare's comic skepticism about love and marriage becomes considerably more cynical in the adaptation. A pastoral flirtation between Corydon and Mopsa, performed for the pleasure of Titania and Bottom, is standard pastoral seduction, but is followed by a nymph who pledges that, if her lover has deceived her, she will do the same to him. Hymen appears at the end of the production, but is so disenchanted with marriage that he is initially reluctant to bless the nuptials.

Purcell's score was lost after his death in 1695, not be rediscovered until the twentieth century. Its disenchanted treatment of love, however, might be seen as setting the tone for stagings of *A Midsummer Night's Dream* throughout the next century. The great success of the musical adaptation of Milton's *Comus*, adapted by the Rev. John Dalton with music by Thomas Arne and first staged in 1738, probably influenced the handling of Shakespeare's play. Although subsequently revised for later versions, this version of *Comus* held the stage throughout the eighteenth and early nineteenth centuries, and was more successful than any version of *A Midsummer Night's Dream* during that period. Certainly influenced by Purcell's collaboration with Dryden in *King Arthur* (Dalton's adaptation featured the spirit Philidel, borrowed from *King Arthur*), the adaptation luxuriated in a strikingly un-Miltonic elaboration of the vicissitudes of love, including pastoral interludes of jaded shepherds and shepherdesses that are reminiscent of both *King Arthur* and Purcell's *Fairy Queen*. (In 1842, an anonymous adaptation of *Comus* borrowed numerous other elements from *King Arthur*, effectively creating a hybrid production.) "By cutting the original and adding scenes of his own the adapter lowered the tone of the piece until it rang no longer with the music of its own spheary chime but echoed and re-echoed the riot and ill-managed merriment of the early eighteenth century stage," complained Alwin Thaler in his survey of productions of Milton during the eighteenth century.[3] Dalton, for example, interrupts Comus's allurements of the Lady with the song of a Pastoral Nymph abandoned by her lover, Damon. Euphrosyne (Mirth), added to Milton's masque from "L'Allegro," responds with a consoling ballad that concludes with a cynical rejoinder to the chaste ideal of the Lady:

Why should they e'er give me pain,
Who to give me joy disdain?

All I hope of mortal man,

Is to love me—whilst he can.[4]

The great success and multiple revivals of this version of Milton's masque probably influenced the handling of Shakespeare's play, which, especially after Purcell, was also seen to be appropriate for musical adaptation. The next significant adaptation of the *Dream*, David Garrick's *The Fairies* (1755), was also musical theater. Garrick cut the mechanicals from the play and emphasized song and dance, interpolating lyrics by Dryden, Lansdowne, Waller, and Milton ("L'Allegro"). "Garrick has produced a detestable English opera," wrote Horace Walpole in a letter to Richard Bentley, "which is crowded by all true lovers of their country. . . . [I]t is Shakespeare's *Midsummer Night's Dream*, which is forty times more nonsensical than the worst translation of any Italian opera-books."[5] Garrick later attempted a full-length treatment of the play in 1763, but it was a miserable failure, lasting only one night. One critic ambivalently remarked that it was "a lively picture of the ungoverned imagination of that great Poet."[6] Garrick's collaborator, George Colman, quickly replaced Garrick's attempt at a full staging with a successful two-act afterpiece, *A Fairy Tale*, which focused on the action of the mechanicals and the fairies. "Dull pantomime," William Hazlitt would later call staged versions of Shakespeare's play. "The boards of a theatre and the regions of fancy are not the same thing."[7] The cultural reversal of Shakespeare's own highly theatrical sense of fairy magic is stunning.

"Libertines of Painting"

A Midsummer Night's Dream's limited success on the eighteenth-century stage, along with its association with the imagination, probably only highlighted its availability to other media, especially the visual arts. Visual artists seem to have taken both *A Midsummer Night's Dream* and *The Tempest* as invitations to explore and to exceed the representational limitations of the stage. Gotthold Lessing's *Laocoon* (1766) had rejected the old alliance between poetry and painting, *ut pictura poesis* (as is painting, so is poetry), and separated the representational media of the two arts: painting works in space, poetry (including drama) in time. The increasing separation of the two arts, however, did not mean that painting relinquished any claims to Shakespeare. Fuseli, in one of his first lectures on painting at the Royal Academy (March 1801), explicitly rejected Lessing's argument for the representation of relatively static subjects, arguing instead for the "momentous energy" of "a moment of apparent kinesis that somehow extends beyond itself, a moment with a readable past and future."[8] Fuseli, that is, wanted painting to be dramatic. The explosion of paintings of Shakespeare's theater in the British art of the later eighteenth century, moreover, suggests that painting in Britain associated its own cultural maturity with its ability to represent, outside the theater, a national icon.

The visual response to the play from the later years of the eighteenth century was to emphasize the imaginative—and interior—landscapes that it produced, often inaccessible to any possible stage production. The opening of John Boydell's Shakespeare Gallery in 1789 marked the moment at which painting temporarily rivaled theater as the natural home of Shakespeare's art. Thomas Banks's sculpture, *Shakespeare Attended by Painting and Poetry* (1789; fig. 4.1), which was prominently displayed at the Shakespeare Gallery, showed Shakespeare poised between the Dramatic Muse and the Genius of Painting. If Shakespeare seems to attend to the music and the laurel crown offered by the Muse, he caresses the arm of the Genius of Painting, who both seductively reveals herself, bare breasted, to the viewer and gestures toward Shakespeare, indicating both her own erotic attractions and her ability to represent Shakespeare's creative power. Although the competitive tension between visual art and theater suggests the conflict between absorption and theatricality in Michael Fried's study of eighteenth-century art theory, "theatricality," as opposed to actual theatrical production, is never far from the visual experience of many of the paintings set in Shakespeare's fairyland.[9] Figures in the paintings consistently solicit the attention of the viewer, unlike the self-enclosed dynamism of the art favored by Denis Diderot and other French critics. Instead of absorption we find that Shakespearean imagination, in the form of his fairies, became the occasion of a visionary art quite different than the French genealogy of modern art, which in some respects continued the Neoclassical insistence on the self-contained autonomy of the dramatic experience. This is especially true of Fuseli and William Blake, who mobilized the Shakespearean supernatural for a form of representation that seems to inaugurate a modern formation of fantasy.

Educated in Zurich by central intellectual figures in the Sturm und Drang and loosely connected with Herder's circle before settling permanently in London in 1779, Fuseli played a significant role in the Shakespeare Gallery and was the first artist to be widely associated with the representation of Shakespeare's fairies. Herder's pamphlet, *On the German Character and Art* (1773), celebrated Shakespeare for his imaginative capacity to transcend empirical actuality, which Herder associated with the restrictions of French Neoclassicism. Fuseli's art extends this critical tradition. His two major paintings of *A Midsummer Night's Dream*, *Titania and Bottom* (1780–1790; fig. 4.2) and *Titania's Awakening* (1785–1789; fig. 4.3), represent the play's fairy plot in completely fantastic terms. This was, as Stuart Sillars astutely remarks, a challenge to theater: "Both immediately declare the absence of the theatrical: the nature of the figures, their relative sizes, and their positioning make any reference

Fig. 4.1. After Thomas Banks, *Shakespeare Attended by Painting and Poetry* (1789);
engraved by Benjamin Smith (1796). By permission of the Folger Shakespeare Library

to the actual world impossible and reveal that this is the product of an imaginative reading of the text."[10] The challenge came from a painter who was also conversant with the London theater. John Knowles, the early biographer of Fuseli, reports that, "Fuseli esteemed the English character more highly than that of any other country, and was much pleased with their amusements. The theatre was a constant source of gratification, and his criticisms on plays and players were usually severe, but generally acute and just."[11] His taste in theater, the Shakespearean supernatural in particular, was shared with some of the primary exponents of the Gothic novel, including Horace Walpole, whose preface to the second edition of *The Castle of Otranto* (1765) included an appeal to Shakespearean precedent for his novelistic practice, and Ann Radcliffe, whose novels often made use of explicitly Shakespearean materials. Like the Gothic novelists, Fuseli took Shakespeare as a model for the exploration of extreme psychological states that would ultimately extend the fairy way of writing into the emergent cultural mode of the fantastic.

In Fuseli's paintings of *A Midsummer Night's Dream*, eroticism is no longer the conventionally pastoral one of theatrical adaptations of Shakespeare, but rather a

Fig. 4.2. After Henry Fuseli, *Midsummer Night's Dream, act IV, scene I* [*Titania and Bottom*] (1780–1790); engraved by John Peter Simon (1796). By permission of the Folger Shakespeare Library

Fig. 4.3. After Henry Fuseli, *Midsummer Night's Dream, act IV, scene I* [*Titania's Awakening*] (1785–1789); engraved by Thomas Ryder and Thomas Ryder, Jr. (1803). By permission of the Folger Shakespeare Library

kind of phantasmagoria, a new form of theatrical spectacle. The phantasmagoria was an entertainment, based on the magic lantern, that became popular shortly after Fuseli's paintings of Shakespeare's plays, but it was anticipated by Philippe Jacques de Loutherbourg's spectacular stage designs and shows in London in the 1770s and 80s, which combined dramatic visual spectacle with supernatural effects. In 1782, de Loutherbourg's Eidophusikon, a miniature theater without actors, presented scenes from Milton. At the same time, he was commissioned by William Beckford, author of *Vathek*, to design his Christmas revels at Fonthill, producing what Beckford described as "that strange, necromantic light which Loutherbourg had thrown over what absolutely appeared a realm of Fairy, or rather, perhaps a Demon Temple deep beneath the earth set apart for tremendous mysteries."[12] Beckford's description is also apt for Fuseli's paintings of *A Midsummer Night's Dream*, both of which seem to participate, through the eroticized "tremendous mysteries" of fairyland, in what Terry Castle has called the "supernaturalizing" of the mind in the period.[13] Both paintings feature a grotesque world of fairy sexuality, in which the central figures are surrounded by impudent fairies that, particularly in the first of the two paintings, actively meet the gaze of the viewer. "It is a scene," remarks Ronald Paulson of the first, "that relates to Fuseli's pornographic drawings of passive spread-eagled men being tortured or in various ways dealt with by terribly active women."[14] Although the connection to Fuseli's pornography is just, it is very difficult to make a clear assessment of just how terrifying this is meant to be. *Titania Awakening* reveals Oberon and Titania bathed in the light of day while the sleeping, and clearly postcoital, Bottom remains heavily shadowed along with much of the world of the fairies, symbolically occupying a dream/nightmare of threatening sexuality. The representation of Oberon and Titania is, Sillars argues, a "serioludic parody of Canova [*Cupid and Psyche*]," allowing the viewer to see the classical eroticism of the central couple—Oberon now occupying the position of standing above and enveloping Titania—along with the monstrous sexuality (the sleeping Bottom, his ass head being removed by fairies at the moment represented in the painting) that continues to complicate this reassertion of classical eroticism.[15] (Bottom is in a different, larger scale than Oberon and Titania.) Bottom seems to represent the darker powers of sexuality, and it is not clear that Fuseli fully believes in the triumphant power of classical masculinity.

Fuseli's contemporaries associated him with the "gothic" energies of his own painting, earning him, for example, the fulsome condemnation of the Reverend R. A. Bromley. In his *Philosophical and Critical History of the Fine Arts* (1793), Bromley associated Fuseli's fantastic style with what the French painter and theorist, Charles du Fresnoy (1611–1688), had termed, in his *De arte graphica*, "Libertines of painting." "[A]s there are libertines of religion, who have no other law but the vehemence of their own inclinations, so these [painters] have no other model, [du Fresnoy] says, but a rodomontado genius, which shews us a wild or savage nature that is not of our acquaintance, but of a new creation."[16] Bromley's disparagement of Fuseli's "new creation" demonstrates something of the continued unsettled nature of literary and artistic "creativity" and "originality" in the period. Fuseli's originality is nothing more than braggadocio, or "rodomontade," associated with Rodomonte, of Ariosto's *Orlando Furioso*; it usurps the authority of God's creation expressed in nature. Although Bromley later accepts the period's approbation of genius and imagination, he also insists on the limits imposed by nature on genius:

> Genius is a creative imagination, which can not only embellish scenes or incidents by the best disposition of concomitant circumstances, but give existence to new ones. It is a gift, by which are poured into the mind with great copiousness the rarest treasures of thought and idea. Consequently it is derived from Nature,

whose stores are as inexhaustible as they are infinitely varied; it is not acquired by labour, which can but give by it's [sic] own scantier measure, and to which in it's best progress Nature has said, "hitherto shalt thou go, and no further." Genius is to the human mind what the Nile is to Egypt, the prolific source of all that has ever embellished and enriched it in every way.[17]

Fuseli's genius, we should understand, remains an unnatural one, and the fantastic here is but one symptom of a more general radicalism that one would, according to Bromley, expect to find in Fuseli: the desire to exceed, or to defy, nature.

Fuseli was, among other things, an early lover of Mary Wollstonecraft and a strong opponent of the British slave trade. "No man," writes Knowles, "was a greater stickler for religious and civil liberty than Fuseli, and no man had a deeper horror of the slave-trade, or a greater dislike to impressing seamen."[18] In the taunting letter to Fuseli with which he begins the first volume (revealing the source of Bromley's antagonism to Fuseli in the personal politics of the Royal Academy), Bromley triumphantly produces as a trump card a possible edition of *Paradise Lost* with Fuseli as the illustrator (perhaps anticipating the Milton Gallery, for which Fuseli executed many paintings in the late 1790s) in order to equate Fuseli and his associates with Milton's satanic subjects:

> That sublime book, never touched but by *learned pens*, was reserved for you to give the genuine spirit to all it's [sic] scenes—*Angels and Devils, Spirits and Substances, bright or obscure, Ministers of Health, and Goblins damned, Gorgons and Hydras, and Chimaeras dire, Hell-hounds with wide Cerberian mouths, Witches eclipsing with their charms the labouring Moon, the snaky Sorceress fast by Hell-gate, Asphaltic pools*, the great *Sorbonian bog, vapours impenetrable, shades of death, darkness visible, chaos in it's eternal night*, these have waited for your hand to give them the reality and effect to which even the Poet's display is not equal. In Pandemonium you cannot possibly have a rival; you have given it to us already as true as the original; repeat but that design, filled with the group of *that industrious crew*, whose machinations you so well understand, and Pandemonium is compleat [sic].[19]

Bromley likens Fuseli to Milton, the political radical, making it clear that Fuseli's fantastic "Satanism" is also political in nature: "a Republican poet can never be brought out so properly as under Republican auspices, if snugly conducted."[20]

Reynolds's Fetus

Fuseli was not the only painter of the period to explore the sexuality of the play, nor was his fantastic version of female sexuality necessarily dominant. At about the same moment as Fuseli was completing his paintings of Titania, Sir Joshua Reynolds painted a portrait of Puck for the Boydell Gallery (1789; fig. 4.4), with a clearly post-coital Titania and Bottom in the background. Puck, meanwhile, who occupies the center of the painting, sitting on very large toadstool, is a leering and impish baby. Early reactions to the painting were troubled by the representation of Puck but said nothing about the background. The *Morning Post* of May 1, 1789, complained that the child Puck was "a portrait of a *foetus* taken from some anatomical preparation."[21] Horace Walpole more forgivingly called Reynolds's Puck "an ugly little imp, but with some character."[22] That character is marked by Puck's sexual knowledge. This mischievous baby seems to direct our attention, through his raised left arm, to the postcoital Bottom and Titania. What this scene discloses about the sexuality of the fairy domain in Shakespeare belies the assumption that the sexuality of the play was a late twentieth-century discovery. Edward Hamilton's Victorian catalogue raisonné of Reynolds engravings passes over the subject in a revealing silence: "A little naked boy, seated on a mushroom; flowers in right hand; both arms raised; landscape, &c."[23] Stuart Sillars notices the clear eroticism of the scene but interprets the Titania in the light of Reynolds's painting of Dido.[24] This reading tends to elide the scene's comic eroticism, which no doubt appealed to the early collectors of the print. If the background of Titania and Bottom is now difficult to discern in the painting itself, it is readily visible in the engraved prints, which are numerous. The Folger Shakespeare Library possesses six different prints of the scene from the early nineteenth century, indicating its continuing popularity with buyers throughout the period.

The comic eroticism of Reynolds's version of Puck was later seen in explicitly theatrical terms. The Victorian art critic Frederic George Stephens said that the portrait was

> not a Puck at all,—as such, indeed, really an absurd picture, and it was probably suggested by that fruitful parent of artistic dishonor the theatre, the occasion being, doubtless, some pantomimic feat with a trap-door, "Hey Presto!" and the like, with which the place of wit is often supplied on the stage. . . . "Puck" here looks as if he had popped up at a prompter's whistle, with "Here we are again!" or what might have been the equivalent phrase.[25]

Stephens simply absorbs Reynolds's Puck into the world of popular performance, much as William Hazlitt had earlier dismissed attempts to stage Shakespeare's play as "dull pantomime." Even if a naked and sexually knowing Puck was unlikely to find his way into any nineteenth-century stage production of the *Dream*, Reynolds's Puck was essentially theatrical, as Stephens quite rightly saw. Unlike Fuseli, whose

Sir J. Reynolds.

Charles Marr.

PUCK.

London, Published Octr 1, 1832, by John Major, 50, Fleet Street.

Fig. 4.4. After Joshua Reynolds, *Puck* (1789); engraved by Charles W. Marr (1832). By permission of the Folger Shakespeare Library

paintings of the play self-consciously exceed the possibilities of a theatrical production, Reynolds continues Shakespeare's own theatrical conception of Puck.

"A Very fairy"

George Romney (1734–1802) consistently engaged Shakespearean subjects, especially the supernatural elements of Shakespeare, throughout his career and was perhaps a moving force behind the Boydell Shakespeare Gallery.[26] Late in his career, he entered an extensive engagement with the figure of Titania as an emblem of female sexuality. Romney was licensed by the fairy sexuality that seems to have permeated the visual—and literary—representations of the period. One significant example was Adeline, the heroine of Ann Radcliffe's popular *The Romance of the Forest* (1791), whose love poetry throughout the book relies on the language, and sometimes the voice, of Titania. "Titania to Her Love" ventriloquizes Titania in an erotic invitation to fairy flight and lounging on the "margin sands."[27] Radcliffe's use of Titania as a kind of seductress in a romantic setting is very close to Romney's use of Titania in the 1790s, and possibly influenced his many experiments with the subject. As with the paintings of Fuseli and Reynolds, *Titania, Puck, and the Changeling* (ca. 1793; fig. 4.5) is clearly a work in which the visual imagination is freed from any reference to the possibility of stage representation. His longtime muse, Emma Hamilton, modeled this Titania, who lies on a beach along with her changeling boy, flirtatiously glancing at the viewer (perhaps her new husband, Sir William Hamilton, but equally serviceable when she took Lord Nelson as her lover). Puck is here much more clearly nonhuman than in Reynolds, and he appears to be placing a ribbon or garter on the leg of the plump changeling boy, whose genitals are fully exposed. In the background, naked spirits seem to emerge out of the light effects playing over the ocean. They are essentially nature spirits who superintend the painting's eroticism.

The seaside, however, is not a setting in *A Midsummer Night's Dream*. Romney perhaps took some inspiration from the speech in which Titania recalls spending time with her votary (the mother of the changeling boy) "on Neptune's yellow sands" (II.i.126), but it is clearly not an attempt to capture any particular scene in the play or even any scene recalled in the play. Adeline's poems from *The Romance of the Forest*, however, make extensive use of Titania in exotic locales, especially seaside ones. The spirits in the background of *Titania, Puck, and the Changeling* are somewhat similar to the "fairy forms" invoked by Adeline in her poem, "Morning, On the Sea Shore": "And fairy forms, of fine aetherial dyes, / Advance with frolic step and laughing eyes."[28] Whether or not Radcliffe directly influenced Romney, his loose appropriation of the figure of Titania is similar in spirit to Radcliffe's. Both the

Fig. 4.5. George Romney, study for *Titania, Puck, and the Changeling* (ca. 1793). By permission of the Folger Shakespeare Library

artist and the novelist transformed Shakespeare's glancing reference to the seashore into the scene of erotic threshold, loosely, if by no means exclusively, associated with female desire, allowing us to see the process of the fairy way of writing transformed into a world of supernatural effects associated with the universe of desire.[29]

The littoral setting of fairy fantasy was important enough to Romney for him to produce a canvas based entirely on Titania's votary, a character who does not even appear in Shakespeare's play. The *Indian Woman* (1793; fig. 4.6) represents the backstory recalled in Titania's explanation of her refusal to yield the changeling boy to Oberon (which involves her strong bond with her votary). In this painting, Romney is particularly concerned with the lines in which Titania describes their mockery of "th'embarkèd traders on the flood":

> When we have laughed to see the sails conceive
> And grow big-bellied with the wanton wind,
> Which she with pretty and swimming gait
> Following, her womb then rich with my young squire,
> Would imitate, and sail upon the land
> To fetch me trifles. . . .
>
> (II.i.127–33)

Romney does not make the Indian woman obviously pregnant, which would have been more daring given the pictorial conventions of the period, but he does picture her holding a piece of cloth in front of her that mirrors the curvature of the ship's sail in the ocean behind her, thus realizing the visual pun of Shakespeare's elegant witticism.

This, moreover, was not the end of his exploration of female sexuality in romantic aquatic settings. Romney's son, John, later wrote an account of his father's career in which Titania seems to have informed Romney's exploration of female sexuality:

> He painted about this time, also, the *Death of Ophelia*, and *Susan*, from the ballad of "When the Seas were roaring"; neither of which was in a finished state. And those various pictures, representing *Titania* under different circumstances, and in different attitudes; one of which, a beautiful naked figure, I regret very much that I did not reserve from the sale. It was, in truth, a very fairy. It represented her reposing in her bower, and in a state of somnolency; and, if I remember rightly, Bottom sleeping by her side.[30]

As with Fuseli and Reynolds, Titania in her bower appears to have become an emblematic occasion for the representation of female sexuality explicitly linked to the

Fig. 4.6. George Romney, *The Indian Woman* (1793). Private collection

supernatural. John Romney's wistful recollection of the image of Titania in her bower as "a very fairy" indicates how strongly this association was felt, even though the surviving images—from Fuseli, Reynolds, or Romney—do very little visually to reinforce our sense that Titania is indeed a fairy. Fuseli and Romney disperse the supernatural effects into the world surrounding Titania.

In a later generation, Louisa Sharpe (1798–1843) transformed the forthright sexuality of Titania into maternal love.[31] A bare bosomed, but discreetly blocked Titania gazes adoringly at the changeling boy, who is crowned with flowers—recalling the immediate source of conflict between Oberon and Titania in the play as her attentions to the boy and her refusal to yield custody of him to Oberon and to the masculine sphere. It seems to announce the Victorian translation of fairy sexuality into familial relations. Romney perhaps anticipated this trajectory with his clear interest in the erotic and the maternal, but there is less suggestion in his representations of Titania and her votary that maternal love is the natural end of female desire. Rather, they exist concurrently and at least partially autonomously.

The conjunction of Shakespearean fairies and proto-Freudian psychopathology awaited Richard Dadd (1817–1866) for its realization. Dadd was the maddest, and most powerful, of the Victorian fairy painters, a strange branch of British painting in the nineteenth century that developed from the Shakespearean visual works of the previous century. It is impossible to disentangle Dadd's artistic development from the course of his madness, which included the delusional murder of his father. From early in his career, Shakespearean fairies seem to have leveraged an ecstatic eroticism that fused and extended elements of Reynolds, Romney, and Fuseli. The central figure of Dadd's *Puck* (1841; fig. 4.7) sits on a toadstool, a clear quotation of the Reynolds Puck, but Dadd also surrounds him with a miniaturized circle of naked fairies, both male and female. The fairy circle, along with the dew-laden plants that partly encircle Puck and reflect the moonlight that originates behind Puck (the painting is itself on a circular canvas), now reveals a self-enclosed world of erotic menace much closer to the world of Fuseli than to the comic lightness of Reynolds. *Come unto These Yellow Sands* (1842; private collection) is loosely based on Ariel's song in the first act of *The Tempest* (I.ii.375–87), but it also transforms the eroticism of Romney's littoral eroticism into something closer to an orgiastic ritual of writhing fairies. After the murder of his father and his confinement in an insane asylum, Dadd's work became an obsessively detailed incarnation of a nightmarish fairyland, including two remarkable canvases: *Contradiction: Oberon and Titania* (1854–1858; Collection of Sir Andrew Lloyd-Webber) and *The Fairy Feller's Master Stroke* (1855–1864; Tate). *Contradiction* proffers a dramatic confrontation of Oberon and Titania, probably based on the statement of the terms of their quarrel in act

PUCK AND THE FAIRIES.

{MIDSUMMER NIGHTS DREAM}

Fig. 4.7. After Richard Dadd, *Puck* (1841); engraved by William Home Lizars. By permission of the Folger Shakespeare Library

2: a kind of nightmare version of the becalmed Victorian family ideal transformed into a fatal struggle between the masculine and the feminine. Titania, apparently inadvertently, crushes one of the fairies underfoot as she faces Oberon.[32]

Blakean Insurrection

William Blake (1757–1827) is the artist of the late eighteenth century with the least explicit interest in the erotic possibilities of *A Midsummer Night's Dream*. Instead, Blake's extraordinary watercolors of the play focus on the domain of the fairies as the place of the imagination and visionary leveling. Oberon and Titania are present in both paintings, and clearly designated as aristocratic figures, but the key figure is Puck, who leads them in flight in *Oberon and Titania, Preceded by Puck* (ca. 1790–1793; fig. 4.8) or mediates their relationship to the fairy circle in *Oberon, Titania and Puck with Fairies Dancing* (ca. 1786; fig. 4.9). Although Blake, like Reynolds, focuses on Puck, the effect could hardly be more different. Reynolds's version of Puck is a leering sexual imp; Blake proposes Puck as the fulcrum of creative energy that seems to proceed from a source other than Oberon and Titania themselves.[33] The fairy circle of *Oberon, Titania and Puck with Fairies Dancing* is completed significantly outside the frame of the picture. (The scale of the image reminds us that these fairies are much smaller than the surrounding plants. This small watercolor is in fact a "life-sized" representation of the fairy world.) Puck mediates between the natural world of the fairy circle—butterflies adorn the dancing fairies—and the aristocratic Oberon and Titania. Puck's body seems to fold itself into the contours of the dancing fairy at the left of the circle while Titania's body bends away from his.

Movement within both of Blake's watercolors derives from a source that, in courtly terms, is lower than Oberon and Titania: the world of fairy courtiers and servants who populate Shakespeare's play. In Shakespeare, Puck represents the imaginative capabilities and growing confidence of the Shakespearean company. Blake is not particularly interested in the theatrical imagination, but he transforms Puck into an emblem of the visionary imagination. Puck's gesture in *Oberon and Titania, preceded by Puck* is toward the viewer rather than the Oberon and Titania who seem passively to follow his flight. The image apparently refers to the moment in act 4 of the play when Oberon releases Titania from the love charm and the two prepare to take flight. In the play, Titania asks for clarification of her "visions" from Oberon but receives instead the blunt dismissal, "Silence a while" (IV.i.79). She later rephrases the request, asking him to provide the explanation on their flight, but we do not learn whether or not Oberon complies. Blake's version of the scene does not seem to grant Oberon so much control over the action and departs significantly from the Shakespearean text by making Puck into their guide. Puck in this image reminds Stuart Sillars of Leonardo's Vitruvian man, but he seems at least as much related to Blake's own images of Albion, Blake's universal man (but also, of course, Britain), especially in *Albion Rose (Glad Day)* (ca. 1796; fig. 4.10).[34] In Blake's symbolic universe, the imagination triumphs along with nationalist imaginings, which is, crucially for Blake, a horizontal (fraternal) rather than vertical (hierarchical) mode of identification.[35] When he produced a black and white etching and engraving of the subject in about 1804, Blake added the lines beneath the image:

Fig. 4.8. William Blake, *Oberon and Titania, Preceded by Puck* (ca. 1790–1793). By permission of the Folger Shakespeare Library

> Albion arose from where he labour'd at the Mill with slaves
> Giving himself for the Nations he danced the dance of Eternal Death[.]

More clearly than other artists of the period, Blake associated Shakespeare's fairies with the revolutionary nationalism emerging in the latter half of the eighteenth century. The emblematic Puck, once a lowly household prankster, now represents a new world of fraternal bonds. In some versions of *Europe: A Prophecy* (1794) Blake included a plate describing the encounter of the poet with a recognizably Puckish fairy. In this version of the poem, according to Jon Mee, Blake "pointedly prefers the riotous spirit of popular tradition to preside over his poem" rather than the Holy Spirit of Milton's *Paradise Lost*.[36]

Late in his career, Blake revisited a version of Puck in his watercolor series of illustrations for *L'Allegro* and *Il Penseroso* (ca. 1816–1820; fig. 4.11). Blake's version of Milton's household goblin, which Milton clearly drew in part from Shakespeare's Puck, explodes out of the bounds of its domestic space. Chauncey Brewster Tinker's commentary on Blake's illustrations of Milton's poems captures this very nicely: "Say

Fig. 4.9. William Blake, *Oberon, Titania and Puck with Fairies Dancing* (ca. 1786). ©Tate, London 2012

what you like of the details, it is the Goblin who fills the scene. . . . Milton suggests a pleasant interior scene, somewhat in the Dutch manner; but Blake will have none of it."[37] If Shakespeare's play produces the horizontal identification of Puck and the Shakespearean audience, Blake's Puck is even more an actively insubordinate force.

The combined effect of the visual images of *A Midsummer Night's Dream* that began to appear, from very different places on the English cultural map, suggests that the play's fairy world was emerging as the scene of erotic and rebellious energies that would transform both the fairy way of writing and the cultural nationalism with which it had been associated since Addison. If the association between Shakespearean fancy and sexuality was a common interest of Fuseli, Reynolds, and Romney, the engagement of Reynolds and Romney remained one concerned with the representation of recognizable forms of sexual seduction and enchantment. Fuseli's representations of fairy sexuality, however, point directly to some dark and dramatic transformation of the quotidian experience of erotic life: a Romantic sexuality. Blake's illustrations connected to Shakespeare's Puck mobilize a nationalist or even revolutionary spirit. Both energies, the sense of a darker, possibly repressed, sexuality and an insurrectionary spirit from below, eventually became central ingredients of a transformed version of the fairy way of writing, whose name itself still

Fig. 4.10. William Blake, *Albion Rose* (ca. 1796). © The Trustees of the British Museum

Fig. 4.11. William Blake, *The Goblin* (ca. 1816–1820). The Pierpont Morgan Library, New York. 1949.4:5. Purchased with the assistance of the Fellows with the special support of Mrs. Landon K. Thorne and Mr. Paul Mellon

suggests a kind of generic oddity within a Neoclassical organization of the system of writing. Of course, the visual artists of the late eighteenth century complicate the concept of a mode of *writing* simply through the insistence of the visual. A complex modern mode, which eventually comes to be called fantasy or the fantastic, emerges across the genres and media of the period, including the phantasmagoria, the Gothic novel, and Shakespearean painting. The visual arts, traditionally associated with the solicitation of desire, thus played a central role in the activation of the fairy way of writing as an ingredient of modern fantasy.

CHAPTER FIVE

Rebellion in Fairyland

The Eve of St. Agnes

There is something exquisitely rich and luxurious in Titania's
saying "since the middle summer's spring" as if Bowers were not
exuberant and covert enough for fairy sports untill [*sic*] their
second sprouting—which is surely the most bounteous over-
whelming of all Nature's goodnesses. She steps forth benignly in
the spring and her conduct is so gracious that by degrees all things
are becoming happy under her wings and nestle against her
bosom: she feels this love and gratitude too much to remain self-
same, and unable to contain herself buds forth the overflowings of
her heart about the middle summer. O Shakespeare thy ways are
just but searchable! The thing is a piece of profound verdure.

—*John Keats, note in his copy of Shakespeare,*
A Midsummer Night's Dream, *II.i.81*[1]

Novel and Lyric

Although the visual art of the Romantic period was fully engaged with the possibilities of Shakespeare's fairy eroticism, including, in the case of Blake, a radicalized
nationalism, the first generation of Romantic poets tended toward some embarrassment when it came to the representation of merely "fanciful" fairies. In this, they
were clearly the inheritors of Johnson's dismissal of Thomas Tickell's enthusiastic
mixture of fairies and classical deities in *Kensington Gardens* (1722) as "exploded beings."[2] Collins, as we have already seen, seems to herald the new demand for a kind
of poetic "fieldwork" into popular superstitions to replace the older poetic habits of
imitation, compelling artists to look elsewhere than previous high literary examples
for their materials. Such fieldwork eventually became pervasive enough to occasion

Thomas Love Peacock's *Four Ages of Poetry* (1820), which excoriates exactly such "research" into the domains of "barbaric manners and supernatural interventions":

> In the origin and perfection of poetry, all the associations of life were composed of poetical materials. With us it is decidedly the reverse. We know too that there are no Dryads in Hyde-park nor Naiads in the Regent's-canal. But barbaric manners and supernatural interventions are essential to poetry. Either in the scene, or in the time, or in both, it must be remote from our ordinary perceptions. While the historian and the philosopher are advancing in, and accelerating, the progress of knowledge, the poet is wallowing in the rubbish of departed ignorance, and raking up the ashes of dead savages to find gewgaws and rattles for the grown babies of the age. Mr. Scott digs up the poachers and cattle-stealers of the ancient border. Lord Byron cruises for thieves and pirates on the shores of the Morea and among the Greek islands. Mr. Southey wades through ponderous volumes of travels and old chronicles, from which he carefully selects all that is false, useless, and absurd, as being essentially poetical; and when he has a commonplace book full of monstrosities, strings them into an epic. Mr. Wordsworth picks up village legends from old women and sextons; and Mr. Coleridge, to the valuable information acquired from similar sources, superadds the dreams of crazy theologians and the mysticisms of German theologians. . . . [3]

Although Peacock acknowledges the centrality of the supernatural and "barbarism" in poetry, or at least the poetry of former ages, he expressly argues that most of his contemporaries have surrendered to what Dr. Johnson had called, with regard to Collins, the "passive acquiescence in popular traditions."[4] Peacock's condemnation registers what we might call the ethnographic character of Romantic poetry as the construction of a national antiquity "in the rubbish of departed ignorance."

Well before Peacock, however, Wordsworth's preface to the second edition of the *Lyrical Ballads* (1800) expressed similar reservations about excessive enthusiasm for romantic incident. Wordsworth denounces the "frantic novels, sickly and stupid German Tragedies, and deluges of idle and extravagant stories in verse" of the early Romantic period, and he was concerned to highlight the rationally "experimental" practice of his poetry in opposition to other writings of the period:

> The First Volume of these Poems has already been submitted to general perusal. It was published, as an experiment which, I hoped, might be of some use to ascertain, how far, by fitting to metrical arrangement a selection of the real language of men in a state of vivid sensation, that sort of pleasure and that quantity of pleasure may be imparted, which a Poet may rationally endeavour to impart.[5]

The language of experiment is carefully chosen and pervasive in the preface. Wordsworth's Romanticism is not a turn away from science, but rather an attempt to adapt some of its protocols, giving us a genealogy of "experimental" writing broader than its usual association with Modernism and Post-Modernism.

Wordsworth's claim to methodological rigor generates a sharp distinction from forms of writing that he considers to have surrendered to a taste for sensationalism, as opposed to the "vivid sensation" that poetry can legitimately aim to produce. Chief, although not unique, among these forms is the Gothic novel, which Wordsworth aligns with the malaise of an urbanized society founded on what we might be inclined to call "information technology":

> For a multitude of causes, unknown to former times, are now acting with a combined force to blunt the discriminating powers of the mind, and unfitting it for all voluntary exertion to reduce it to a state of almost savage torpor. The most effective of these causes are the great national events which are daily taking place, and the increasing accumulation of men in cities, where the uniformity of their occupations produces a craving for extraordinary incident, which the rapid communication of intelligence hourly gratifies. To this tendency of life and manners the literature and theatrical exhibitions of the country have conformed themselves. The invaluable works of our elder writers, I had almost said of Shakespeare and Milton, are driven into neglect by frantic novels, sickly and stupid German Tragedies, and deluges of idle and extravagant stories in verse.[6]

Wordsworth and Peacock both reject popular sensationalism, but Wordsworth insists upon his own, properly experimental, methodology of approaching sensation. Anticipating later critiques of mass culture, Wordsworth views the entertainments of an urban and industrial class as sensationalist exploitation.

More than a century later, Walter Benjamin's great essay "The Storyteller" uses terms similar to those of Wordsworth in order to describe the impossibility of the recovery of the world of the tale in the context of "information": "Every morning brings us news of the globe, and yet we are poor in noteworthy stories. This is because no event any longer comes to us without already being shot through with explanation. In other words, by now almost nothing that happens benefits storytelling; almost everything benefits information."[7]

Benjamin's argument rests on the novel as essentially modern in character. It invades and disrupts the domain of the tale:

> The earliest symptom of a process whose end is the decline of storytelling is the rise of the novel at the beginning of modern times. What distinguishes the novel

from the story (and from the epic in the narrower sense) is its essential dependence on the book. The dissemination of the novel became possible only with the invention of printing. What can be handed on orally, the wealth of the epic, is of a different kind from what constitutes the stock in trade of the novel. What differentiates the novel from all other forms of prose literature—the fairy tale, the legend, even the novella—is that it neither comes from oral tradition nor goes into it. This distinguishes it from storytelling in particular. The storyteller takes what he tells from experience—his own or that reported by others. And he in turn makes it the experience of those who are listening to his tale.[8]

If, from Benjamin's point of view, the novel is the form that declares the death of the storyteller, this does not mean that the two forms of narration do not intersect and overlap in their long history. The novelistic forms of Wordsworth's lifetime—Gothic novel, national tale, historical novel—often self-consciously emulated the effects of the oral tales and popular print tales.

The prominence of the ballad in the title of *Lyrical Ballads*, meanwhile, was a strong indication of Wordsworth and Coleridge's shared commitment to the ballad in order to convey the effect of an authentic oral and popular form. Wordsworth was, as we have seen, particularly concerned that the "lyrical" aspect of the ballads should distance them from the "deluges of idle and extravagant stories in verse." This concern extended to the shape of the *Lyrical Ballads* itself. As Coleridge reports the original plan of the volume in *Biographia Literaria* (1817), he and Wordsworth would effectively divide between them the two elements associated with the fairy way of writing—the supernatural and the domestic:

> It was agreed that my endeavours should be directed to persons and characters supernatural, or at least romantic; yet so as to transfer from our inward nature a human interest and a semblance of truth sufficient to procure for these shadows of imagination that willing suspension of disbelief for the moment, which constitutes poetic faith. Mr Wordsworth, on the other hand, was to propose to himself as his object to give the charm of novelty to things of every day, and to excite a feeling analogous to the supernatural, by awakening the mind's attention from the lethargy of custom and directing it to the loveliness and the wonders of the world before us.[9]

Coleridge's "willing suspension of disbelief" thus appears in the context of a recharged version of the fairy way of writing: "shadows of imagination" even echoing Puck's "if we shadows have offended" in the epilogue to *A Midsummer Night's Dream* (V.i.414). However, Wordsworth's increasing hostility to what he considered to be populist sensationalism led to his demotion, in the 1800 edition, of Coleridge's *Rime of the Ancient Mariner* to the conclusion of the volume and the excision of *Christabel* from the same volume.[10]

Wordsworth was contending with the success of both the Gothic novel and the Gothic ballad. The Gothic novel, from at least Radcliffe onward, retained verse as a means of conveying both extreme forms of subjectivity and the experience of the supernatural. Matthew Gregory "Monk" Lewis's wildly successful *The Monk*, first published in 1796, included a number of Gothic ballads, and was widely considered to have popularized the form. Lewis, moreover, brought out *Tales of Wonder*, a collection of supernatural and Gothic ballads widely associated with German sensationalism, and which Lewis termed his "hobgoblin repast," in late 1800, making it roughly contemporary with the second volume of *Lyrical Ballads*. The association of verse with supernatural threshold experiences survived at least through the novels of Scott. In Walter Scott's novel, *The Monastery* (1820), for example, the White Lady of Avenel, is a supernatural spirit "of the race of Ariel" who only speaks in riddling verse.

The ballad and the Gothic novel, more generally, appear to have established the interface between prose and verse during the period. Scott and James Hogg moved from the collection of ballads to tales and novels. Hogg's *Winter Evening Tales* (1820) was his most successful prose work during his own lifetime. Lewis, as we have seen, moved in the opposite direction. The canonical Romantic poets, however, generally scorned any exchange with the novel and were more tempted to emulate the stage, with its Shakespearean prestige, rather than the novel. Still, the success of "frantic novels" had an effect on the poetry, most noticeably in the narrative poems that borrowed motifs and strategies from the Gothic novel. This often produced backhanded tributes to the novelistic forms the poets disdained. As he finished off *Endymion*, for instance, Keats lampooned Radcliffe's style for his friend John Reynolds:

> Buy a girdle—put a pebble in your Mouth—loosen your Braces—for I am going among Scenery where I intend to tip you the Damosel Radcliffe—I'll cavern you, and grotto you, and waterfall you, and wood you, and water you, and immense-rock you, and tremendous sound you, and solitude you.[11]

In the following year, in a letter to his brother and sister-in-law in America, Keats remains jocular about "mother Radcliff," but also more willing to acknowledge his own debt to her: "In my next Packet . . . I shall send you the Pot of Basil, S[t] Agnes eve, and if I should have finished it a little thing call'd the 'eve of S[t] Mark' you see what fine mother Radcliff names I have—it is not my fault—I did not search for them."[12] He did not search, but he discovered a legacy—bequeathed by a mother

(Keats consistently emphasizes Radcliffe's femininity—"damosel," "mother") associated with a popular form. This passage, however, is preceded by one that perhaps indicates Keats was more actively interested in the legacy of popular romance: "I was surprised to hear from Taylor the amount of Murray the Booksellers last sale—what think you of [£] 25,000? He sold 4000 coppies [*sic*] of Lord Byron."[13] Keats is referring to the fourth and last canto of Byron's *Childe Harold*, one of the bestsellers of Romantic poetry, but he could have just as easily been thinking of Radcliffe herself, probably the most highly paid novelist of the period.[14] The fairy way of writing, as it enters the Romantic period, is a form determined as much by the emergence of the Gothic novel as it is by the vernacular tradition of Spenser and Shakespeare that it more readily acknowledges.

This Pleasant Tale

The return to a strong version of fairy sexuality marks Keats's most distinctive revision to the fairy way of writing. Through his reading of Shakespeare and Spenser, Keats glances back at the medieval world of fairy eroticism, which, probably more than any other English poet of the period, he recuperates for the experience of the modern reader. Keats's early interest in Spenser, then, often runs counter to Spenser's accommodation of fairy sexuality to the discipline of Protestant marriage. "Calidore," for example, seems to turn the tables on Spenser's Calidore, who disturbs Colin Clout, who is piping in the midst of what appears to be a fairy circle. In Keats's version, Calidore and his fellow knights unknown to *The Faerie Queene*, pick up some damsels, who maintain a strangely detached indifference to the men:

He [Calidore] gave each damsel's hand so warm a kiss,
And had such manly ardour in his eye;
That each at other look'd half staringly;
And then their features started into smiles
Sweet as blue heavens o'er enchanted isles.[15]

These fairies, unlike the ones that Calidore encounters in Spenser's poem, seem finally unperturbed by his seductions, even as their own attractions take on increasingly other-worldly form: smiles that link them to enchanted, possibly perilous isles.

The seductive encounter with another level of being is a central motif of Keats's poetry. He accessed the medieval romance through the sometimes stern gaze of Spenser, especially the episode of the Bower of Bliss in Book II of *The Faerie Queene*, but in using Spenser, he also seems to glance behind Spenser to the fairy seductions that populate the world of the medieval romance. A charming early sonnet, "This pleasant tale is like a little copse," describes the experience of reading *The Flower and the Leaf,* which in the early nineteenth century was still ascribed to Chaucer. The speaker of the sonnet exclaims on his own desire to come to rest in the rich medieval verse as *locus amoenus*:

> This pleasant tale is like a little copse;
>   The honied lines do freshly interlace,
>   To keep the reader in so sweet a place,
> So that he here and there full hearted stops;
> And oftentimes he feels the dewy drops
>   Come cool and suddenly against his face,
>   And by the wandering melody may trace
> Which way the tender-legged linnet hops.
> Oh! what a power has white simplicity!
>   What mighty power has this gentle story!
>   I, that do ever feel athirst for glory,
> Could at this moment be content to lie
>   Meekly upon the grass, as those whose sobbings
>   Were heard of none beside the mournful robbins.

The dilemma suggested by the poem is the conflict between the poetic ambition of the speaker who does "ever feel athirst for glory" and the desire to rest indolently in the world so seductively represented in *The Flower and the Leaf.* If the occasion is now "Chaucer," the conflict remains Spenserian: Keats fashions himself as Guyon visiting the "copse" of luxurious medieval courtly allegory, as alluring as the Spenserian Bower of Bliss.

For the early Keats, the sensuousness he celebrates is also the languorous sense of duty evaded. The poem enacts the conflict between duty—poetic (epic) vocation— and pleasure—the readerly seductions of poems such as *The Flower and the Leaf.* James Thomson's earlier imitation of Spenser, *The Castle of Indolence* (1733–1734), remains clearly in the background of Keats's own appropriation of Spenser, even if Keats seems less willing than Thomson (or Spenser himself, for that matter) to abandon pleasure for duty.[16] In this respect, he is perhaps the most unconsciously anti-Spenserian of all of the great English readers of Spenser. Like the "swinish" Grylle (borrowed from the Circe episode in *The Odyssey*) at the conclusion of Guyon's destruction of the Bower of Blisse in Book II of *The Faerie Queene*, Keats would no doubt have "repyned greatly" at the destruction of the bower.[17]

Old and New Romance

Perhaps partly for this reason, Keats's various attempts to fill out the Virgilian epic *cursus* remain unsatisfactory or incomplete: *Endymion, Hyperion, The Fall of Hyperion*. Sleep, the apogee of indolent luxury, emerges in the early Keats—*Sleep and Poetry, Endymion*—as the domain of poetic freedom, even though Keats also recognizes that the dreaming imagination is insufficient in itself to obtain the palm. If *Endymion* does not entirely lose the adolescent quality associated with the dream-quest, *The Eve of St. Agnes* succeeds so powerfully because the eruption of dream into waking, sexualized reality is so abrupt and invasive. As one of Keats's own canonical remarks on the imagination had put the matter just before the completion of *Endymion* in 1817, "What the imagination seizes as Beauty must be truth—whether it existed before or not—for I have the same Idea of all our Passions as of Love they are all in their sublime, creative of essential Beauty. . . .The Imagination may be compared to Adam's dream—he awoke and found it truth."[18] The lines gloss Milton's description of Adam's dream of the creation of Eve in *Paradise Lost* without any mention of the intervention of the divine in this sensuous creation of what is, after all, a love mate. Keats's poetry consistently reconceives the Miltonic imagination in terms of a sensuous medieval romance. By the time of *The Eve of St. Agnes* he was also ready to switch the gender of the imaginative dreamer.

The popular superstition that the eve of St. Agnes's feast day (January 21) would provide a maiden with a vision of her future husband was long established in England, but, as Robert Gittings argues, "Keats made the central part of his poem differ from the folk-lore tale. It was not a vision his heroine received, but the physical presence of her love, who had found his way into her room to see her sleeping."[19] Gittings, however, perhaps underestimates the extent to which the popular tradition of the eve of St. Agnes was already quite robustly sexual. A chapbook derived from Madame d'Aulnoy's English persona, *Mother Bunch's Closet Newly Broke Open*, first published around 1765 and reissued four times in the late eighteenth and early nineteenth centuries, featured ribald advice for young men and women on both the eve of St. Agnes and Midsummer eve. The instructions to the maid on the former are suggestive of the frankly erotic handling of the story in Keats:

[A]nd when thou liest down, lay thy right Hand under thy Head, saying these Words, *Now the God of Love send me my Desire*; and make sure to sleep as soon as thou canst, and thou shalt be sure to dream of him who shall be thy Husband and see him stand before thee; and thou wilt take great notice of him and his complexion; and if he offers to salute thee do not deny him, but shew as much favour unto him as thou canst; but if he offers to be uncivil to thee, be sure to hold thy Legs together."[20]

More canonical sources for the poem were almost equally bawdy. Henry Noble MacCracken long ago argued that *The Eve of St. Agnes* was essentially the blend of a story from Boccaccio's *Filocolo* with the popular superstition concerning the eve of St. Agnes.[21] MacCracken's argument has languished in recent years, partly because Keats's reading of the *Filocolo* remains unsubstantiated.[22] Although Keats was no doubt influenced by several sources, including, considerably closer to hand than Boccaccio, Coleridge's *Christabel* and Radcliffe's *Mysteries of Udolpho*, Boccaccio highlights the sexual bravura of Keats's design. Moreover, Keats had been engaged with John Reynolds in a proposed sequence of poems based on *The Decameron* (and was learning to read in Italian in order to do so), which had produced *Isabella*, so we need not so completely rule out Boccaccio's typically frank handling of sexual cunning as an influence on Keats. In *Filocolo* a young lover convinces his beloved's nurse to hide him in her room while she undresses for bed and goes to sleep. Florio, the lover, attempts to awaken Biancofiore while she simultaneously dreams of him. His words do not succeed in doing so, so he resorts to more direct measures:

> He uncovered her and looked with loving eye at her tender bosom, and with a longing hand touched her rounded breasts, kissing them many times. He reached his hands into her private parts, which love had never let him know in his more simple years, and as he touched them he finally came to that place where all sweetness is enclosed; and touching her tender parts in this way he took such delight that his happiness seemed to exceed the realms of the gods.[23]

MacCracken was himself appalled by Boccaccio's handling of sexual seduction: "It is much to Keats's credit that he substitutes here for Boccaccio's debased picture, the poetic device of the lute playing," he comments on the crucial scene of awakening into the arms of her lover.[24] Whether or not he is a version of Boccaccio's Florio, Porphyro's design clearly possesses its sources in medieval fabliaux and romance, both of which were ripe with erotic possibility for Keats. This erotic landscape was no doubt also connected for Keats with *Romeo and Juliet*, with the nurse Angela representing the earthy Italianate motif of the nurse/confidante that Keats, like Shakespeare before him, adopts. Keats, however, significantly strips her of her bawdry. This is a poem in which sexuality is focused on the central couple, not refracted, as so often in Shakespeare, onto the lower orders more generally.

The name Porphyro, moreover, suggests both the Neoplatonic philosopher and opponent of Christianity, as well as Porphyrion, the classical giant who attacked the

Olympians.[25] Titans such as Porphyrion were often associated, by Milton among others, with the Celtic gods, and thus indirectly with the fairy domain that lends its atmosphere to the poem.[26] The purplish stone porphyry was mined in Egypt and used in both the Roman and Byzantine empires; it remained an elusive and exotic source of interest in Keats's lifetime. Napoleon's expedition to Egypt in 1798 had searched for the ancient quarry without success. (It was discovered by the English explorers James Burton and Sir John Wilkinson in 1823, shortly after Keats's death.) The richness of the color of porphyry monuments was no doubt suggestive in a poem in which color is so important. The name Porphyry thus carries Eastern, anti-Christian, anti-aristocratic, and even Celtic associations. As a romance hero, he is a direct ancestor of Heathcliff, whose dark features are consistently associated with blackness in *Wuthering Heights*, and the heroes of popular romance in our own time. The name Madeline, derived from Mary Magdalene, places her more clearly in the domain of Christianity, even if as a penitent "fallen" woman (the patristic interpretation of her status in the New Testament).

There is every reason to believe, then, that Porphyro's designs on Madeline were intended by Keats himself to be as disruptive as possible to Christian morality and aristocratic society of his own time. Keats's own friends reacted to Keats's revisions to the poem, which made the seduction of Madeline even clearer than in the final printed version, in terms similar to MacCracken's response to Boccaccio's narrative. John Taylor and Richard Woodhouse exchanged their own apprehensions about Keats's revisions to the poem, which made the sexual consummation in lines 314–22 more explicit.[27] Woodhouse wrote, "I do apprehend it will render the poem unfit for ladies, & indeed scarcely to be mentioned to them among the 'things that are.'" Keats himself remained defiant, at least up to the point of publication, telling Woodhouse that he wrote for men and "that he sh^d despise a man who would be such a eunuch in sentiment as to leave a maid, with that Character about her, in such a situation: & sho^d despise himself to write about it &c &c &c—and all this sort of Keats-like rhodomontade."[28]

Woodhouse's exasperation fails to register Keats's more accurate sense of the full impact of the poem, even if in terms that are as likely to offend our sensibilities as much as those of Regency England. Nowhere has the sexuality of Keats's poetry occupied such a central, and controversial, position in his canon and its reception. Keats's defiance of contemporary norms in this matter was perhaps rodomontade (he seems to have relented for the purposes of publication), but it also suggested his own sense of the imaginative impact of the poem. He was, after all, not simply representing the sexual fulfillment of his two central characters; he was also using the fairy way of writing to revise the possibilities of the romance as a genre. "Rodomontade" was also assigned to Fuseli's painting, as we have seen, and the shared attribute suggests something about the rebellious relationship of both men to the sexuality morality of the period.

Keats consciously sets the poem in the world of medieval romance as filtered through both the English Gothic novel and the Pope's *Rape of the Lock* (which itself has Shakespeare clearly in its own hinterland). The poem begins with a return to Pope's "all the Nurse and all the Priest have taught," but now filled out as characters in a narrative—the beadsman and Angela, the nurse. Keats's beadsman is not the innocuous priest of Pope, but rather a version of living death:

> Numb were the Beadsman's fingers, while he told
> His rosary, and while his frosted breath,
> Like pious incense from a censer old,
> Seem'd taking flight for heaven, without a death,
> Past the sweet Virgin's picture, while his prayer he saith.   (5–9)

The "sculptur'd dead" of the chapel—"knights, ladies, praying in dumb orat'ries"— meanwhile, "seem to freeze" (14–15). Against this backdrop of the frozen world of Catholicism and antique aristocracy enters the living "argent revelry" of the riotous young aristocracy:

> At length burst in the argent revelry,
> With plume, tiara, and all rich array,
> Numerous as shadows haunting fairily
> The brain, new stuff'd, in youth, with triumphs gay
> Of old romance.   (37–40)

Although described as a kind of *jeunesse dorée*, they represent the values of "old romance" still "haunting fairily" the imagination. Their revelry is "argent," which, in heraldic terms, is represented by the color white—cold and frozen in the world of the poem. Old romance is the purely aristocratic domain of the medieval romance, though of course readily applicable to the Regency world of dandies and rakes.

"These let us wish away" (40), the narrator immediately declares after the phrase "old romance," moving for the first time to a direct use of first-person (plural) narration. This breaks with the tale-like narrative voice that, Christine Gallant has remarked, marks the poem from the very first line ("St. Agnes' Eve—Ah bitter chill it was!").[29] The narrative voice itself is alternately that of the oral tale, with its "ahs" and "ays," and the Standard English of its normative first person plural. This combination suggests the historical moment of the poem: a collective, even national voice responding to the "argent revelry" of Regency England in the year of the Peterloo Massacre. The poem was written before the massacre, but Keats's "rodomontade" about his proposed revisions to the poem occurred in the months after Peterloo, which perhaps lent urgency to his desire to bring forward the sexual rebellion in the poem. This was, moreover, a matter of more than sexual morality. Keats had originally assigned Angela the Beldam interjections of "Christ" and "Jesu" that would have both connected her even more closely to Juliet's nurse. His publishers, Gittings remarks, "careful to avoid religious as well as sexual offence in the poem," removed them.[30] The combination of elements that troubled the publishers reveals the kind of effect Keats wanted for the poem: an old wives' tale meant to have pungency for his own historical moment.

The poem concludes with a reminder of the poem's fiction of orality; the final stanza begins, "And they are gone: ay, ages long ago" (370). Benjamin says that the world of the storyteller "is by definition outside all real historical categories."[31] This appears to be true of the storyteller narrator of Keats's poem, who remembers the chill of a particular Eve of St. Agnes, which, it turns out, belongs to the time out of mind of the old tales. The poem's conclusion thus suggests the ahistorical temporality of the folktale, as well as the radically unworldly temporality that was traditionally ascribed to fairies. These traditional forms seem here to license a radical, even utopian break with modern, novelistic temporality.

La Belle Dame

Madeline's status in the poem is one of its greatest interpretative dilemmas. I think that it is crucial not to read her as a novelistic character, just as the implied temporality of the poem should not be rendered in journalistic terms. Probably the most influential reading of the poem in the past fifty years has been Jack Stillinger's "The Hoodwinking of Madeline" (1961), proposing a kind of battle of the sexes between Porphyro and Madeline rather than a "spiritual pilgrimage" (the reading of Earl Wasserman) that had been the dominant reading of the poem at the time Stillinger first published his essay.[32] Stillinger usefully de-idealized the poem, but he opened the door to a novelistic psychology of Porphyro and Madeline.[33] Instead, we can read Madeline in terms of the generic clues provided by Keats.

After describing the rout of the aristocratic old romance, the narrator quickly turns our attention to the old wives' tale of the eve of St. Agnes as a possible alternative:

> These let us wish away,
> And turn, sole-thoughted, to one Lady there,

Whose heart had brooded, all that wintry day,

On love, and wing'd St. Agnes' saintly care,

As she had heard old dames full many times declare.   (41–45)

Like the lady herself, it would seem, the reader remains "sole-thoughted"—turned from the aristocratic old romance and toward the popular world of the legend surrounding the eve of St. Agnes:

They told her how, upon St. Agnes' Eve,

Young virgins might have visions of delight,

And soft adorings from their loves receive

Upon the honey'd middle of the night,

If ceremonies due they did aright;

As, supperless to bed they must retire,

And couch supine their beauties, lily white;

Nor look behind, nor sideways, but require

Of heaven with upward eyes for all they desire.   (46–54)

The narrator describes Madeline as "hoodwink'd with faery fancy" and thus "all amort / Save to St. Agnes and her lambs" (69–70), apparently dismissing "faery fancy" as mere superstition alongside the death-in-life of empty Catholic ritual. Madeline is, however, no Catholic saint, and her deathlike devotion to St. Agnes is clearly eroticized: her virginal "visions of delight" revise Pope's "Virgins visited by Angel Pow'rs." The "honey'd middle" of St. Agnes' Eve is certainly suggestive enough in this regard. Porphyro dismisses such Catholic enchantments when he hears of her obsequies to St. Agnes: "he scarce could brook / Tears, at the thought of those enchantments cold, / And Madeline asleep in lap of legends old" (133–35). When, however, Madeline does awaken, to Porphyro singing "La belle dame sans mercy," his physical intrusion into her chamber confirms her dream: "Her eyes were open, but she still beheld, / Now wide awake, the vision of her sleep" (298–99).

The nurse associates Porphyro's audacity with elfin confidence, but even more striking is her sense of Madeline as conjurer:

Thou must hold water in a witch's sieve,

And be liege-lord of all the Elves and Fays,

To venture so: it fills me with amaze

To see thee, Porphyro!—St. Agnes' Eve!

God's help! my lady fair the conjurer plays

This very night: good angels her deceive!"   (120–25)

The strange sense that the poem produces—that Porphyro the trickster remains under the enchantment of his "victim"—echoes through the allusive language of his seduction of Madeline.[34]

His initial plan, like that of Iachimo in *Cymbeline*, is simply to see her in the "privacy" (165) of her chamber:

> That he might see her beauty unespied,
> And win perhaps that night a peerless bride,
> While legion'd fairies pac'd the coverlet,
> And pale enchantment held her sleepy-eyed.
> Never on such a night have lovers met,
> Since Merlin paid his Demon all the monstrous debt.   (166–71)[35]

The "legion'd fairies" still seem to inhabit the world of Belinda's boudoir from *The Rape of the Lock*. Merlin's "monstrous debt," whatever it might actually be—most suitable to the reading I propose here is the life that Merlin owes to his fairy lover, Vivien—suggests the perilous nature of Porphyro's erotic quest.[36] This sense of the impending doom of the male who has been embraced by a fairy lover thus hangs over the rather more mundane seduction of the innocent Madeline, creating a counterplot in which it is Madeline who is the unwittingly supernatural agent of a perilous seduction.

The "ancient ditty" of "La belle dame sans mercy," which is Porphyro's means of awakening Madeline, only heightens the effect of her own uncanny power. Although "long since mute" in *The Eve of St. Agnes*, Keats himself soon after produced his own version, "La Belle Dame Sans Merci: A Ballad," based on the traditional ballad, "Thomas Rymer," which had been printed in Robert Jamieson's *Popular Ballads* (1806) and, in a somewhat embellished version, in Walter Scott's *Minstrelsy of the Scottish Border* (1802–1803). In Keats's version, the ballad shifts to a dialogue in which, crucially, the knight can retell his own story as if he were, at least at the beginning, the principal actor in it. The lesson of "La Belle Dame" is quite explicitly that the apparent seduction of the lady is rather the reverse. In *The Eve of St. Agnes*, of course, this potential meaning is muted enough to allow for a reading that emphasizes the "hoodwinking" of Madeline rather than the "enchantment" of Porphyro. Perhaps, though, Keats wrote "La Belle Dame" at least partially as a kind of retrospective elaboration of the crucial situation of seduction in his earlier poem. One hint to that effect is that the Belle Dame "look's at me as she did love, / And made sweet moan" (19–20). Madeline, when she hears "La belle dame sans mercy" responds in her sleep with "a soft moan" (294). Madeline is not a *fée fatale* along the lines of the belle dame—her own desire is genuine enough—but she does occupy a place that is neither that of victim nor predator: the place of enchantment. Keats's mobilization of the domain of fairy is simultaneously represented as simultaneously innocent and uncanny.[37]

When Porphyro finally does "melt" into Madeline's dream (320), an image both sexual and oneiric—Keats's fully eroticized version of Adam's dream—enchantment becomes physical reality. The two escape the dragon's lair of romance tradition, in the shape of the drunken revelers: "there were sleeping dragons all around, / At glaring watch, perhaps, with ready spears" (353–54). Keats twice repeats the phrase "like phantoms" (361–62) to describe their progress through this dragon's lair. A poem which begins with Porphyro's rejection of old "faery fancy" concludes with Porphyro and Madeline absorbed into what Porphyro himself calls "an elfin storm from faery land" (343).

Searchable Shakespeare

Keats also surrounds the conclusion of the poem with the distinctive penumbra of Shakespearean tragedy. The "bloated wassaillers . . . drown'd all in Rhenish" (346, 349) suggests *Hamlet*; the poem's Porter, lying "in uneasy sprawl" (363), appears to be a cameo appearance from *Macbeth*. The storm of "flaw-blown sleet" (325) and gusts that "still rave and beat" (327) recalls the magnificent tempests of *King Lear*.[38] Keats's sonnet on *King Lear*, written about a year before *The Eve of St. Agnes*, suggests that Shakespeare was very much on his mind as a means of transforming the old "golden-tongued Romance" into something more powerful:

> O golden-tongued Romance, with serene lute!
>   Fair plumed syren, queen of far-away!
>   Leave melodizing on this wintry day,
> Shut up thy olden pages, and be mute.
> Adieu! for, once again, the fierce dispute
>   Betwixt damnation and impassion'd clay
>   Must I burn through; once more humbly assay
> The bitter-sweet of this Shaksperean fruit.
> Chief Poet! and ye clouds of Albion,
>   Begetters of our deep eternal theme!
> When through the old oak forest I am gone,
>   Let me not wander in a barren dream:
> But, when I am consumed in the fire,
> Give me new phoenix wings to fly at my desire.   (10–14)

The sonnet replaces the medieval romance with the bracing "modern" instance of *King Lear*. *Lear* is itself a play with a pronounced interest in the relationship between romance, fairy tale (the Cinderella story of Cordelia, Edgar's invocation of the old English tale of "Childe Roland"), and tragedy: a combination of ingredients that Keats seems to have found congenial at the time of writing *The Eve of St. Agnes*. The sestet places the speaker inside the domain of romance—wandering in a forest, potentially consumed by fire (and thus sexual desire). This, however, is not "golden-tongued Romance," which has been muted by the poem, but romance that has been "assayed" in the fire of Shakespearean tragedy. The hope of the sonnet is that Keats as reader of Shakespeare—and perhaps under the "enchantment" of Shakespeare—will not suffer the fate of the knight of "La Belle Dame," wandering "in a barren dream." In fact, the allusive presence of Shakespeare in the conclusion of *The Eve of St. Agnes* suggests that the essential distinction for Keats remains one between barren dream and fruitful romance: the question of poetic strength for which Shakespeare appears to offer a compelling imaginative landscape and testing ground.[39]

The visual power of *The Eve of St. Agnes*, which so many readers have noticed in its striking sensuality (although the other senses, particularly hearing, are by no means neglected), emblematizes what Keats considers a new romance ready to stand the test of Shakespeare's *Lear*. At the crucial moment of her undressing before the hidden Porphyro, the painted glass of her windows stunningly casts its glow over her own form of "enchantment":

> A casement high and triple-arch'd there was,
> All garlanded with carven imag'ries
> Of fruits, and flowers, and bunches of knot-grass,
> And diamonded with panes of quaint device,
> Innumerable of stains and splendid dyes,
> As are the tiger-moth's deep-damask'd wings;
> And in the midst, 'mong thousand heraldries,
> And twilight saints, and dim emblazonings,
> A shielded scutcheon blush'd with blood of queens and kings.
>
> Full on this casement shone the wintry moon,
> And threw warm gules on Madeline's fair breast,
> As down she knelt for heaven's grace and boon;
> Rose-bloom fell on her hands, together prest,
> And on her silver cross soft amethyst,
> And on her hair a glory, like a saint:
> She seem'd a splendid angel, newly drest,

Save wings, for heaven:—Porphyro grew faint:

She knelt, so pure a thing, so free from mortal taint.   (208–25)

As with the moon of *A Midsummer Night's Dream*, virginal and barren in itself, but apparently sponsoring the topsy-turvy world of desire, the cold "wintry moon" here seems to create something entirely new as it shines through the medieval decorations: the sudden illumination of Madeline's body as it receives the new light cast by the heraldry and religious imagery. (The implication, that the light shining through the stained glass would actually color Madeline's body, is symbolically powerful if technically incorrect about the effect of stained glass.) The generation of new desire and new romance here clearly emerges out of the dialectical exchange of the old order: virginal moon and the radiant emblems of the feudal/Catholic order. Madeline becomes the living embodiment of this synthesis: angelic but no longer virginal, devoted to her lover, and radiant with a new "blush" of desire given to her by moonlight.

A similar combination appears to occur in the case of Porphyro, in an even more expansive sensory range. As he approaches her bedside, the reader suddenly "hears" the clamor from the other rooms:

The boisterous, midnight, festive clarion,

The kettle-drum, and far-heard clarionet,

Affray his ears, though but in dying tone:—

The hall door shuts again, and all the noise is gone.   (258–61)

When Porphyry shuts the door again, the "dying tone" of the revelry is also the passing of the feudal (and Regency) aristocracy. He proceeds to load her bedside table with sweets and exotic foods from the East, reminding us of the Middle Eastern connections signaled by his name. Like the stained glass of Madeline's room, they suddenly produce a new source of sensory richness as they fuse with Madeline's Christian world:

These delicates he heap'd with glowing hand

On golden dishes and in baskets bright

Of wreathed silver: sumptuous they stand

In the retired quiet of the night,

Filling the chilly room with perfume light. . . .   (271–75)

The romance of Porphyro and Madeline represents a synthesis of the medieval elements of *The Eve of St. Agnes*, fusing them into eroticized rebellion.[40] This perhaps also lies behind the sense that they are forever "lost" to that world in the "elfin-storm." The medieval world they leave behind collapses into "ashes cold" (378), the last words of the poem. Indeed, Keats has effectively plundered the medieval romance in order to revise and revivify its essential ingredients in a new poetic form, if one that remains recognizably indebted to the fairy way of writing.

The colouring of St Agnes eve

As the marvellous [*sic*] is the most enticing and the surest guarantee of harmonious numbers I have been endeavouring to persuade myself to untether Fancy and let her manage for herself—I and myself cannot agree about this at all. Wonders are no wonders to me. I am more at home amongst Men and women. I would rather read Chaucer than Ariosto—The little dramatic skill I may as yet have however badly it might show in a Drama would I think be sufficient for a Poem— I wish to diffuse the colouring of St Agnes eve throughout a Poem in which Character and Sentiment would be the figures to such drapery—Two or three such Poems, if God should spare me, written in the course of the next six years, would be a famous gradus ad Parnassum altissimum—I mean they would nerve me up to the writing of a few fine Plays—my greatest ambition—when I do feel ambitious. I am sorry to say that is very seldom.[41]

Keats himself recognized the power of *The Eve of St. Agnes* in visual terms—its "colouring" and "drapery"—which he hoped to diffuse throughout future poetic projects, but with the addition of "character" and "sentiment." What this letter balances is the "marvellous" and the dramatic. Keats wants both in a kind of Shakespearean synthesis: the world of the "marvelous" and that of Chaucerian "Men and women." The rest of the letter remarks on his reading of Holinshed's *Chronicles*, strongly suggesting the Shakespearean character of his dramatic ambition.

Whether or not Keats's early death robbed him of an ambition that, if realized, would have made him unique among the English Romantic poets—a fully dramatic artist—the great success of *The Eve of St. Agnes* was in the visual arts rather than on the stage: a medium that lent its own coloring to the portrayal of desire and rebellion. With some collaboration from John Everett Millais, William Holman Hunt painted *The Flight of Madeline and Porphyro during the Drunkenness Attending the Revelry* (1848; Guildhall Art Gallery, London) in the same year that Keats was widely rediscovered through the biography of Richard Monckton Milnes and revolution broke out across continental Europe. Dante Gabriel Rossetti saw and praised the painting, and the Pre-Raphaelite Brotherhood was formed shortly thereafter. Millais's own painting, *Isabella* (1848–1849; Walker Art Gallery), based on the Keats poem, effectively announced his own adherence to Pre-Raphaelitism, and he went on to paint two striking versions of *The Eve of St. Agnes* (second version, 1862–1863; Royal Collection), both of which place the viewer in the position of Porphyro watching his lover undress. His version of Tennyson's *Marianna* (1850–1851; Tate Britain), on the other hand, borrows Keats's motif of female desire colored by its proximity to the stained glass of medieval religion and heraldry. For Millais, the connection between Keats and Shakespeare in the domain of sexuality and fantasy was apparently natural enough. Shortly after *Marianna*, Millais produced *Ophelia* (1851–1852; Tate Britain), an obsessive representation of a naturalized (and fatal) female desire that continues to adorn many a dorm room in the English-speaking world.

Keats's early reputation as a sensual poet largely remained with him throughout the century, which also made him particularly available to literary and artistic movements that vaunted the spirit of youth—and the erotic rebellion that seemed to be intimately aligned with youth—from Tennyson and the Pre-Raphaelites to Wildean aestheticism. William Butler Yeats paid Keats the tribute of exempting his work from the general run of insipid English fairies: "Shakespeare and Keats had the folklore of their own day, while Shelley had but mythology."[42] Yeats also understood Keats's version of the lamia (in the poem of the same name) to be a strong version of the Celtic fairy lover.

Ultimately, however, the fairy way of writing was largely excluded from Modernist culture, and marginalized along two different cultural fronts. The innocuous fairies of Tickell passed into the nineteenth century as the material of children's stories. By the time of J. M. Barrie's *Peter Pan* (1904), the world of fairies was already linked to a kind of self-exile from the demands of adulthood.[43] Modernism would forgive neither Barrie nor later, in a different fashion, J. R. R. Tolkien their failure to adhere to the protocols of cultural adulthood. By the end of the nineteenth century, moreover, the word "fairy" had acquired the secondary meaning of an effeminate male homosexual, at least in New York City, and possibly spreading outward from there.[44] There is little clear evidence about the early use of the term, but it is possible that it drew on the older association of the fairy with seductive femininity also mobilized by Keats. The "fairy" as homosexual was thought to have refused adult masculinity, which linked the male homosexual to the permanent childhood of Barrie. Fairies thus entered the twentieth century with a set of associations hardly likely to grant them much cultural prestige.

CHAPTER SIX

Before and after Literature
J. R. R. Tolkien

Belief

If the early modern history of the fairy way of writing is part of the disenchantment of the world, self-consciously appropriating discredited forms of enchantment, the modern history of fantasy returns to precisely the problem of belief seemingly jettisoned by early modern fantasy. From the German Romantics—in particular the Catholic Novalis (1772–1801)—onward, the fairy tale, and then the fantastic more generally, became favored vehicles for expressing religious and sacramental belief.[1] By the middle of the nineteenth century, the English fairy tale could be made to bear the weight of Christian, if heterodox, truth in the stories of George MacDonald (1824–1905), a literary follower of Novalis.

The conjunction of the literary fairy tale and Christianity measured something of the disenchantment of Christian belief itself in the period. G. K. Chesterton (1874–1936), who was an important precursor for the Christian appropriation of fantasy in twentieth-century English literature, described the Victorian age as a period when unbelief or agnosticism became more or less the official creed of the educated, who retained their religion as a matter of social formality or moral instruction. "A solemn friend of my grandfather used to go for walks on Sunday carrying a prayer-book, without the least intention of going to church. And he calmly defended it by saying with uplifted hand: 'I do it, Chessie, as an example to others.' "[2] In response, the essential trick of Chesterton's own orthodoxy was to break ranks with elite norms and embrace the beliefs of the uneducated, returning to the domain of the old wives' tales *as a believer*. In this he continued, in the new and somewhat surprising domain of Christian apologetics, the fairy way of writing. For this reason, the early engagement of William Butler Yeats with the myths of Ireland was a particularly important influence on the young, pre- or proto-orthodox, Chesterton:

> Now against this drab background of dreary modern materialism, Willie Yeats was calmly walking about as the Man Who Knew the Fairies. Yeats stood for

enchantment; exactly where [St. John] Hankin stood for disenchantment. But I very specially rejoiced in the fighting instinct which made the Irishman so firm and positive about it. He was the real original rationalist who said that the fairies stand to reason. He staggered the materialists by attacking their abstract materialism with a completely concrete mysticism; "Imagination!" he would say with withering contempt; "There wasn't much imagination when Farmer Hogan was dragged out of bed and thrashed like a sack of potatoes—that they did, they had 'um out;" the Irish accent warming with scorn; "they had 'um out and thumped 'um; and that's not the sort of thing that a man wants to imagine." But the concrete examples were not only a comedy; he used one argument which was sound, and I have never forgotten it. It is the fact that it is not abnormal men like artists, but normal men like peasants, who have borne witness a thousand times to such things; it is the farmers who see the fairies. It is the agricultural labourer who calls a spade a spade who also calls a spirit a spirit; it is the woodcutter with no axe to grind, except for woodcutting, who will say he saw a man hang on a gallows and afterwards hang round it as a ghost. It is all very well to say we ought not to believe in the ghost on an ignorant man's evidence. But we should hang the man on the gallows on the same man's evidence.[3]

It is clear that Chesterton never forgot the lesson of Yeats, since so much of his championing of Christianity was in effect the championing of the beliefs of the common people over those of their betters. If the later Anglo-American, Eliotic brand of High Church Anglicanism, so prominent in British Modernism of the 1920s and 1930s, seems continuous with Chesterton, the two were culturally of quite distinctive forms. Eliot created out of cultural disenchantment a select community of hierophants; Chesterton never really stopped being a prolific journalist-essayist and popularizer of a late Victorian and Edwardian variety. His amicable disputations with George Bernard Shaw indicate something of his cultural position; like Shaw, he was a public controversialist. As later with C. S. Lewis (1898–1963), he understood himself to be attacking elite prejudices on behalf of the basic common sense of Christian belief. Gabriel Syme, protagonist of *The Man Who Was Thursday* (1908), thus finds himself looking down on the "sprawling eccentricities" of the cultural elite "from the starry pinnacle of the commonplace."[4]

Although Chesterton's Christian populism sometimes drifted into the anti-Semitism shared by his brother, Cecil, and his close friend, Hillaire Belloc, it also produced fantasy fiction that both dissented from British imperialism in the wake of the Boer War and anticipated some of the nightmares of the managed society of the coming century (and beyond). *The Napoleon of Notting Hill* (1904) is an early science fiction (set in the future of 1984) with a touch of the fairy way of writing. King Auberon (Oberon) of Britain perversely responds to what we might identify as a globalized, managerial society with the re-enchantment of London, creating a medieval domain of fiefdoms out of the city's individual neighborhoods. Despite its visionary conclusion, *The Man Who Was Thursday* is subtitled "A Nightmare," partly because of its Kafkaesque imagining of a world of seemingly unlimited surveillance.

The difference between the Modernists and those more directly indebted to Chesterton—the "Inklings," the Oxford coterie of the 1930s and 1940s that included C. S. Lewis and J. R. R. Tolkien (1892–1973)—was consequential for the history of Anglo-American literature in the twentieth century, but it was not a difference that can be fully described in terms of religious or political belief. T. S. Eliot, after all, converted to Christianity *before* C. S. Lewis (although Eliot was older at the time of his conversion), and Eliot and Pound were more reactionary politically than most of the individual members of the Inklings. The literary genealogy of the Inklings prominently included the Victorian progressivism of George MacDonald and William Morris (1834–1896). MacDonald, whose work is suffused with Christian mysticism, was a heterodox clergyman and protofeminist, who wrote to earn a living after being ousted by his congregation for his heterodox views. Morris's fantasies, which strongly influenced Tolkien, were written in the same period as his socialist classic, *News from Nowhere* (1890). The Inklings themselves, however, did not inherit the visionary progressivism of MacDonald and Morris, and their Christianity was Modernist to the extent that it was self-consciously defiant of a secularizing modernity.[5]

The crucial difference between the Modernists and the Inklings was cultural, expressed in the allotment of cultural capital. The Modernists insisted on exclusion and autonomy; the Inklings attempted an end-run around Bloomsbury and Eliot with attempts to speak to a general readership in terms that only guaranteed their marginalization in twentieth-century high literary culture. The Inklings were aware, and resentful, of this distribution of cultural capital. As early as 1926, before the Inklings existed, Lewis was already attempting to put together a collective parody of Eliot, to be submitted to Eliot's own *Criterion*, under the pseudonym of a brother and a sister, Rollo and Bridget Considine. "Bridget is the elder," wrote Lewis in his diary, "and they are united by an affection so tender as to be almost incestuous."[6] If Franco Moretti is correct that Modernism was "the last *literary season* of Western culture," it was also the moment that firmed up distinctions between the autonomous work of the "literary" artist and the heteronomous appeal to the marketplace of the "middlebrow" or popular writer.[7] The Inklings were generally demoted to the latter camp.

The Inklings' programmatic engagement with fantasy was, of course, central to their middlebrow status, an early consequence of the widening gulf between "serious" and "genre" fiction in the early years of the century. Although I do not wish simply to reinforce this division, it does seem reasonable to examine the efficacy of the program of Christian fantasy. Did the Inklings succeed in undoing the disenchantment of the world, or did they repeat the Victorian displacement of enchantment to the nursery? In Lewis, in particular, the proselytizing aspect of the *Chronicles of Narnia* sometimes has the unintended effect of making Christian revelation look like a substitute for a more powerful experience of childhood fantasy. At the conclusion of *The Voyage of the "Dawn Treader"* (1952), Aslan explains to Edmund and Lucy that they are now too old to enter his world (Narnia), which is clearly the world of the child's tale:

> "Dearest," said Aslan very gently, "you and your brother will never come back to Narnia."
>
> "Oh, *Aslan!*" said Edmund and Lucy both together in despairing voices.
>
> "You are too old, children," said Aslan, "and you must begin to come close to your own world now."
>
> "It isn't Narnia, you know," sobbed Lucy. "It's *you*. We shan't meet *you* there. And how can we live, never meeting you?"
>
> "But you shall meet me, dear one," said Aslan.
>
> "Are—are you there too, Sir?" said Edmund.
>
> "I am," said Aslan. "But there I have another name. You must learn to know me by that name. This was the very reason why you were brought to Narnia, that by knowing me here for a little, you may know me better there."[8]

Here, Christianity appears to struggle with the Victorian cult of the child, and it is not clear that the association of full Christian belief with adulthood is a net gain for Christian doctrine. Aslan is the child's version of Christ, but the older children must now learn to recognize him in the adult world rather than in the world of tales. But is this adult world of Christian belief more than weak compensation for the loss of primary childhood belief? Both Lewis and Tolkien were powerfully gripped by the largely pagan Germanic literature of "the North" as young readers, and there is little biographical sense of an equivalent early engagement with the Bible or Biblical literature. Lewis frankly attributed his own early hesitations about accepting Christianity to the fact that "the *spontaneous* appeal of the Christian story is so much less to me than that of Paganism."[9] One certainly senses the residual version of this childhood preference in *Narnia*, however much the series is meant to guide children to Christian adulthood.

Fiction and Disbelief

Unlike Lewis, Tolkien consistently refused the attempt to allegorize Christian belief in fantasy form. Tolkien's essay "On Fairy-Stories" (first presented as a lecture in 1939) concludes with an epilogue that engages with the relationship between fairy tale and Christianity in terms more nuanced than those of Lewis. For Tolkien, the power of Christianity is its fusion of the "Primary World" of human experience and history with the "Secondary World" of fairy tales and stories of all kinds. Christianity is in effect the fairy tale realized in history. "The Gospels contain a fairy-story, or a story of a larger kind which embraces all the essence of fairy-stories. . . . But this story has entered History and the primary world; the desire and aspiration of sub-creation has been raised to the fulfillment of Creation."[10] "Sub-creation" is Tolkien's term for artistic production generally, since he knew very well that the power of "creation" had once been thought to belong to God alone. The concept of "sub-creation" thus resituates artistic creation in the context of the larger divine act of creation; humans create because they have in them something of God's original creative act. In this, he followed MacDonald, whose essay, "The Imagination," both insists on the power of the imagination and encloses literary creation within God's creation.[11]

As befits, however, a reader shaped by the pagan literature of the North, Tolkien is less interested than either Lewis or MacDonald in the truth of the tale than in the truth of the *form*. The tale itself is the form that, in the New Testament, bears the burden of Christian truth and is then itself redeemed in all of its incarnations:

> In God's kingdom the presence of the greatest does not depress the small. Redeemed Man is still man. Story, fantasy, still go on, and should go on. The Evangelium has not abrogated legends; it has hallowed them, especially the "happy ending" . . . . All tales may come true; and yet, at the last, redeemed, they may be as like and as unlike the forms that we give them as Man, finally redeemed, will be like and unlike the fallen that we know.[12]

Tolkien clearly hopes and expects to meet his beloved, and often pagan, literature of the North in heaven—not necessarily reformed, but simply understood in its complete relationship to Christian revelation. He can expect this because the Christian eucatastrophe is itself a kind of fairy tale, which God has chosen, says Tolkien, because "God redeemed the corrupt making-creatures, men, in a way fitting to this aspect, as to others, of their strange nature."[13]

Unlike Lewis in *Narnia*, Tolkien fiercely rejects turning the fairy story into something like the child's version of Christianity. It has for Tolkien its own independent existence, if an existence that is in some *final* sense reconcilable with Christian truth: "true" because understood as part of the subcreative process that reflects God's original "creative process" and because the Christian mythos takes the form of a fairy story. That reconciliation was for Tolkien a diminishment if it attempted to allegorize itself in terms of Christian belief. The question of allegory was the primary literary disagreement between Tolkien and Lewis, and I think that Tolkien's reservations about allegory can be boiled down to a fundamental reservation about any literary practice that reduces the autonomy of the tale. This can also be measured in the literary reputation of the two writers. Adult readers of Lewis's fantasy tend to be enthusiastic Christians, for whom *Narnia* represents the literary practice of the theory contained in his Christian apologetics. Tolkien's huge "fan base" includes everything from heavy metal enthusiasts to W. H. Auden. Christian belief is largely secondary, or nonexistent, for much of his readership.

The basis for this distinction between the two writers can already be found in "On Fairy-stories." Although Tolkien's epilogue to the essay emphasizes the final truth of the fairy tale in the context of Christianity, he is generally much more insistent in the essay on the radically separate nature of the kind of "truth" that is produced in the Secondary World of the tale. For this reason, he challenges Coleridge in the context of addressing the question of whether children are the best audience for the fairy tale:

> Children are capable, of course, of *literary belief*, when the story-maker's art is good enough to produce it. That state of mind has been called "willing suspension of disbelief." But this does not seem to me a good description of what happens. What really happens is that the story-maker proves a successful "sub-creator." He makes a Secondary World which your mind can enter. Inside it, what he relates is "true": it accords with the laws of that world. You therefore believe it, while you are, as it were, inside. The moment disbelief arises, the spell is broken; the magic, or rather art, has failed. You are then out in the Primary World again, looking at the little abortive Secondary World from outside. If you are obliged, by kindliness or circumstance, to stay, then disbelief must be suspended (or stifled), otherwise listening and looking would become intolerable. But this suspension of disbelief is a substitute for the real thing, a subterfuge we use when condescending to games or make-believe, or when trying (more or less willingly) to find what virtue we can in the work of an art that has for us failed.[14]

Coleridge himself associated the "willing suspension of disbelief" with his own supernatural and "romantic" contributions to *The Lyrical Ballads*. The result is what he terms "poetic faith," which probably struck Tolkien as pretty thin gruel, the literary equivalent of Coleridge's early Unitarianism. For Tolkien, however, such a "willing suspension" implies indulgence in rather than engagement with a fiction, roughly the same as an adult's patronizing attitude toward a child's tale. Tolkien's language here is that of magic, but without sharing the Victorian enthusiasm for the child's naïve "enchantment" by the fairy story. Tolkien does not fundamentally distinguish between child and adult readers in this respect; both share a capacity for what Tolkien calls "literary belief," but this is not the unquestioning faith usually ascribed to young children. The literary sub-creator must be able to solicit belief from tough-minded readers, whether adults or children. The "magic" of Tolkien's concept of the Secondary World depends on its adherence to its own internal logic as a coherent world, and it must be capable of casting the temporary "spell" of belief over a reader who enters its domain.

Tolkien's ambition here is not merely to quibble with Coleridge, but to overturn an attitude toward fiction that lies behind Coleridge, including almost the entire literary edifice of the fairy way of writing, which always depended on a form of suspended disbelief and thus disenchantment. As William Nelson has argued, Renaissance writers had already adumbrated the essentials of Coleridge's suspension of disbelief:

> Renaissance makers of fiction . . . seek to delight or instruct their readers, not to delude them. . . . Representation of reality is scarcely a major concern . . . and the fictional character of the tale is not really in doubt. Recognition that the story is play and not history lies at or near the surface of awareness, not deep beneath it, for the author parodies the role of historian rather than assumes it, and he does not want his reader to think him so unscrupulous as to tell false for true or so foolish as to play a child's game with the seriousness of a child.[15]

Tolkien, however, wants to play a child's game with the seriousness of an adult, and Nelson's formulation of the self-conscious playfulness of Renaissance fictions allows us to see something of the distance between Tolkien's fiction and the fairy way of writing as it was construed after Shakespeare. It is easy to see why Tolkien's personal canon of English literature ended with Chaucer.

Despite his own literary tastes, however, Tolkien might be better understood as in some respects essentially modern in his approach to fiction. His own fiction attempts to elicit—and, unusually, often gains—the "total immersion" of the reader in the reality of the fictive world, which Nelson argues is characteristic of modern fictions:

Once we have opened the pages of a novel we do not wish to be reminded that the events recorded are not true history. For the space of our reading we expect to be captivated, to find the characters "convincing," the plot (however fantastic) within its terms believable. Henry James accuses the author who betrays the unreality of his story and so breaks his own bubble of committing "a terrible crime."[16]

Tolkien's comment, cited earlier, makes a similar point in the domain of magic: "The moment disbelief arises, the spell is broken; the magic, or rather art, has failed." If it is uncommon to find Tolkien placed alongside James, it is also indicative of the ambitious task he is already setting for fantasy fiction in his essay: to produce a convincing fiction about a fabulous world for modern readers, even when measured against the realist or psychological novel.

Theater and Camp

If the disagreement with Coleridgean aesthetics is perhaps to be expected from Tolkien, it is a measure of the audacity of the essay that it includes a stern negative assessment of Shakespeare, as well as pretty much all of English literature after Chaucer, for which Shakespeare serves as synecdoche:

> In human art Fantasy is a thing best left to words, to true literature. In painting, for instance, the visible presentation of the fantastic image is technically too easy; the hand tends to outrun the mind, even to overthrow it. Silliness or morbidity are frequent results. It is a misfortune that Drama, an art fundamentally distinct from Literature, should so commonly be considered together with it, or as a branch of it. Among these misfortunes we may reckon the depreciation of Fantasy. For in part at least this depreciation is due to the natural desire of critics to cry up the forms of literature or "imagination" that they themselves, innately or by training, prefer. And criticism in a country that has produced so great a Drama, and possesses the works of William Shakespeare, tends to be far too dramatic. But Drama is naturally hostile to Fantasy. Fantasy, even of the simplest kind, hardly ever succeeds in Drama, when that is presented as it should be, visibly and audibly acted. Fantastic forms are not to be counterfeited. Men dressed up as talking animals may achieve buffoonery or mimicry, but they do not achieve Fantasy.[17]

The appeal to "true literature" is directed against both the theater of Shakespeare and the visual tradition that probably includes, for Tolkien, the "morbidity" of Fuseli and the "silliness" of Victorian fairy painting.

Tolkien's attention turns quickly from Shakespeare to the dismal "failure of the bastard form, pantomime."[18] Although Shakespeare remains great and pantomime low, there is also the sense that the trajectory set in place by Shakespearean theater, particularly regarding supernatural beings, almost inevitably leads to pantomime. Shakespeare has clearly, in any case, exercised too great an influence over English literature, producing a literature dominated by theater. This is especially true, of course, in the domain of fairy stories, but Tolkien manages to avoid any real discussion of Shakespeare's most extended excursion into the domain of fairies, *A Midsummer Night's Dream*. (It appears only in a footnote devoted to the history of the word "elf" in German.) The reason for this avoidance of Shakespeare's version of "Faërie" (Tolkien's term for the imaginative domain he associates with fairy stories) takes us down a detour in seventeenth-century literature, and to a poem rather than a play:

> Drayton's *Nymphidia* [1627] is, considered as a fairy-story (a story about fairies), one of the worst ever written. The palace of Oberon has walls of spider's legs. . . . The knight Pigwiggen rides on a frisky earwig, and sends his love, Queen Mab, a bracelet of emmets' eyes, making an assignation in a cowslip-flower. But the tale that is told amid all this prettiness is a dull story of intrigue and sly go-betweens; the gallant knight and angry husband fall into the mire, and their wrath is stilled by a draught of the waters of Lethe. It would have been better if Lethe had swallowed the whole affair.[19]

Michael Drayton's poem is an easier target than Shakespeare's play: it is a lesser work. It is also strongly influenced by Shakespeare's erotic treatment of Faërie in the *Dream* and Mercutio's fantasia upon Queen Mab in *Romeo and Juliet*. Tolkien, as we have already seen, is not afraid to take Shakespeare to task for his perceived faults, but in this instance, Tolkien deflects the double charge of wantonness and diminishment from Shakespeare to Drayton—where it is indeed more prominent. There remains an unspoken but strong sense in Tolkien's essay that Shakespeare's delinquency, partly erotic, in the domain of Faërie has reduced the possibilities of fantasy to mere pantomime, in the form of either child's play or erotic romp.

The long Victorian tradition of rendering Shakespearean fantasy in the form of luscious stage spectacles probably did little to endear theatricalized fantasy to Tolkien. The signal production of *A Midsummer Night's Dream* in his own childhood, directed by Sir Herbert Beerbohm Tree in 1900, was simply the most extravagant of a long line of spectacles:

> In the forest scenes, mechanical birds sounded in English beeches, and the moon sent silver light through traceries of branches to light a fairy troupe of children, who danced in a fairy ring to Mendelssohn. . . . Titania was sung to sleep in a honeysuckle bower by forty-seven fairies, one of whom hovered in the air above her,

amid hanging boughs, while moonlight played on a background sea. . . . Tree's costume chart lists ten "special flying fairies, 4 fireflies, 9 imps, 4 sea urchins, 8 wood elves, [and] 2 wood fairies." Some fairies could switch on battery-operated glow lamps which they wore at such moments as Puck's incantation over the sleeping lover. [Julia] Neilsen as Oberon wore an electrically lighted breastplate and crown.[20]

Tree's 1911 revival of the play famously added live rabbits to the forest scenes, following a trail of bran around the stage. As Gary Jay Williams remarks, "By the end of the first decade of the twentieth century, productions of the play were overripe with novelties."[21]

Even the Modernist productions of the play that triumphed in Tolkien's early adulthood retained the long-standing tradition of rendering the play with a maximum of spectacle. A production inflected by Expressionist theater made its way to Hollywood in the 1935 version directed by Max Reinhardt, whose stage productions of the play in Germany and the Anglophone world were already famous, and William Dieterle. The merger of the *Dream* with the great "dream factory" that dominated the culture of the twentieth century is a notable event in itself, and it appeared only a few years before Tolkien first presented his lecture on fairy tales. Tolkien claimed to have no knowledge of or interest in cinema, and there is no particular reason to assume that he saw the film. In any case, Tolkien would have probably seen it as simply a more spectacular version of the general problem of presenting invented beings on the stage, a problem that Tolkien no doubt most closely associated with Shakespeare's *Dream*:

> Drama has, of its very nature, already attempted a kind of bogus, or shall I say at least substitute, magic: *the visible and audible presentation of imaginary men in a story.* That is in itself an attempt to counterfeit the magician's wand. To introduce, even with mechanical success, into this quasi-magical secondary world a further fantasy or magic is to demand, as it were, an inner or tertiary world. It is a world too much.[22]

Tolkien's criticism recognizes, backhandedly, the strong relationship between magic and theater in Shakespeare's play—its "bogus" magic—but it clearly possesses no sympathy for the self-referential and playful magic of Shakespearean theater. As I have already argued, Shakespeare stakes a claim to theatrical magic in *A Midsummer Night's Dream*, but it is not a claim that relies on the audience's absorption in the world of the supernatural entities presented in the spectacle. Shakespeare's theatrical magic relies on disenchantment: a sophisticated audience trained to see the fairy world and its supernatural events as alienated versions of its own world. The play mocks excessive absorption through the representation of the mechanicals, whose understanding of theatrical performance is naïvely literal.

The priority of disbelief, to borrow Tolkien's terms, remains widely associated with the experience of theater. William Nelson states the argument against what he considers to be excessive emphasis on the believability of fiction in terms that are intriguingly theatrical: "But when the distinction between make-believe and real is obscured—when disbelief is shut out rather than suspended or held back—a voice from the balcony calls out to warn the stage heroine of the approach of the villain."[23] Nelson's theatrical analogy describes the urbane playfulness shared by an elite Renaissance culture. Since the Renaissance, self-referential artifice and theatricality have often appeared to go hand in hand, eliciting the opposition between absorption and theatricality proposed by Michael Fried for eighteenth-century French painting. Although Fried does not extend this opposition to the literary experience of the novel, Tolkien's clear antitheatricality, as we shall see, will suggest a model of novelistic absorption.[24]

Tolkien's dislike of the farcical overextension of stage magic brings another term into play. It is difficult now to watch the Reinhardt/Dieterle Hollywood version of *A Midsummer Night's Dream* without the concept of "camp" as the appropriate aesthetic lens for the full appreciation of the film: its over-the-top rendition of the "course of true love" of the various lovers from Shakespeare's play, along with Mickey Rooney, as Puck, hamming it up, as Robertson Davies later remarked, like the son of Tarzan.[25] "Tinseltown" in its heyday was perhaps never more succinctly represented than in the forest scenes of the play: stage sets draped with cellophane hanging from trees and sparkling gauzy costumes for the fairies. The combination of camp and magic made its mark on at least one young filmgoer of the 1930s: Kenneth Anger. Anger, in fact, claims to have played the changeling prince in the film. Whether or not the claim is true, it shows that Anger's eagerness to locate the powerful filmic iconography of his *Magick Lantern Cycle* in a specific Hollywood genealogy that also reflects some of the problems of theatrical magic. If the camp mayhem of the forest scenes of the Reinhardt/Dieterle film version of the play might seem to take us very far away from Shakespeare, it nevertheless remains closer to a Shakespearean sense of magic than a Tolkienian one. Anger's films clearly borrowed from the over-the-top Hollywood Shakespeare, if not from Shakespeare himself. (The Hollywood *Dream* perhaps provided Anger with all that he needed from Shakespeare.) Anger's own very serious interest in magic, of course, followed a very different path than Tolkien's: into the domain of Aleister Crowley's occult practice, which provided most of his films with their looming sexual peril in the service of personal regeneration. The combination of peril, mysticism, and camp defines Anger's films. However much they differ in almost every other respect, Anger and Tolkien share an interest in what Tolkien called "the Perilous Realm" of Faërie.[26]

Novelistic Fantasy

The role of magic might be seen, from Romanticism onward, as part of a larger project of self-emancipation: the creator as a kind of magus. Figures such as Crowley and Anger belong to this post-Romantic appropriation of magic. As a cultural conservative, Tolkien was, as we have already seen, cautious about the idea of creative magic, and repelled by self-emancipation, but his equally strong concern with the attempt to capture something of the power of the "Perilous Realm" betrayed his own Romantic attempt at re-enchantment, using fantasy and the novel as the arduous skills required of the modern magus. It is indicative of Tolkien's own ambitions in this regard that he conceives of this as a task beyond the scope of Shakespeare, the bard of the English supernatural for three centuries. Although the Shakespeare of *King Lear* and *Macbeth* appealed to Tolkien more than *A Midsummer Night's Dream*, even the great tragedies are compromised by their theatricality. "*Macbeth*," he remarks in "On Fairy-Stories," "is indeed a work by a playwright who ought, at least on this occasion, to have written a story, if he had the skill or patience for that art."[27] Given the strong presence of *Macbeth* in *The Lord of the Rings*, much more noticeable than any other Shakespeare play, Tolkien perhaps thought of himself as completing that demanding task in place of the mercurial Shakespeare. If, for example, Shakespeare only has Birnam Wood come to Dunsinane Castle in synecdochic fashion—the branches carried as camouflage by the English and Scottish forces allied against Macbeth—Tolkien goes Shakespeare one better: the forest of Fangorn moves itself to edge of Helm's Deep in order to do battle with the Orcs in *The Lord of the Rings*.[28] The novel allows for the imaginative realization of movement on this scale. Stage versions of *Macbeth* can get by with a half-dozen men carrying branches, but the stage would be hard pressed to present Tolkien's equivalent with any degree of conviction.

Tolkien's version of tragedy, moreover, is essentially modern. Instead of the tragic fall of a severely compromised figure of greatness, Tolkien portrayed the costs of a tragic victory over evil on the part of a character, Frodo, who makes no claim to greatness. The powerful historicity of the novel is equally modern. Tolkien's great artistic triumph, as Tom Shippey has so persuasively argued, is intimately connected to his scholarly commitment to the philology of the Northern languages and literatures of Europe. This, Shippey argues, lies in the creative elaboration of what he calls the "asterisk-reality" of philological speculation (the use of an asterisk to mark a conjectural word not otherwise supported by textual evidence) in order to create an entire narrative apparatus surrounding his own hunches about words and the world that produced them.[29] This combination of philological excavation and fantasia gives the novel its very powerful sense of a mythological world whose completeness is conveyed, not by the exhaustive outline of its history and structure, but rather by the fragmentary, archeological nature of its representation. This is in fact the signal accomplishment of Tolkien as a fantasist. The "reality-effect" of Tolkien's fantasy is the sense, shared by readers and the novel's own characters, especially, but not only, the hobbits, that they are themselves confronted by a world whose history they know only in fragments and old tales.

C. S. Lewis's review *of The Lord of the Rings* on its first appearance (1954) makes this point in terms that once again remind us of the largely negative role of theater in defining Tolkien's project. Most fantasy since the Renaissance, writes Lewis, portrays an essentially theatricalized world without any convincing sense of its ongoing existence:

> One would have supposed that diurturnity was the quality least likely to be found in an invented world. And one has, in fact, an uneasy feeling that the worlds of the *Furioso* or *The Water of the Wondrous Isles* weren't there at all before the curtain rose. But in the Tolkienian world you can hardly put your foot down anywhere from Esgaroth to Forlindon or between Ered Mithrin and Khand, without stirring the dust of history. Our own world, except at certain rare moments, hardly seems so heavy with its past. This is one element in the anguish which the characters bear. But with the anguish there comes also a strange exaltation. They are at once stricken and upheld by the memory of vanished civilizations and lost splendour.[30]

Diurturnity, the sense of existence over an expansive period of time, is indeed Tolkien's central achievement in his trilogy, although it certainly builds on the achievement of the historical novel, Sir Walter Scott in particular, in constructing the encounter between quotidian time and the sense of a deep time of "lost splendour." The experience of Tolkien's diurturnity is also, Lewis indicates, the material of tragedy, of both anguish and exaltation. This sense of lost splendor is built, as Lewis argued, on an extraordinary *personal* mythology unlike any of its medieval precursors. In contrast to Sir Thomas Malory's *Morte d'Arthur* (1485), which "comes largely from the great weight of other men's work built up century by century . . . [t]he utterly new achievement of Professor Tolkien is that he carries a comparable sense of reality unaided."[31] If Lewis acknowledges the *originality* of Tolkien, then Tolkien at least partly writes from an internalized source of creativity: a stance fundamentally foreign to the texts Tolkien loved and studied. Tolkien himself, excellent philologist that he was, must have been quite aware of the essentially modern nature of his relationship to the texts and languages that were the ingredients of his own creative endeavor.

Tolkien's representation of mythic history also begs for assessment in the context of the absorptive function of the novel. The inaugural gesture of the novel is the reader's pleasure in Don Quixote's failure to distinguish between the world of romance and his own actual world. Quixote, we might say, is the ultimate absorbed reader, and, if this is so, then the history of the novel, including the fantasy novel, after Cervantes is partly the attempt to discover modes of absorption appropriate to the skeptical novelistic universe. As a fantasist, Tolkien might appear to belong to a prenovelistic world of medieval adventure romance—an aspect of the trilogy thoroughly exploited by Peter Jackson in his movie version—but the encounter of epic action with the lowness, both in height and in prestige, of its central characters, the hobbits, is the generic confrontation of epic romance and the domestic novel. The Shire is quite recognizable as the rural England of Tolkien's childhood, the hobbits themselves thoroughly immersed in its domestic world. It takes Tolkien much of *The Fellowship of the Ring*, the first book of Tolkien's trilogy, simply to get the hobbits out of the Shire in the first place.[32] The Shire is outside of the adventure time that constitutes most of the trilogy, and the narrative dilation of the Shire establishes the contrast between its "low" world and the "high" world of much of the rest of Tolkien's fantasy. Tolkien assumes that his readers more or less recognize and share the Englishness of the Shire, and share as well both the resistance and the fascination of the hobbits as they begin to encounter the great events and long history of Middle Earth, which they know only dimly. The "realist" or domestic quality attached to the Shire lends Tolkien's fiction some of its persuasive power for modern readers, modeling the reader's own encounter with the fragments of the deep history of Middle Earth.

Return to Faërie

The novelistic experience of the readers of *The Lord of the Rings* leads us back to the fairy tale: a genre that, it turns out, the characters of the Shire—and elsewhere in Middle Earth—also know. These characters find themselves in the very recognizable "modern" position of trying to make sense of old and largely discredited tales—tales that come to reassert their old power in new circumstances. In this respect, Tolkien has not attempted to "shut out" disbelief, as Nelson puts it; his recognition of the problem of believing incredible old tales is very much in the tradition of the Shakespeare of *The Winter's Tale*. At the beginning of *The Fellowship of the Ring*,

Sam Gamgee, who embodies some of the virtues of traditional (and superstitious) Hobbitry, defends the old tales against the dismissal of the Ted Sandyman, the miller's son:

"Queer things you do hear these days, to be sure," said Sam.

"Ah," said Ted, "you do, if you listen. But I can hear fireside-tales and children's stories at home, if I want to."

"No doubt you can," retorted Sam, "and I daresay there's more truth in some of them than you reckon. Who invented the stories anyway? Take dragons now."

"No thank 'ee," said Ted, "I won't. I heard tell of them when I was a youngster, but there's no call to believe in them now. There's only one Dragon in Bywater, and that's Green," he said, getting a general laugh.

"All right," said Sam, laughing with the rest. "But what about these Tree-men, these giants, as you might call them? They do say that one bigger than a tree was seen up away beyond the North Moors not long back."[33]

Sam, of course, is the one proven correct by the events of the novel, including the arrival of the tree-men, or Ents, in *Two Towers*. In that book, the wizard Gandalf confirms from above, as it were, what Sam had dimly suspected from below. He explains the Ents, not now to a skeptical village miller but to Théoden, King of Rohan:

"Is it so long since you listened to tales by the fireside? There are children in your land who, out of the twisted threads of story, could pick the answer to your question. You have seen Ents, O King, Ents out of Fangorn Forest, which in your tongue you call the Entwood. Did you think that the name was given only in idle fancy? Nay, Théoden, it is otherwise: to them you are but the passing tale; all the years from Eorl the Young to Théoden the Old are of little count to them; and all the deeds of your house but a small matter."

The king was silent. "Ents!" he said at length. "Out of the shadows of legend I begin a little to understand the marvel of the trees, I think. I have lived to see strange days. Long we have tended our beasts and fields, built our houses, wrought our tools, or ridden away to help in the wars of Minas Tirith. And that we called the life of Men, the way of the world. Songs we have that tell of these things, but we are forgetting them, teaching them only to children, as a careless custom. And now the songs have come down among us out of strange places, and walk visible under the Sun."[34]

Tolkien's trilogy often produces this uncanny sense of the old tales and songs suddenly walking in the sunlight, as the Ents at Isengard do, dismantling the fortifications of the great wizard, Saruman (which is no doubt a Tolkienian allegory, much as he rejected the concept, of the relationship between the legendary world of old wives' tales and that of supposedly wise men). Gandalf's words to the king, "to them you are but the passing tale," transform the solid world of men into the shadow of the old legends. It is also an allegory of reading Tolkien's fantasy. As with all powerful effects of literary absorption, the effect of literary enchantment temporarily reverses reality and fiction: the Primary World of the reader is diminished in relation to the Secondary World of the author, temporarily less real than the spell of the story. This is partly because the skepticism of a Ted Sandyman or King Théoden is recognizable to a novel reader; both characters come to appear rather commonplace and thus realistic in comparison to the marvels they doubt. This Tertiary World of the fantasy brings the Secondary World of most of the characters of *The Lord of the Rings* closer to the Primary World of the reader. (Tolkien, as we have seen, rejected the tertiary world of theatrical fantasy, but its novelistic, absorptive possibilities were entirely congenial to him.) Beyond this, moreover, the powerful diurturnity of the novel, noticed by Lewis, belongs to this Tertiary World. Even the heroic world of Théoden pales by comparison. If for Théoden, then certainly for the quotidian world of the reader, "Our own world . . . hardly seems so heavy with its past," as Lewis argued. The historicity of Middle Earth has produced a seemingly endless market for the posthumous publication of Tolkien's own elaborations of the history of Middle Earth. As we saw in the previous chapter, Walter Benjamin's essay "The Storyteller" described the falling away of the oral world of the tale at the hands of the novel and the rationalizing world that lies behind it. The great success of Tolkien among readers, however, suggests a myth of countermodernity: the use of novelistic absorption to suggest the larger reality of the old fireside tales.

Even that counter myth, however, is enfolded within a narrative that in its elegiac quality looks surprisingly like Benjamin's. The realization of the old tales is not a full recuperation, but rather the twilight of the great beings who once inhabited Middle Earth and who know, or suspect, that even triumph against Mordor entails the quietus of their powers in the world. The full consciousness of this is most powerfully expressed by the Great Elf-lords: Elrond and Galadriel. The latter is of particular interest to the fairy way of writing because she is one of the very few significant female characters in the trilogy, and because Tolkien clearly establishes her as the *precursor* of the mysterious and enchanting fairies who entered the mainstream of European literature with the medieval romance. Her domain, Lothlórien, is clearly understood by the men of the Middle Earth as the "perilous realm" associated by Tolkien with Faërie more generally. Both Boromir of Gondor and Éomer of Rohan respond in a similar fashion to the "peril" of Lorien. "'And now we must enter the Golden Wood, you say,'" says Boromir to Aragorn. "'But of that perilous land we have heard in Gondor, and it is said that few come out who once go in; and of that few none have escaped unscathed.' "[35] Éomer's response upon hearing that Aragorn, Gimli, and Legolas have been in Lothlórien is similar: " 'Then there is a Lady in the Golden Wood, as old tales tell!' he said. 'Few escape her nets, they say. These are strange days! But if you have her favour, then you are also net-weavers and sorcerers, maybe.' "[36]

The female fairy of medieval romance was often a sexual enchantress, and this tradition is, I think, obscurely represented in the suspicions of Boromir and Éomer regarding the "nets" of Galadriel. Boromir and Éomer are seen to misrecognize Galadriel as a version of the fairy enchantress of romance, but purged of the sexual peril that so often comes with the fairy enchantress. She is indeed perilous, we are constantly reminded, but only to those who bring their own peril with them. The peril, then, is closer to something like self-revelation, which is indeed the function of Galadriel's mirror. (By extension, the suggestion would seem to be that the old European legends of the fairy seductress reflect the nature of the legend makers more than that of the fairies themselves.) She tests the other characters, but the erotic nature of the test, so often prominent in the medieval romance, largely disappears.

She herself sees more clearly than anyone the future of the Elves, and that future, we might say, is to become *fairies*. " 'Do you not see now whereof your coming is to us as the footstep of Doom?' " she says to Frodo. " 'For if you fail, then we are laid bare to the Enemy. Yet if you succeed, then our power is diminished, and Lothlórien will fade, and the tides of Time will sweep it away. We must depart into the West, or dwindle to a rustic folk of dell and cave, slowly to forget and to be forgotten.' "[37] The Elves will pass away or become "a rustic folk of dell and cave": the ingredients of fairy tales. Tolkien does not use the word "fairy" in *The Lord of the Rings* because he associates the word with the disenchanted *future* of Middle Earth. Tolkien's fantasy, then, is not so much a medieval world, but rather the Ur-medieval world as imagined by a medievalist. "Fairy" has a French etymology, from the Old French *fae* (*fée*), and Tolkien no doubt considered it a late-comer, as it is in English, where the Germanic "elf" was used in Old English and "fairy" only after the Norman invasion. Tolkien probably associated the eroticized fairy enchantress with the French romance tradition. It is the fate of Galadriel, she knows, to fade and be misrecognized as one of these seducers. Her "perilous realm," meanwhile, will diminish into the fragmentary, rustic existence of the fairies of fairy tales and romances. She rules the domain, in effect, which the modern reader can only reconstruct from the traces of those "later" forms. Through characters like Galadriel, we are made to feel that we have witnessed the old legends and myths before they become the diminished traditions handed down to us. Like Milton in *Paradise Lost*, Tolkien transforms his own belated relationship to tradition into temporal priority.

Sexuality and Utopia

Terminological insistence on Elves rather than fairies is one form of shielding the enchantments of Middle Earth from both adult sexual fantasy as well as childish diminishment. In this sense, Tolkien radically extracts the fairy from the fairy way of writing. As I have argued before in this book, the sexuality of the fairy is certainly one part of that tradition: highlighted in some instances (Shakespeare, the visual tradition, Keats), more subdued in others. The transformation of the older medieval traditions regarding this aspect of fairies begins in English with Spenser and Shakespeare. Tolkien's essay on fairy stories is quite aware, as I have already argued, of the all-pervasive erotic playfulness of Shakespeare's *Dream* and largely avoids direct discussion of the play. Hostile as he clearly is to the idea that the Victorian nursery is the natural home of Faërie, he leaves this aspect of the Victorian fairy in place.

The de-sexualization of Faërie must then stand as one aspect of Tolkien's legacy to fantasy. In this, he has certainly not gone unchallenged. Angela Carter was not engaged by Tolkien's writing in particular, but she can be seen as attempting to reactivate the sexual current of fairy writing. Philip Pullman's *His Dark Materials* (1995–2000) is an attempt, and not the only one, to confront Tolkien on the terrain of fantasy with a trilogy (already a mark of Tolkien's influence) that is resolutely anti-Christian and erotic in its trajectory. The televised version of *Game of Thrones*, moreover, extends an eroticized version of fantasy into soft-core pornography. In general, there is no lack of grounds on which Tolkien's work can be attacked: racism, sexism, and so forth. Tolkien's literary reputation might survive these charges, but, in the contemporary literary system, there is one charge only that casts Tolkien outside the domain of "literature": it is infantile.

Edmund Wilson made this charge in a review of *The Lord of the Rings* in 1956, and it has—partially—stuck.[38] In fact, the cultural position of *The Lord of the Rings* is not among children's literature, as Wilson clearly conceived it, but rather as a rite of passage for the reading adolescent (a strange, or perhaps fitting, fate for a book that so rigorously excised sexuality from its domain). Shippey's *J. R. R. Tolkien: Author of the Century* (2000) has combated this cultural assignation of Tolkien's work by situating him alongside some of the central figures of twentieth-century literature, and in particular those who responded acutely to the trauma of the First World War. There is much that is persuasive in Shippey's argument. Still, I wish here to highlight some of the ways in which Tolkien is not fully assimilable to literature, at least as literature has come to be defined by the realist and modernist/postmodernist novel.[39] In the contemporary North American bookstore, "literature" or "fiction" means the novel; fantasy, a different section, means essentially Tolkien and the followers of Tolkien. (Tolkien does not lack precursors, but they are not generally included on the shelves of fantasy.) Tolkien is in effect the inventor of a genre, the genre of fantasy as we now know it. This genre belongs to the larger section of "genre fiction"—science fiction, romance, mystery, thriller—but not to literature. Tolkien himself could be defensive about this aspect of his reputation, but it is really part of his genuine interest. Tolkien is both "before" and "after" literature: "before" in the sense that Tolkien mines the world of saga and legend from a period well before the modern conceptualization of literature that began in the seventeenth and eighteenth centuries, and which eventually became an account of literature defined by the centrality of the novel; "after" in the sense that Tolkien's vast readership suggests that fantasy might outlive or transform the increasingly brittle literary system organized around the novel, realist or experimental. Beginning around the end of the Second World War, "serious" literature increasingly took refuge in the academy, particularly in American-style creative programs, where its claim to cultural centrality has steadily diminished. What's left outside the academy is dominated by "genre" fiction, including fantasy.

Tolkien has thrived in a new literary landscape suffused with mass culture. *The Lord of the Rings* belongs to the literary canon of the youth culture of the 1960s and 1970s. Tolkien's own conservatism makes this success difficult to explain in terms of manifest political message. First and foremost, his fiction testifies to the continuing nostalgia for aristocracy—blood really does tell much of the story in Tolkien.[40] However, there can be few other ecological fictions as influential as Tolkien's. His greatest, and most tragic, creations—the Elves, the Ents (the "tree shepherds" in some late effusion of the pastoral tradition)—are creatures absolutely bound to the natural world. This aspect of Tolkien was, however, part and parcel of his conservatism. As Françoise Meltzer has recently argued, the Romantic elaboration of the idea of nature in Germany and France was often accompanied by the revival of a Catholic medievalism, and Tolkien certainly belongs to this aspect of the Romantic legacy.[41]

Perhaps even more important for Tolkien's reception in the 1960s, however, was his relationship to cultural magic. Youth culture did not hesitate to grant Tolkien the status of magus, featuring him prominently in its syncretism of various forms of magic and mysticism: Aleister Crowley, Glastonbury, Hobbits, hippies, and Radical Fairies. Middle Earth plays a prominent role in Led Zeppelin's lyrics, perhaps the most clearly overextended attempt to establish the rock star as a new form of sexualized magus. Taking his measure of the moment, a very different creative magus and follower of Crowley, Kenneth Anger, engaged Led Zeppelin's Jimmy Page to score his masterpiece-in-waiting, *Lucifer Rising* (without finally using Page's work). What remains fascinating in this apparent incoherence is the cultural moment in which Tolkien and Anger might briefly occupy the same stage. Erik Davis sums up this conjunction very nicely in his book on the album, *Led Zeppelin IV*: "But Zeppelin is a special sort of *Lord of the Rings*, one where you get to *root for both sides*."[42] After Led Zeppelin, the rock star began to recede to a more discreet place on the cultural horizon. It is unlikely, however, that this represents a permanent recession of the desire for cultural magic. If the long early modern history of the fairy way of writing is part of the "disenchantment" of the world, the twentieth-century history of fantasy is partly the attempt to re-enchant it.

For Tolkien himself, the desire for cultural magic is answered in the domain of story, which, as we have seen, possesses for him its own autonomous forms of enchantment. If those forms are ratified in the New Testament, according to Tolkien, they do not depend upon even Christian truth. The "Cauldron of Story" or, alternatively, the "Pot of Soup," as he terms the concept and process of story making in "On Fairy-stories," suggests traditionally female labor, with perhaps a hint of witchcraft (thinking, as most English speakers do, of the bubbling cauldron of the Weird Sisters in *Macbeth*). The cauldron lacks a magus, possessing instead its own deep history, structurally and ontologically prior to the events of human history, which are essentially tossed into the ongoing soup. (He insists that historical figures associated with tales and legends are in fact secondary to those stories, which precede, and outlast, whatever historical elaboration they assume.) Even Christianity's "hallowing" of the soup is retrospective and does not necessarily change the nature of the soup itself. It "has always been boiling, and to it have continually been added new bits, dainty and undainty."[43] The "bits" are the pieces of human history, tossed together in unexpected forms:

> I wish to point to something else that these traditions contain: a singularly suggestive example of the relation of the "fairy-tale element" to gods and kings and nameless men, illustrating (I believe) the view that this element does not rise or fall, but is there, in the Cauldron of Story, waiting for the great figures of Myth and History, and for the yet nameless He or She, waiting for the moment when they are cast into the simmering stew, one by one or all together, without consideration of rank or precedence.[44]

The final phrase is a very striking one in Tolkien's works, which are not usually noted for their egalitarian qualities. In some respects, it anticipates the epilogue to his essay, in which he argues for the structural anticipation of the Gospel in the world of magical stories. Here, however, the potential Christian interpretation is muted. The Cauldron of Story is like Christianity in its insistence on a kind of final leveling, if only at the level of story. But Tolkien points us to no utopia at this particular moment in the essay, not even a Christian one. Instead, story itself is the place of leveling.

Introduction

1. Bond, *Spectator*, no. 419, 3: 570.
2. See Cocking, *Imagination*; Engell, *Creative Imagination*.
3. Dryden, *Works*, 16:7.
4. Coleridge, *Biographia Literaria*, 168–69.
5. For more on the fantastic as a modern literary mode, see Todorov, *Fantastic*.
6. Burke, *Popular Culture*, 3–22.
7. For an extensive discussion of this process, see McKeon, *Secret History*.
8. Nicholas Hudson argues that the conceptualization of a traditional oral culture was a product of the eighteenth century ("Oral Tradition," 161–76). However, the *practice* of intellectual interest in, and use of, oral culture goes back to the sixteenth century, as the work of Natalie Zemon Davis (*Society and Culture*, 227–67) demonstrates. See also the essays in the collection edited by Mary Ellen Lamb and Karen Bamford (*Oral Traditions*).
9. Guillory, "Genesis," 324.
10. B. Anderson, *Imagined Communities*, 15.
11. Ibid., 37–46. In the end, this process "created languages-of-power of a different kind from the older administrative vernaculars. Certain dialects inevitably were 'closer' to each print-language and dominated their final forms" (*Imagined Communities*, 45).
12. Stewart, *Crimes of Writing*, esp. 66–131.
13. Bottigheimer, *Fairy Tales*. For accounts that emphasize the continued interdependence of orality, literacy, and print long after the advent of print, see Fox, *Oral and Literate Culture*, and the essays in Fox and Woolf, *The Spoken Word*.
14. See in particular McLane, *Balladeering*, esp. 16–43.
15. Diane Purkiss, for example, refers to Shakespeare "unblushingly strip-mining both popular culture and every learned text he can lay his hands on for the sake of creating an arresting stage event." Such spectacle becomes "less appealing once the listener is conscious of the female voices suppressed" (*Witch in History*, 207).
16. Burke, *Popular Culture*, 15.
17. Aubrey, *Three Prose Works*, 290.
18. Hardy, *Tess of the D'Urbervilles*, 22.
19. Burke, *Popular Culture*, 286.

20. McLane, *Balladeering*, 33–43.
21. Trilling, "Fate of Pleasure," 67.
22. Maureen Duffy's impressive survey, *The Erotic World of Faery*, remains invaluable for this aspect of fairy writing.
23. For other recent examples of feminist and psychoanalytic scholarship along these lines, see Purkiss, *At the Bottom of the Garden*, and the essays in Haase, *Fairy Tales and Feminism*.
24. Burke, "Afterward," 210.

Chapter 1 • *The Fairies' Farewell: Shakespeare's Old Wives' Tales*

1. P. Anderson, *Lineages*, 48.
2. Auerbach, *Literary Language*, 96.
3. Ibid., 98–99.
4. Jacques Le Goff argues for the rejection of folk culture by the clergy, but he allows for some overlap in areas of spirit belief and miracles ("Culture cléricale," 780–91). For the church's active participation in the carnivalesque inversion of its own official culture, see Gurvich, (*Medieval Popular Culture*, esp. 179–80) and Davis (*Society and Culture*, 97–123).
5. Ziolkowski, *Fairy Tales*, 34–43.
6. Bloch, *Feudal Society*, 1:80.
7. Guillory, *Cultural Capital*, 73. See also Le Goff, "Culture cléricale," 788–89; Davis, *Society and Culture*, 232 ff.
8. Auerbach, *Mimesis*, 130.
9. Chrétien de Troyes, *Arthurian Romances*, 298.
10. Ibid., 299.
11. Chaucer, *Complete Poetry*, lines 859–61.
12. Ibid., lines 864–81.
13. Burke, *Popular Culture*, 70.
14. By Shakespeare's time, as Helen Cooper notes, romance had already obtained broad popular appeal. *Bevis of Hampton* and *Guy of Warwick* "get a handful of mentions each in the broad corpus of Shakespeare's work, with a casualness that again shows how universal a knowledge of the work could be assumed at every social level of his characters and his audience" (*English Romance*, 31).
15. Thomas, *Religion*, 45.
16. Ibid., 610. See also Buccola, *Fairies*, esp. 23–28.
17. Warner, *Albion's England*, 367.
18. Scott, *Minstrelsy*, 2:337.
19. MacCulloch, "Fairy and Witch Beliefs," 227–44; Scott, *Minstrelsy*, 3:337–46.
20. Rowse, *Simon Forman*, 303.
21. Clark, "Protestant Demonology," 59.
22. Scot, *Discoverie of Witchcraft*, 164.
23. Bacon, *Works*, 3:288; cited by Fox, *Oral and Literate Culture*, 175–76.
24. Wooton, "Scott," q.v.
25. For the wide variety of magical uses associated with holy water, see Thomas, *Religion*,

29–30. Eamon Duffy (*Stripping of the Altars*) is particularly attentive to the popular attachment to the Catholic sacraments, which lasted into the Elizabethan Settlement.

26. Stephen Greenblatt similarly argues that this moment in the play reinvests old Catholic practice with "the charismatic magic of the theater" ("Resonance and Wonder," 14).

27. Scot, *Discoverie of Witchcraft*, xxii.

28. Davis, *Society and Culture*, 233. See Pocock on the French legal scholarship of the same period, which began the rediscovery of a native and customary law that "may have furnished one of the roots of European romanticism" (*Ancient Constitution*, 15). It seems reasonable to infer affiliations between legal and cultural developments of the period.

29. Nashe, *Works*, 1:347.

30. Spenser, *Faerie Queene*, VI.x.7, 668n.

31. Woodcock, *Fairy in The Faerie Queene*, 43–50. For the barriers to Spenser's use of popular materials, see Lamb, *Popular Culture*, 163–93.

32. Scott, *Minstrelsy*, 2:350, 2n.

33. Briggs, *Anatomy of Puck*, 6.

34. Spenser, *Works*, 628.

35. See Mary Ellen Lamb's reading of the play in the context of the developing interest in the old wives' tales (*Popular Culture*, 45–62).

36. Lyly, *Endymion*, IV.iii.33–36.

37. Ibid., IV.iii.45.

38. Jan Kott emphasizes the ongoing carnivalesque tradition, stemming from Apuleius (*Bottom Translation*, 29–68).

39. According to E. J. Kenney, Milesian stories were "anecdotes, more often than not scabrous, culled from the illimitable subliterary repertoire of traditional popular storytelling and embellished for an educated audience" (Kenney, "Introduction," ix–x).

40. As Stephen Orgel notes, however, the name Titania classicizes her, connecting her with the great classical enchantress, Circe: "Shakespeare took [the name] from Ovid, where it appears four times as a name for Circe, and once for Diana, thereby embodying both aspects of the power of transformation in the play, the seductive and the protective, the licentious and the chaste" (*Imagining Shakespeare*, 97).

41. In this respect, the central insight of Louis Montrose's pathbreaking essay on the play retains its interpretive power: Titania is a displaced version of Elizabeth, linked to issues of sexuality and social power in a courtly context ("Shaping Fantasies"). A modified version of this argument appears in Montrose's book, *The Purpose of Playing*.

42. Lamb, *Popular Culture*, 108.

43. I have elsewhere discussed the role of imagination in the play at greater length (Pask, "Engrossing Imagination").

44. See Michael D. Bristol's argument for an early version of a "culture industry" in Elizabethan London (*Big-Time Shakespeare*, 30–41).

45. Wall, *Staging Domesticity*, 112.

46. For the larger historical view of the dismantling of the patriarchalist analogy, see McKeon, "Historicizing Patriarchy." For the Stuarts, see Goldberg, "Fatherly Authority."

47. The classic account is Mauss, *The Gift*.

48. See Lamb, "Virtual Audiences," 127–28.

49. Stephen Orgel makes the strong case for the relationship between theater and magic in the play ("Introduction," *The Winter's Tale*, 57–62).

50. Orgel, "Introduction," *The Winter's Tale*, 79. Valerie Traub also stresses the muteness and submissiveness of Hermione at the end of the play (*Desire and Anxiety*, 45–46). For the contrary view, in psychoanalytic terms, see Adelman, *Suffocating Mothers*, 220–36.

51. The best account of the temporality of the play is Michael Bristol's, which argues persuasively for a polarization of the play's action around the solstices of Christmas and Mid-summer (*Big-Time Shakespeare*, 147–74). In *A Midsummer Night's Dream*, however, Midsummer often seems to incorporate a loose sense of both the period of maying (spring) and early summer. Perdita herself, on the other hand, specifies that the flowers of spring have already come and gone: a sharper distinction between spring and solstice than in the earlier play.

52. Bate, *Shakespeare and Ovid*, 231.

53. In Gellner's account, agrarian society, unlike national culture, tolerates strong vertical stratification according to status as well as the lateral insulation of agricultural communities from one another (*Nations and Nationalism*, 8–18).

54. Richard Helgerson (*Forms of Nationhood*) and Claire McEachern (*English Nationhood*) have advanced strong claims for an emergent nationalism in the English writing of the period.

55. Kumar, *English National Identity*, esp. 89–120; Greenfield, *Nationalism*, 27–88.

56. P. Anderson, *Lineages*, 39.

57. For a discussion of the role of "fraternity" in a more fully formed nationalism, that of the United States in the nineteenth century, see B. Anderson, *Imagined Communities*, 202–3.

58. For the fullest account of this historical process, see Cressy, *Bonfires and Bells*. For the participation of Shakespeare and other writers of the period, see Laroque (*Shakespeare's Festive World*) and Marcus (*Politics of Mirth*).

Chapter 2 · *Caliban's Masque: Drollery, Concupiscence, Creativity*

1. Jonson, *Ben Jonson*, ed. Herford and Simpson, 6:16–17.

2. Dryden, *Works*, 13:239.

3. Ibid., 13:240.

4. H. Smith, *Shakespeare's Romances*, 143–44. The *Oxford English Dictionary* indicates that the verb was primarily used for God's creation, before acquiring secondary regal and legal usages in the late medieval and Early Modern period. Dryden, however, had precursors in Philip Sidney and George Puttenham, both of whom compared the poet as maker to God's creation although they did not use the verb "create" to describe the poetic process.

5. Bond, *Spectator*, 2:586–87.

6. Murphy, *Tempest*, 80.

7. Hazlitt, *Selected Writings*, 1:149.

8. L. Smith, *Four Words*, 21. Smith himself points out the example of Caliban in the criticism from Dryden onward.

9. Dryden, *Works*, 16:7.

10. Craig, "Jonson," 184.

11. Gilman, "All Eyes," 214–30. However, Glynne Wickham ("Masque and Anti-Masque,"

1–14) and Stephen Orgel ("Introduction," *Tempest*, 47) both argue that the true antimasque to Prospero's masque is the disappearing banquet of act 3, scene 3.

12. Bevington, "*The Tempest*," esp. 231; Orgel, "Marginal Jonson," 144.

13. From *Love Restored* onward, the printed editions of Jonson's masques regularly name the King's Men as the performers of the professional parts (Orgel, "Introduction," *Tempest*, 43).

14. Jonson, *Complete Masques*, 14. Subsequent quotations from Jonson's masques refer to this edition by line number (prose by page number).

15. Milton, *Complete Poems*, lines 115–22. For a fuller account of Shakespeare's pervasive presence in *Comus*, see Guillory, *Poetic Authority*, 68–93.

16. E. A. J. Honigmann persuasively argues that Shakespeare uses *The Winter's Tale* to respond to Jonsonian criticism (*Shakespeare's Impact*, 109–20), and *The Tempest* seems to me to continue his late engagement with Jonson.

17. In fact, Orgel observes, Shakespeare's imitation of a Jonsonian form might have directly influenced Jonson himself: "If Jonson had an English model for such pastoral masques as *The Golden Age Restored* (1615), *The Vision of Delight* (1617), and *Pan's Anniversary* (1620), works in which royal power is conceived as power over nature and the seasons, it can only have been Prospero's masque—there are Continental analogues, but no other English examples" ("Introduction," *Tempest*, 46). See also Levin, "Two Magian Comedies," 210–31.

18. Orgel, "Introduction," *Tempest*, 50.

19. Wheeler offers a more fully psychoanalytic account than my own, one in which "Prospero's repressed sexual desire for his daughter is purged by his projection of it onto the loathsome Caliban" ("Fantasy and History," 314).

20. Knight, *Crown of Life*, 245.

21. See Goldberg, "Under the Covers," 105–28. John Kirke's *Seven Champions of Christendome* (1638) offered another take on this aspect of Caliban by revisiting the character as Suckabus, clownish son of the enchantress Calib and the devil Tarpax. Suckabus is a compendium of scatological humour.

22. Pask, "Prospero's Counter-Pastoral," 389–404.

23. Knight, *The Crown of Life*, 255.

24. Cohen, "Prerevolutionary Drama," 129–30.

25. Norbrook, "What Cares These Roarers?" 35.

26. This was clearly the dramatic center of interest for seventeenth-century audiences, as indicated by Thomas D'Urfey's adaptation of *The Sea Voyage* as *A Common-Wealth of Women* (1685).

27. Beaumont and Fletcher, *Dramatic Works*, II.ii.199.

28. The best discussion of the role of a natural sexuality in both this play and in the Dryden-Davenant *Tempest* is Miner, "The Wild Man," 87–114. Miner assimilates Caliban to the European "wild man," and observes that seventeenth-century revisions of *The Tempest* were interested less in Caliban himself than in the exploration of European behavior in the wild.

29. Dryden, *Works*, 10:3–4. Subsequent quotations of Dryden's *Tempest* refer to this edition (by act, line, and scene number when referring to the play itself; by line number when referring to the prologue; and by page number when referring to the preface).

30. Dobson, *National Poet*, 47.

31. Maus, "Arcadia Lost," 77.

32. Ibid.

33. Ibid., 84.

34. Pepys, *Diary*, 8:522. Joseph Roach's comments on Pepys and the Restoration *Tempest* are particularly instructive in this regard ("The Enchanted Island," 67).

35. Dabydeen, "Hogarth and the Canecutter," 258.

36. This is the modern discourse of sexuality described by Michel Foucault, *History of Sexuality*.

37. Gumbrecht, *Making Sense*, 201, 261. See also Niklas Luhmann's discussion of the incorporation of sexuality into the European discourse of love (*Love as Passion*, 109–20).

Chapter 3 • *The Fairy Way of Writing*

1. "Only through the modern valorization of the actual—of the factual, the empirical, the historical—does the ancient and equivocal whole of 'fiction' become resolvable into separate and unequivocal parts: falsehood and fiction, deceit and the aesthetic mode of truth, what is made up and what is made" (McKeon, *Secret History*, 109).

2. Marvell, *Andrew Marvell*, lines 7–8.

3. Spingarn, *Critical Essays*, 2:58–59.

4. Dryden, *Works*, 11:12.

5. Shaftesbury, *Characteristics*, 25, 26.

6. For an argument which convincingly demonstrates the close proximity of empirical science and eighteenth-century aesthetics, see McKeon, "Mediation as Primal Word."

7. Dryden, *Works*, 17:55.

8. Dryden, *Works*, 10:6, lines 21–26.

9. See Marcie Frank's reassessment of the significance of Dryden's adaptation of Milton (*Origins of Criticism*, 42–63).

10. Dryden, *Works*, 12:95.

11. Milton, *Complete Poems*, 210.

12. Dryden, *Works*, 12:96.

13. Ibid., 16:7.

14. Sermain, *Le Conte de fées*, 46–47. See also Scholar, "La force de l'imagination."

15. Bacon, *Works*, 4:516–17; cited by Daston, "Marvelous Facts," 112.

16. Cited by Daston, "Marvelous Facts," 118.

17. For the equally important *positive* association of melancholy and imaginative genius, which has a genealogy that goes back at least as far as Ficino, see Klibansky, et al., *Saturn and Melancholy*.

18. Locke, *Educational Writings*, 242–43.

19. Fox, *Oral and Literate Culture*, 193–94.

20. Tuveson, *Imagination*, 72–91; Engell, *Creative Imagination*, 17–21.

21. Engell, *Creative Imagination*, 27.

22. For an account of Locke's influence on the development of children's literature, see Pickering, *John Locke*.

23. See, for example, the interest in the question of "second sight" by prominent virtuosi—including Samuel Pepys, John Evelyn, Robert Boyle, and Aubrey (Hunter, *Occult Laboratory*).

24. See Fox (*Oral and Literate Culture*, 179, 203) for a strong statement of the value of Aubrey's work, including its "anthropological interest" in popular materials.

25. Aubrey, *Three Prose Works*, 132. Buchanan-Brown's introduction notes the skeptical tendency of the *Remaines* to equate Christian and pagan rituals (*Three Prose Works*, xxxiv–xxxv). If this was potentially damaging to Christian belief, it simultaneously allowed Aubrey his anthropological perspective on popular culture.

26. Ibid., 132.

27. Ibid., 204.

28. Ibid.

29. Ibid., 290. For an account of Aubrey and print, see Dragstra, " 'Before women were Readers,' " 41–53.

30. Burke, *Popular Culture*, 15.

31. Ibid., 270–81.

32. Ibid., 286.

33. Collier, *Short View*, 188–89.

34. Dryden had himself already raised the same problem in "The Author's Apology." Horace, writes Dryden, "would have blam'd any Author, who was a *Christian*, had he introduc'd into his Poem Heathen Deities, as *Tasso* is condemn'd by *Rapin* on the like occasion: and as *Camoens*, the Author of the *Lusiads*, ought to be censur'd by all his Readers, when he brings in *Bacchus* and Christ into the same Adventure of his Fable" (*Works*, 12:97). The Horatian concern expressed here, however, is one of the internal logic and consistency of the epic machinery.

35. Collier, *Short View*, 191.

36. McKeon, *Secret History*, 101.

37. Bond, *Spectator*, no. 419, 3:570. Subsequent quotations from *The Spectator* refer to this edition.

38. Broadus, "Addison's Influence," 123–34.

39. Empson, *Some Versions of Pastoral*, 253–94.

40. Gellner, *Nations and Nationalism*, 37–38.

41. Ibid., 61.

42. Jacob, *Works*, 424.

43. Walter Cohen has recently traced motifs that Shakespeare borrowed from Boccaccio back to their origins in Sanskrit literature ("Shakespeare as World Literature").

44. Sermain, *Le conte de fees*, 54. Burke, however, argues that the discovery of popular culture largely on the cultural periphery of Europe reflects both the greater distance of intellectuals from popular culture in areas with long-established national literatures as well as the greater investment in the Renaissance and classicism in the European core (Burke, *Popular Culture*, 13–14).

45. Bottigheimer, *Fairy Tales*, 53–74.

46. Sévigné, *Correspondance*, 41–42.

47. Ibid., 516.

48. Cited by DeJean, "Transnationalism, 43.

49. Ibid., 43–44.

50. This also complicates the history of the French fairy tale in England since d'Aulnoy's tales were often revised and printed as those of "Mother Bunch," as opposed to Perrault's "Mother Goose." As Pickering remarks of Mother Bunch, "Unfortunately for the reputation of the fairy tale, Mother Bunch was the most famous Miss Lonelyhearts in eighteenth-century chapbooks" (Pickering, *John Locke*, 54).

51. Perrault, *Contes*, 50.

52. Ibid., 52; cited by Sermain, *Le conte de fees*, 34 (my translations throughout).

53. Perrault, *Contes*, 154.

54. Ibid. As Collinet notes of the passage, the alternative moral contradicts Arnolphe in Molière's *L'École des femmes*: Votre sexe n'est là que pour la dépendance: / Du côté de la barbe est la toute-puissance" (Your sex is made to cower; / With the beard lies all power), *Théâtre complet*, III.ii.699–700.

55. Auerbach, "*La Cour et la Ville*," 179.

56. Marc Fumaroli brilliantly elucidates Lhéritier's investment in rhetorical eloquence in her (earlier) version of the tale ("Les Fées," 153–86). However, although Fumaroli is no doubt correct in his insistence that there is no real "folk" in Perrault's tales, I believe that he underestimates the significance of Perrault's radical simplification of Lhéritier's version of the tale, which leaves almost no trace of Lhéritier's emphasis on the heroine's reading and her eloquence when confronted by the fairies. Fumaroli thus overestimates Perrault's investment in the culture of rhetorical eloquence. In his preface to the verse tales, Perrault explicitly distinguishes his own tales from "l'élégance et les agréments dont les Grecs et les Romains ont orné leurs Fables" ("the elegance and charm with which the Greeks and Romans have ornamented their fables," Perrault, *Contes*, 51).

57. See Susan Stewart on the "distressing" of vernacular genres, including the ballad and the fairy tale, in order to provide them with the aura of antiquity and authenticity (*Crimes of Writing*, 66–101).

58. For a contrary view, see Levine, *Between the Ancients and the Moderns*.

59. Kramnick, *Making the English Canon*.

60. Rogers, *Essays on Pope*, 84.

61. Pope, *The Rape of the Lock*, lines 29–34. Subsequent quotations from the poem refer to this edition by line number.

62. Ibid., 380, 2n; cited by Rogers, *Essays on Pope*, 75.

63. "The sylphs have embodied frivolity, heedlessness, the 'lighter' impulses of women. The gnomes, on the other hand, represent what might be briefly termed biology" (Rogers, *Essays on Pope*, 78). Rogers goes on to suggest that spleen was commonly associated with menstruation. Helen Deutsch sees Pope himself as identified with this feminine diminishment of the classical machinery (*Resemblance and Disgrace*, 40–82).

64. Cited by Abrams, *The Mirror and the Lamp*, 289.

65. Woodhouse, "Poetry of Collins," 96.

66. Lonsdale, *Poems*, line 39. Subsequent quotations of Collins's poetry refer to this edition by line number.

67. Ibid., 431, 29n.

68. Wasserman, "Collins' 'Ode,'" 92–115.

69. McKeon, "Tacit Knowledge," 195.

70. Woodhouse, "Collins and the Creative Imagination," 76–77.

71. For Collins's distancing of the supernatural poetic motifs, see Spacks, *Insistence of Horror,* 70–75.

72. Johnson, *Lives of the English Poets,* 3:337.

Chapter 4 • Painting Shakespearean Fantasy

1. "Ein Originalschriftsteller in hohen Sinne der Alten ist, wenige Beispiele ausgenommen, beständig ein Nationalautor" (Herder, *Werke,* 1:584; quoted by Kind, *Edward Young,* 44).

2. Spacks, "Ev'ry Woman," 38.

3. Thaler, "Milton in the Theater," 291.

4. Dalton, *Comus,* 45.

5. Walpole, *Correspondence,* 35:209–10. Walpole himself, however, was not above participating in a leisurely aristocratic entertainment based on the *Dream,* an extended flirtation conducted in letters between "Oberon" and "Titania" which he records in a later letter (*Correspondence,* 10:113–18).

6. Williams, *Our Moonlight Revels,* 70.

7. Hazlitt, *Selected Writings,* 1:157–58.

8. Meisel, *Realizations,* 19.

9. Fried, *Absorption and Theatricality.*

10. Sillars, *Painting Shakespeare,* 228.

11. Knowles, *Henry Fuseli,* 1:377.

12. Cited by Warner, *Phantasmagoria,* 152. For more on the connections between Fuseli, the Phantasmagoria, and the Gothic novel, see Myrone, "Fuseli and Gothic Spectacle."

13. Castle, *Female Thermometer,* 161.

14. Paulson, *Book and Painting,* 135. Nicola Bown also emphasizes the role of female domination in the painting, which, she argues, signals Fuseli's general mistrust of the imagination (*Fairies,* 21–24).

15. Sillars, *Painting Shakespeare,* 233.

16. Bromley, *Critical History,* 1:37; cited by Knowles, *Henry Fuseli,* 1:184.

17. Bromley, *Critical History,* 1:42.

18. Knowles, *Henry Fuseli,* 1:376.

19. Bromley, *Critical History,* 1:xxvi.

20. Ibid.

21. Cited by Sillars, *Painting Shakespeare,* 208.

22. Cited by Hamilton, *Catalogue Raisonné,* 154.

23. Ibid.

24. Sillars, *Painting Shakespeare,* 206–13.

25. Stephens, *English Children,* 36.

26. Dixon, *"Designs from Fancy."*

27. Radcliffe, *Romance of the Forest,* 284–85. See Frank, "Fairy Time," 103–17.

28. Radcliffe, *Romance of the Forest*, 290.

29. See Terry Castle's chapter on *The Mysteries of Udolpho* (1794), in which she demonstrates Radcliffe's displacement of supernatural effects into the domain of dreams and desires (*Female Thermometer*, 120–39). Radcliffe's explicit use of Shakespearean fairies in *The Romance of the Forest* seems to anticipate this aspect of the later novel.

30. Romney, *George Romney*, 234.

31. Print by John Samuel Agar (1829), after painting by Louisa Sharpe (location unknown). Collection of the Folger Shakespeare Library, ART File S528m5 no. 6.

32. For a fuller interpretation of Dadd's fairy painting than can be provided here, see Bown, *Fairies*, 78–82, 150–62.

33. W. Moelwyn Merchant, on the other hand, argues that Blake's Puck "has something of grace, something of the sinister infant Puck of Reynolds's painting" ("Blake's Shakespeare," 243).

34. Sillars, *Painting Shakespeare*, 175. Anthony Blunt linked Blake's colored print of Albion to another version of the Vitruvian man, a figure from Scamozzi's *Idea dell'Architectura Universale* of 1615 ("Blake's 'Glad Day,' " 65–68). Blunt later proposed an alternative source: two engravings in *De' Bronzi di Ercolano* (1767–1771) showing the front and back of a bronze faun (*The Art of William Blake*, 34, plates 6a, b). The potentially mixed heritage of idealized Vitruvian man and wild faun is itself suggestive for Blake's conceptualization of Albion and his potential connections to Puck.

35. See Ferber, "Blake's Idea of Brotherhood."

36. Mee, *Dangerous Enthusiasm*, 118.

37. Tinker, "Note," 11.

Chapter 5 • Rebellion in Fairyland: The Eve of St. Agnes

1. Spurgeon, *Keats's Shakespeare*, 52.

2. Johnson, *Lives*, 2:311.

3. Peacock, *Works*, 8:19–20.

4. Johnson, *Lives*, 3:337.

5. Coleridge and Wordsworth, *Lyrical Ballads*, 177, 171.

6. Ibid., 177.

7. Benjamin, *Illuminations*, 89.

8. Ibid., 87.

9. Coleridge, *Biographia Literaria*, 168–69.

10. Gamer, *Romanticism*, 123–26.

11. Keats, *Letters*, 1:245.

12. Ibid., 2:62.

13. Ibid.

14. William St. Clair estimates a total of 100,000 copies of the cantos of *Childe Harold* printed during the entire period, compared to 1,500 copies of all of Keats's printed editions, and only 500 of those copies sold at unremaindered prices (*Reading Nation*, 217). In the fourth canto of the poem, Byron explicitly acknowledges his debt to Radcliffe, and allusively borrows from her description, in *The Mysteries of Udolpho*, of Venice as a fairyland:

I lov'd her from my boyhood—she to me
Was as a fairy city of the heart,
Rising like water columns from the sea,
Of joy the sojourn, and of wealth the mart;
And Otway, Radcliffe, Schiller, Shakespeare's art
Had stamp'd her image in me . . . (canto 4, lines 154–59)

15. Keats, *Complete Poems*, lines 147–51. Further quotations of Keats's poetry refer to this edition by line number.

16. See Kucich, *Keats*, 56–62. Kucich notes the strong influence of Thomson's poem on the Romantics. "Wordsworth annotated his copy of *The Castle of Indolence* with a Spenserian poem about his own conflicting attractions to imaginative luxury and intellectual responsibility" (62).

17. Spenser, *The Faerie Queene*, II.xii.86.

18. Keats, *Letters*, 1:184–85.

19. Gittings, *John Keats*, 277.

20. *Mother Bunch's Closet*, 5.

21. MacCracken, "Source," 145–52.

22. According to Gittings, however, Keats had access to a collection of three modern French *romans* in the *Bibliothèque Universelle des Dames* (vol. 9, 1785), one of which, *Flores et Blanche-Fleur*, derived from the medieval romance that was Boccaccio's source for *Il Filocolo*. Gittings, however, argues that Keats made less use of *Flores* than of the other two (*John Keats*, 277–78). In any case, Boccaccio's handling strikes me as closer in spirit to Keats than the Count de Tressan's courtly romances.

23. Boccaccio, *Il Filocolo*, 337–38.

24. MacCracken, "Source," 150, 5n.

25. Gilbreath, "Etymology," 20–25.

26. Gallant, *Keats*, 93.

27.   See, while she speaks his arms encroaching slow,
         Have zoned her, heart to heart,—loud, loud the dark winds blow!

For on the midnight came a tempest fell;
More sooth, for that his quick rejoinder flows
Into her burning ear: and still the spell
Unbroken guards her in serene repose.
With her wild dream he mingled, as a rose
Marrieth its odour to a violet.
Still, still she dreams, louder the frost wind blows. . . .
                                     (Keats, *Complete Poems*, p. 457).

28. Keats, *Letters*, 2:162–63.

29. Gallant, *Keats*, 95.

30. Gittings, *John Keats*, 279.

31. Benjamin, *Illuminations*, 97.

32. Stillinger, *Hoodwinking of Madeline*, 67–93.

33. More recently, Fleming McClelland has turned the tables on Stillinger's reading, producing a Madeline cunningly luring Porphyro into marriage ("Does Madeline Sleep?" 31–34). Needless to say, this seems like an interpretative step backward, but it does demonstrate some of the limitations of reading the poem as a fully psychologized battle of the sexes.

34. For a similar argument, see Arseneau, "Madeline," 227–43.

35. Algernon Swinburne noted the connection between Imogen and Madeline in his essay on Keats in *The Encyclopeædia Britannica* (14:23).

36. See Harvey, "Merlin," 83–94.

37. In this respect, Madeline can be seen as part of the process, described by Terry Castle, in which the eighteenth century "invented" the uncanny in a fashion that anticipated Freud's mobilization of the term for psychoanalysis (*Female Thermometer*, esp. 3–20). Castle's own examples are generally drawn from representations of female sexuality and desire.

38. Gittings, *John Keats*, 279.

39. R. S. White argues that "intensity" is the primary quality Keats draws from *King Lear* (*Keats*, 176–84).

40. As Daniel Watkins argues, Keats disrupts "every detail in the feudal life even as he sets them down as its constituent features" (*Keats's Poetry*, 71).

41. Keats, *Letters*, 2:234.

42. Yeats, "The Message of the Folk-lorist" (1883), in *Uncollected Prose*, 1:288; cited in Gallant, *Keats*, 38.

43. The Kensington Gardens setting is common to Tickell's and Barrie's fairy world. Although no doubt an accident of literary history, it does suggest just how much the fairy world had become part of the furnishings of a fashionable London household.

44. The *Oxford English Dictionary* gives, as its first entry for this usage of fairy, a description from *The American Journal of Psychology* in 1895: "This coincides with what is known of the peculiar societies of inverts. Coffee-clatches, where the members dress themselves with aprons, etc., and knit, gossip and crotchet; balls, where men adopt the ladies' evening dress, are well known in Europe. 'The Fairies' of New York are said to be a similar secret organization." George Chauncey tracks the development of the term in New York from the early years of the twentieth century, where it was consistently associated with effeminacy (*Gay New York*, 47–63).

Chapter 6 • Before and after Literature: J. R. R. Tolkien

1. The literary fairy tale in Germany was itself influenced by the fairy way of writing in its English formation. Ludvig Tieck's influential fairy tales, among the first literary fairy tales written in German, were directly connected to his engagement with Shakespeare (Hubbs, "Romantic Fairy Tales").

2. Chesterton, *Autobiography*, 20.

3. Ibid., 147. St. John Hankin was a well-known dramatist of the period, who Chesterton associates with skepticism and cultural pessimism.

4. Chesterton, *Man Who Was Thursday*, 64.

5. This shared defiance enabled what would have once been unthinkable, as late as the

nineteenth century: the homogenization of very different versions of Christianity, such as Lewis's sometimes pugnacious and anti-Catholic Ulster Protestantism, Eliot's High Anglicanism, and Tolkien's Anglo-Catholicism, into a generalized Christian identity.

6. Carpenter, *Inklings*, 21.

7. Moretti, *Signs*, 209. The distinction between autonomous and heteronomous is taken from the work of Pierre Bourdieu (*Règles de l'art*). The *Oxford English Dictionary* lists the first appearance of the term "middlebrow" in *Punch* in 1925. Virginia Woolf is the first writer widely associated with using the term.

8. Lewis, *Voyage*, 215–16.

9. Carpenter, *Inklings*, 47.

10. Tolkien, *Fairy-stories*, 77–78.

11. "[T]he fact that there is always more in a work of art—which is the highest human result of the embodying imagination—than the producer himself perceived while he produced it, seems to us a strong reason for attributing to it a larger origin than the man alone—for saying at the last, that the inspiration of the Almighty shaped its ends" (MacDonald, *Imagination*, 25).

12. Tolkien, *Fairy-stories*, 78–79.

13. Ibid., 77–78.

14. Ibid., 52.

15. Nelson, *Fact or Fiction*, 67.

16. Ibid., 66.

17. Tolkien, *Fairy-stories*, 61.

18. Ibid., 61.

19. Ibid., 30.

20. Williams, *Our Moonlight Revels*, 133–35.

21. Ibid., 141.

22. Tolkien, *Fairy-stories*, 62.

23. Nelson, *Fact or Fiction*, 66.

24. Fried, *Absorption and Theatricality*. Fried does, however, discuss a number of visual representations of scenes of reading in his book, suggesting the applicability of the argument to the literary field.

25. Davies, "*A Midsummer Night's Dream*," 181; cited by Williams, *Our Moonlight Revels*, 179.

26. Tolkien, *Fairy-stories*, 32.

27. Ibid., 62.

28. See Tom Shippey's illuminating discussion of Tolkien's literary engagement with Shakespeare, which often revolved around his engagement with *Macbeth* (*Tolkien*, 192–96).

29. Shippey, "Creation from Philology," 286–316. This paper is much expanded in the argument of *The Road to Middle-Earth*, rev. ed. (Boston: Houghton Mifflin, 2003).

30. Lewis, *Other Worlds*, 115–16.

31. Ibid., 112.

32. Adam Gopnik has captured the novel's combination of English domesticity and adventure as Tolkien's "arranged marriage between the Elder Edda and *The Wind in the Wil-*

lows—big Icelandic romance and small-scale, cozy English children's book. The story told by *The Lord of the Rings* is essentially what would happen if Mole and Ratty got drafted into the *Nibelungenlied*" ("Dragon's Egg," 86–87).

33. Tolkien, *Fellowship*, 53.

34. Tolkien, *Two Towers*, 155.

35. Tolkien, *Fellowship*, 352.

36. Tolkien, *Two Towers*, 35.

37. Tolkien, *Fellowship*, 380.

38. Wilson, "Orcs," 326–32.

39. Burton Raffel systematically elaborates the nonliterary status of *The Lord of the Rings*, primarily with reference to the canon of the modern British and American novel ("Literature," 218–46).

40. W. H. Auden appears to have gently challenged Tolkien on this question, querying Tolkien about whether the representation of the Orcs as an irredeemably wicked race was not "heretical" (Tolkien, *Letters*, 355). Tolkien's response in the published letters appears to be incomplete.

41. Meltzer, "Fairy Tree," 493–520.

42. Davis, *Led Zeppelin*, 61.

43. Tolkien, *Fairy-stories*, 44–45.

44. Ibid., 46.

Quotations from the three Shakespeare plays discussed at length in this book—*A Midsummer Night's Dream*, *The Winter's Tale*, and *The Tempest*—are taken from the individual editions of those plays listed below. Quotations from Shakespeare's other plays are from *The Riverside Shakespeare* as listed below.

Abrams, M. H. *The Mirror and the Lamp: Romantic Theory and the Critical Tradition*. New York: W. W. Norton, 1958.

Adelman, Janet. *Suffocating Mothers: Fantasies of Maternal Origins in Shakespeare's Plays, Hamlet to The Tempest*. New York: Routledge, 1992.

Anderson, Benedict. *Imagined Communities: Reflections on the Origin and Spread of Nationalism*. Rev. ed. London: Verso, 1991.

Anderson, Perry. *Lineages of the Absolutist State*. London: NLB, 1974.

Arseneau, Mary. "Madeline, Mermaids, and Medusas in 'The Eve of St. Agnes.'" *Papers on Language and Literature* 33 (1997): 227–43.

Aubrey, John. *Three Prose Works*. Edited by John Buchanan-Brown. Fontwell, Sussex: Centaur, 1972.

Auerbach, Erich. "*La Cour et la Ville*." In *Scenes from the Drama of European Literature*. Minneapolis: University of Minnesota Press, 1984.

———. *Literary Language and Its Public in Late Latin Antiquity and in the Middle Ages*. Translated by Ralph Manheim. Princeton: Princeton University Press, 1993.

———. *Mimesis: The Representation of Reality in Western Literature*. Translated by Willard Trask. Princeton: Princeton University Press, 1968.

Bacon, Francis. *The Works of Francis Bacon*. Edited by James Spedding, Robert Leslie Ellis, and Douglas Denon Heath. 15 vols. Boston, 1860–1864.

Barber, C. L. *Shakespeare's Festive Comedy: A Study of Dramatic Form and Its Relation to Social Custom*. Princeton: Princeton University Press, 1959.

Bate, Jonathan. *Shakespeare and Ovid*. Oxford: Clarendon Press, 1993.

Beaumont, Francis, and John Fletcher. *The Dramatic Works in the Beaumont and Fletcher Canon*. Vol. 9. Edited by Fredson Bowers. Cambridge: Cambridge University Press, 1994.

Benjamin, Walter. *Illuminations*. Edited by Hannah Arendt. Translated by Harry Zohn. New York: Schocken, 1968.

Bettelheim, Bruno. *The Uses of Enchantment: The Meaning and Importance of Fairy Tales.* New York: Knopf, 1976.

Bevington, David. "*The Tempest* and the Jacobean Court Masque." In Bevington and Holbrook, eds.

Bevington, David, and Peter Holbrook, eds. *The Politics of the Stuart Court Masque.* Cambridge: Cambridge University Press, 1998.

Bloch, Marc. *Feudal Society.* Translated by L. A. Manyon. 2 vols. Chicago: University of Chicago Press, 1970.

Blunt, Anthony. *The Art of William Blake.* New York: Columbia University Press, 1959.

———."Blake's 'Glad Day.' " *Journal of the Warburg Institute* 2 (1938): 65–68.

Boccaccio, Giovanni. *Il Filocolo.* Translated by Donald Cheney and Thomas G. Bergin. New York: Garland, 1985.

Bond, Donald F., ed. *The Spectator.* 5 vols. Oxford: Clarendon Press, 1965.

Bottigheimer, Ruth B. *Fairy Tales: A New History.* Albany: State University of New York Press, 2009.

Bourdieu, Pierre. *Les règles de l'art: genèse et structure du champ littéraire.* Paris: Seuil, 1992.

Bown, Nicola. *Fairies in Nineteenth-Century Art and Literature.* Cambridge: Cambridge University Press, 2001.

Briggs, K. M. *The Anatomy of Puck: An Examination of Fairy Beliefs among Shakespeare's Contemporaries and Successors.* London: Routledge and Kegan Paul, 1959.

Bristol, Michael D. *Big-Time Shakespeare.* London: Routledge, 1996.

Broadus, Edmund K. "Addison's Influence on the Development of Interest in Folk-Poetry in the Eighteenth Century." *Modern Philology* 8 (1910): 123–34.

Bromley, Robert Anthony. *A Philosophical and Critical History of the Fine Arts.* 2 vols. London, 1793–1795.

Buccola, Regina. *Fairies, Fractious Women, and the Old Faith: Fairy Lore in Early Modern British Drama and Culture.* Selinsgrove, PA: Susquehanna University Press, 2006.

Burke, Peter. "Afterward." In *Literature and Popular Culture in Early Modern England*, edited by Matthew Dimmock and Andrew Hadfield. Farnham, Surrey: Ashgate, 2009.

———. *Popular Culture in Early Modern Europe.* London: Temple Smith, 1978.

Carpenter, Humphrey. *The Inklings: C. S. Lewis, J. R. R. Tolkien, Charles Williams and Their Friends.* London: HarperCollins, 2006.

Carter, Angela. *The Bloody Chamber.* New York: Harper & Row, 1979.

Castle, Terry. *The Female Thermometer: Eighteenth-Century Culture and the Invention of the Uncanny.* New York: Oxford University Press, 1995.

Chaucer, Geoffrey. *The Complete Poetry and Prose of Geoffrey Chaucer.* Edited by John H. Fisher. New York: Holt, Rinehart and Winston, 1977.

Chauncey, George. *Gay New York: Gender, Urban Culture, and the Makings of the Gay Male World, 1890–1940.* New York: Basic Books, 1994.

Chesterton, G. K. *Autobiography.* London: Hutchinson, n.d.

———. *The Man Who Was Thursday: A Nightmare.* New York: Modern Library, 2001.

Chrétien de Troyes. *Arthurian Romances.* Translated by William W. Kibler. London: Penguin, 1991.

Clark, Stuart. "Protestant Demonology: Sin, Superstition, and Society." In *Early Modern*

European Witchcraft: Centres and Peripheries, edited by Bengt Ankarloo and Gustav Henningsen. Oxford: Clarendon Press, 1990.

Clarke, Charles, and Mary Cowden Clarke. *Recollections of Writers*. Fontwell, Sussex: Centaur, 1969.

Cocking, J. M. *Imagination: A Study in the History of Ideas*. London: Routledge, 1991.

Cohen, Walter. "Prerevolutionary Drama." In *The Politics of Tragicomedy: Shakespeare and After*, edited by Gordon McMullan and Jonathan Hope. New York: Routledge, 1992.

——. "Shakespeare as World Literature." Paper presented at the annual meeting of the Shakespeare Association of America, Dallas, Texas, 2008.

Coleridge, Samuel Taylor. *Biographia Literaria*. London: Dent, 1975.

Coleridge, Samuel Taylor, and William Wordsworth. *Lyrical Ballads, 1798 and 1800*. Edited by Michael Gamer and Dahlia Porter. Peterborough, Ontario: Broadview Press, 2008.

Collier, Jeremy. *A Short View of the Immorality and Profaneness of the English Stage*. New York: Garland, 1972.

Cooper, Helen. *The English Romance in Time: Transforming Motifs from Geoffrey of Monmouth to the Death of Shakespeare*. Oxford: Oxford University Press, 2004.

Craig, Hugh. "Jonson, the Antimasque and the 'Rules of Flattery.'" In Bevington and Holbrook, eds.

Cressy, David. *Bonfires and Bells: National Memory and the Protestant Calendar in Elizabethan and Stuart England*. London: Weidenfeld and Nicolson, 1989.

Dabydeen, David. "Hogarth and the Canecutter." In Hulme and Sherman, eds.

[Dalton, John]. *Comus: A Masque*. London, 1760.

Daston, Lorraine. "Marvelous Facts and Miraculous Evidence in Early Modern Europe." *Critical Inquiry* 18 (1991): 93–124.

Davies, Robertson. "*A Midsummer Night's Dream*." In *The Stratford Scene, 1958–1968*, edited by Peter Raby. Toronto: Clarke, Irwin, 1968.

Davis, Erik. *Led Zeppelin IV*. New York: Continuum, 2007.

Davis, Natalie Zemon. *Society and Culture in Early Modern France*. London: Duckworth, 1975.

DeJean, Joan. "Transnationalism and the Origins of the (French?) Novel." In *The Literary Channel: The Inter-National Invention of the Novel*, edited by Margaret Cohen and Carolyn Dever. Princeton: Princeton University Press, 2002.

Deutsch, Helen. *Resemblance and Disgrace: Alexander Pope and the Deformation of Culture*. Cambridge, MA: Harvard University Press, 1996.

Dixon, Yvonne Romney. "*Designs from Fancy*": *George Romney's Shakespearean Drawings*. Washington, DC: Folger Shakespeare Library, 1998.

Dobson, Michael. *The Making of the National Poet: Shakespeare, Adaptation, and Authorship, 1660–1769*. Oxford: Clarendon Press, 1992.

Dragstra, Henk. "'Before Women Were Readers': How John Aubrey Wrote Female Oral History." In Lamb and Bamford, eds.

Dryden, John. *The Works of John Dryden*. Edited by Edward Niles Hooker, H. T. Swedenberg, and Vinton A. Dearing. 20 vols. Berkeley: University of California Press, 1956–2000.

Duffy, Eamon. *The Stripping of the Altars: Traditional Religion in England, c. 1400–c. 1580*, 2nd ed. New Haven: Yale University Press, 2005.

Duffy, Maureen. *The Erotic World of Faery*. London: Hodder and Stoughton, 1972.

During, Simon. *Modern Enchantments: The Cultural Power of Secular Magic*. Cambridge, MA: Harvard University Press, 2002.

Empson, William. *Some Versions of Pastoral*. 1935. Reprint. New York: New Directions, 1974.

Engell, James. *The Creative Imagination: Enlightenment to Romanticism*. Cambridge, MA: Harvard University Press, 1981.

Ferber, Michael. "Blake's Idea of Brotherhood," *PMLA* 93 (1978): 438–47.

Foucault, Michel. *The History of Sexuality: An Introduction*. Translated by Robert Hurley. Vol. 1. New York: Vintage, 1990.

Fox, Adam. *Oral and Literate Culture in England, 1500–1700*. Oxford: Oxford University Press, 2000.

Fox, Adam, and Daniel Woolf, eds. *The Spoken Word: Oral Culture in Britain, 1500–1850*. Manchester: Manchester University Press, 2002.

Frank, Marcie. "Fairy Time: From Shakespeare to Scott." In *Shakespeare and the Eighteenth Century*, edited by Peter Sabor and Paul Yachnin. Aldershot, Hampshire: Ashgate, 2008.

———. *Gender, Theatre, and the Origins of Criticism from Dryden to Manley*. Cambridge: Cambridge University Press, 2003.

Fried, Michael. *Absorption and Theatricality: Painting and Beholder in the Age of Diderot*. Berkeley: University of California Press, 1980.

Fumaroli, Marc. "Les enchantements de l'éloquence: 'Les Fées' de Charles Perrault ou De la littérature." In *Le statut de la littérature: mélanges offerts à Paul Bénichou*, edited by Marc Fumaroli. Geneva: Droz, 1982.

Gallant, Christine. *Keats and Romantic Celticism*. Basingstoke, Hampshire: Palgrave Macmillan, 2005.

Gamer, Michael. *Romanticism and the Gothic: Genre, Reception, and Canon Formation*. Cambridge: Cambridge University Press, 2000.

Gellner, Ernest. *Nations and Nationalism*. Ithaca: Cornell University Press, 1983.

Gilbreath, Marcia. "The Etymology of Porphyro's Name in Keats's 'Eve of St. Agnes.'" *Keats-Shelley Journal* 37 (1988): 20–25.

Gilman, Ernest R. "'All Eyes': Prospero's Inverted Masque." *Renaissance Quarterly* 33 (1980): 214–30.

Gittings, Robert. *John Keats*. London: Heinemann, 1968.

Goldberg, Jonathan. "Fatherly Authority: The Politics of Stuart Family Images." In *Rewriting the Renaissance*, edited by Margaret W. Ferguson, Maureen Quilligan, and Nancy Vickers. Chicago: University of Chicago Press, 1986.

———. "Under the Covers with Caliban." In *Margins of the Text*, edited by D. C. Greetham. Ann Arbor: University of Michigan Press, 1997.

Gopnick, Adam. "The Dragon's Egg: High Fantasy for Young Adults." *The New Yorker*, 5 December 2011, 86–89.

Greenblatt, Stephen. "Resonance and Wonder." *Bulletin of the American Academy of Arts and Sciences* 43 (1990): 11–34.

Greenfield, Liah. *Nationalism: Five Roads to Modernity*. Cambridge, MA: Harvard University Press, 1992.

Guillory, John. *Cultural Capital: The Problem of Literary Canon Formation.* Chicago: University of Chicago Press, 1993.

———. "Genesis of the Media Concept." *Critical Inquiry* 36 (2010): 321–62.

———. *Poetic Authority: Spenser, Milton, and Literary History.* New York: Columbia University Press, 1983.

Gumbrecht, Hans Ulrich. *Making Sense in Life and Literature.* Translated by Glen Burns and Wlad Godzich. Minneapolis: University of Minnesota Press, 1992.

Gurvich, Aron. *Medieval Popular Culture: Problems of Belief and Perception.* Translated by Janos M. Bak and Paul A. Hollingsworth. Cambridge: Cambridge University Press, 1988.

Haase, Donald, ed. *Fairy Tales and Feminism: New Approaches.* Detroit: Wayne State University Press, 2004.

Hamilton, Edward. *A Catalogue Raisonné of the Engraved Works of Sir Joshua Reynolds, P.R.A.* London, 1884.

Hardy, Thomas. *Tess of the D'Urbervilles.* London: Random House, 2008.

Harvey, Karen J. "The Trouble about Merlin: The Theme of Enchantment in 'The Eve of St. Agnes.'" *Keats-Shelley Journal* 34 (1985): 83–94.

Hazlitt, William. *The Selected Writings of William Hazlitt.* Edited by Duncan Wu. 9 vols. London: Pickering & Chatto, 1998.

Helgerson, Richard. *Forms of Nationhood: The Elizabethan Writing of England.* Chicago: University of Chicago Press, 1992.

Herder, Johann Gottfried. *Werke in zwei Bänden.* 2 vols. Munich: Carl Hanser, 1953.

Honigman, E. A. J. *Shakespeare's Impact on His Contemporaries.* London: Macmillan, 1982.

Hubbs, V. C. "Tieck's Romantic Fairy Tales and Shakespeare." *Studies in Romanticism* 8 (1969): 229–34.

Hudson, Nicholas. "'Oral Tradition': The Evolution of an Eighteenth-Century Concept." In *Tradition in Transition: Women Writers, Marginal Texts, and the Eighteenth-Century Canon,* edited by Alvaro Ribeiro, SJ, and James G. Basker. Oxford: Clarendon Press, 1996.

Hulme, Peter, and William H. Sherman, eds. *The Tempest and Its Travels.* Philadelphia: University of Pennsylvania Press, 2000.

Hunter, Michael, ed. *The Occult Laboratory: Magic, Science and Second Sight in Late Seventeenth-Century Scotland.* Woodbridge, Suffolk: Boydell, 2001.

Jacob, Hildebrand. *Works of Hildebrand Jacob, Esq.* London, 1735.

Johnson, Samuel. *Lives of the English Poets.* Edited by George Birkbeck Hill. 3 vols. 1905. Reprint. New York: Octagon Books, 1967.

Jonson, Ben. *Ben Jonson.* Edited by C. H. Herford and Evelyn Simpson. 11 vols. Oxford: Clarendon Press, 1925–1952.

———. *Ben Jonson: The Complete Masques.* Edited by Stephen Orgel. New Haven: Yale University Press, 1969.

Keats, John. *Complete Poems.* Edited by Jack Stillinger. Cambridge, MA: Harvard University Press, 1978.

———. *The Letters of John Keats.* Edited by Hyder Edward Rollins. 2 vols. Cambridge, MA: Harvard University Press, 1958.

Kenney, E. J. "Introduction." *The Golden Ass,* by Apuleius. London: Penguin, 1998.

Kind, John Louis. *Edward Young in Germany.* 1906. Reprint, New York: AMS Press, 1966.

Klibansky, Raymond, Erwin Panofsky, and Fritz Saxl. *Saturn and Melancholy: Studies in the History of Natural Philosophy, Religion, and Art.* New York: Basic, 1964.

Knight, G. Wilson. *The Crown of Life: Essays in Interpretation of Shakespeare's Final Plays.* London: Methuen, 1948.

Knowles, John. *The Life and Writings of Henry Fuseli.* 3 vols. London, 1831.

Kott, Jan. *The Bottom Translation: Marlowe and Shakespeare and the Carnival Tradition.* Translated by Daniela Miedzyrzecka and Lillian Vallee. Evanston, IL: Northwestern University Press, 1987.

Kramnick, Jonathan. *Making the English Canon: Print-Capitalism and the Cultural Past, 1700–1770.* Cambridge: Cambridge University Press, 1998.

Kucich, Greg. *Keats, Shelley, and Romantic Spenserianism.* University Park, PA: Pennsylvania State University Press, 1991.

Kumar, Krishan. *The Making of English National Identity.* Cambridge: Cambridge University Press, 2003.

Lamb, Mary Ellen. *The Popular Culture of Shakespeare, Spenser, and Jonson.* Abingdon, Oxfordshire: Routledge, 2006.

———. "Virtual Audiences and Virtual Authors: *The Winter's Tale, The Tempest,* and Old Wives' Tales." In *Staging Early Modern Romance: Prose Fiction, Dramatic Romance, and Shakespeare,* edited by Mary Ellen Lamb and Valerie Wayne. New York: Routledge, 2009.

Lamb, Mary Ellen, and Karen Bamford, eds. *Oral Traditions and Gender in Early Modern Literary Texts.* Aldershot, Hampshire: Ashgate, 2008.

Laroque, François. *Shakespeare's Festive World: Elizabethan Seasonal Entertainment and the Professional Stage.* Cambridge: Cambridge University Press, 1991.

Le Goff, Jacques. "Culture cléricale et traditions folkloriques dans la civilisation mérovingienne." *Annales ESC* 22 (1967): 780–91.

Levin, Harry. "Two Magian Comedies: *The Tempest* and *The Alchemist.*" In *Shakespeare and the Revolution of the Times.* New York: Oxford University Press, 1976.

Levine, Joseph. *Between the Ancients and the Moderns: Baroque Culture in Restoration England.* New Haven: Yale University Press, 1999.

Lewis, C. S. *Of This and Other Worlds.* Edited by Walter Hooper. London: Collins, 1982.

———. *The Voyage of the "Dawn Treader."* New York: Collier, 1970.

Locke, John. *The Educational Writings of John Locke.* Edited by James L. Axtell. Cambridge: Cambridge University Press, 1968.

Lonsdale, Roger, ed. *The Poems of Thomas Gray, William Collins, Oliver Goldsmith.* Harlow, Essex: Longmans, 1969.

Luhmann, Niklas. *Love as Passion: The Codification of Intimacy.* Translated by Jeremy Gaines and Doris L. Jones. Stanford: Stanford University Press, 1998.

Lyly, John. *Endymion.* Edited by David Bevington. Manchester: Manchester University Press, 1996.

MacCracken, Henry Noble. "The Source of Keats's 'Eve of St. Agnes.'" *Modern Philology* 5 (1907): 145–52.

MacCulloch, J. A. "The Mingling of Fairy and Witch Beliefs in Sixteenth and Seventeenth-Century Scotland." *Folklore* 32 (1921): 227–44.

MacDonald, George. *The Imagination and Other Essays*. Boston: Lothrop, [1883].

Marcus, Leah S. *The Politics of Mirth: Jonson, Herrick, Milton, Marvell and the Defense of the Old Holiday Pastimes*. Chicago: University of Chicago Press, 1986.

Marvell, Andrew. *Andrew Marvell*. Edited by Frank Kermode and Keith Walker. Oxford: Oxford University Press, 1990.

Maus, Katharine Eisaman. "Arcadia Lost: Politics and Revision in the Restoration *Tempest*." *Renaissance Drama* n.s. 13 (1982): 189–200. Reprint. *Critical Essays on John Dryden*, edited by James A. Winn. New York: G. K. Hall, 1997.

Mauss, Marcel. *The Gift: The Form and Reason for Exchange in Archaic Societies*. Translated by W. D. Halls. New York: Routledge, 1990.

McClelland, Fleming. "Does Madeline Sleep, or Does She Wake? The Hoodwinking of Porphyro." *The Keats-Shelley Review* 10 (1996): 31–34.

McEachern, Claire. *The Poetics of English Nationhood, 1590–1612*. Cambridge: Cambridge University Press, 1996.

McKeon, Michael. "Historicizing Patriarchy: The Emergence of Gender Difference in England, 1660–1760." *Eighteenth-Century Studies* 28 (1995): 295–322.

———. "Mediation as Primal Word: The Arts, the Sciences, and the Origins of the Aesthetic." In *This Is Enlightenment*, edited by Clifford Siskin and William Warner. Chicago: University of Chicago Press, 2010.

———. *The Secret History of Domesticity: Public, Private, and the Division of Knowledge* Baltimore: Johns Hopkins University Press, 2005.

———. "Tacit Knowledge: Tradition and Its Aftermath." In *Questions of Tradition*, edited by Mark Salber Phillips and Gordon Schochet. Toronto: University of Toronto Press, 2004.

McLane, Maureen N. *Balladeering, Minstrelsy, and the Making of British Romantic Poetry*. Cambridge: Cambridge University Press, 2008.

Mee, Jon. *Dangerous Enthusiasm: William Blake and the Culture of Radicalism in the 1790s*. Oxford: Clarendon Press, 1992.

Meisel, Martin. *Realizations: Narrative, Pictorial, and Theatrical Arts in Nineteenth-Century England*. Princeton: Princeton University Press, 1983.

Meltzer, Françoise. "Reviving the Fairy Tree: Tales of European Sanctity." *Critical Inquiry* 35 (2009): 493–520.

Merchant, W. Moelwyn. "Blake's Shakespeare." In *The Visionary Hand: Essays for the Study of William Blake's Art and Aesthetics*, edited by Robert N. Essick. Los Angeles: Hennessey and Ingalls, 1973.

Milton, John. *Complete Poems and Major Prose*. Edited by Merritt Y. Hughes. Indianapolis: Bobbs-Merrill, 1957.

Miner, Earl. "The Wild Man through the Looking Glass." In *The Wild Man Within: An Image in Western Thought from the Renaissance to Romanticism*, edited by Edward Dudley and Maximillian E. Novak. Pittsburgh: University of Pittsburgh Press, 1972.

Molière. *Théâtre complet de Molière*. Edited by Robert Jouanny. 2 vols. Paris: Garnier, 1960.

Montrose, Louis. *The Purpose of Playing: Shakespeare and the Cultural Politics of the Elizabethan Theatre*. Chicago: University of Chicago Press, 1996.

———. " 'Shaping Fantasies': Figurations of Gender and Power in Elizabethan Culture." *Representations* 2 (Spring 1983): 61–94.

Moretti, Franco. *Signs Taken for Wonders*. London: Verso, 1983.

Mother Bunch's Closet Newly Broke Open. Newcastle, n.d.

Murphy, Patrick M., ed. *The Tempest: Critical Essays*. New York: Routledge, 2001.

Myrone, Martin. "Fuseli and Gothic Spectacle." *Huntington Library Quarterly* 70 (2007): 289–310.

Nashe, Thomas. *The Works of Thomas Nashe*. Edited by Ronald B. McKerrow. With corrections by F. P. Wilson. 5 vols. Oxford: Basil Blackwell, 1958.

Nelson, William. *Fact or Fiction: The Dilemma of the Renaissance Storyteller*. Cambridge, MA: Harvard University Press, 1973.

Norbrook, David. "'What Cares These Roarers for the Name of King?': Language and Utopia in *The Tempest*." In *The Politics of Tragicomedy: Shakespeare and After*, edited by Gordon McMullan and Jonathan Hope. New York: Routledge, 1992.

Orgel, Stephen. *Imagining Shakespeare: A History of Texts and Visions*. Basingstoke, Hampshire: Palgrave Macmillan, 2003.

———. "Introduction." *The Tempest*, by William Shakespeare. Oxford: Oxford University Press, 1987.

———. "Introduction." *The Winter's Tale*, by William Shakespeare. Oxford: Oxford University Press, 1996.

———. "Marginal Jonson." In Bevington and Holbrook, eds.

Pask, Kevin. "Engrossing Imagination: *A Midsummer Night's Dream*." *The Shakespearean International Yearbook* 3 (2003): 172–92.

———. "Prospero's Counter-Pastoral," *Criticism* 44 (2002): 389–404.

Paulson, Ronald. *Book and Painting: Shakespeare, Milton and the Bible: Literary Texts and the Emergence of English Painting*. Knoxville: University of Tennessee Press, 1982.

Peacock, Thomas Love. *The Works of Thomas Love Peacock*. Edited by H. F. B. Brett-Smith and C. E. Jones. 10 vols. 1924. Reprint. New York: AMS, 1967.

Pepys, Samuel. *The Diary of Samuel Pepys*. Edited by Robert Latham and William Matthews. 11 vols. Berkeley: University of California Press, 1974.

Perrault, Charles. *Contes: suivis du Miroir ou la Métamorphose d'Orante, de La peinture, Poème et du Labyrinthe de Versailles*. Edited by Jean-Pierre Collinet. Paris: Gallimard, 1981.

Pickering, Samuel F., Jr. *John Locke and Children's Books in Eighteenth-Century England*. Knoxville: University of Tennessee Press, 1981.

Pocock, J. G. A. *The Ancient Constitution and the Feudal Law: A Study of English Historical Thought in the Seventeenth Century*. 2nd ed. Cambridge: Cambridge University Press, 1987.

Pope, Alexander. *The Rape of the Lock and Other Poems*. Edited by Geoffrey Tillotson. Vol. 2 of *The Twickenham Edition of the Poems of Alexander Pope*. General editor, John Butt. 2nd ed. London: Methuen; New Haven: Yale University Press, 1954.

Purkiss, Diane. *At the Bottom of the Garden: A Dark History of Fairies, Hobgoblins, and Other Troublesome Things*. New York: New York University Press, 2003.

———. *The Witch in History: Early Modern and Twentieth-Century Representations*. London: Routledge, 1996.

Radcliffe, Ann. *The Romance of the Forest*. Oxford: Oxford University Press, 1986.

Raffel, Burton. "*The Lord of the Rings* as Literature." In *Tolkien and the Critics: Essays on J.R.R. Tolkien's "The Lord of the Rings,"* edited by Neil D. Isaacs and Rose A. Zimbardo. Notre Dame: University of Notre Dame Press, 1968.

Roach, Joseph. "The Enchanted Island: Vicarious Tourism in Restoration Adaptations of *The Tempest*." In Hulme and Sherman, eds.

Rogers, Pat. *Essays on Pope*. Cambridge: Cambridge University Press, 1993.

Romney, John. *Memoirs of the Life and Works of George Romney*. London, 1830.

Rowse, A. L. *Simon Forman: Sex and Society in Shakespeare's Age*. London: Weidenfeld and Nicolson, 1974.

Scholar, Richard. "La force de l'imagination de Montaigne: Camus, Malebranche, Pascal." *Littératures Classiques* 45 (2002): 127–38.

Scot, Reginald. *The Discoverie of Witchcraft*. Edited by Brinsley Nicholson. Totowa, NJ: Rowman and Littlefield, 1973.

Scott, Walter. *Minstrelsy of the Scottish Border*. Edited by T. F. Henderson. 4 vols. Edinburgh: Blackwood, 1902.

Sermain, Jean-Paul. *Le conte de fées: du classicisme aux Lumières*. Paris: Desjonquères, 2005.

Sévigné, Marie de Rabutin-Chantal, marquise de. *Correspondance*. Edited by Roger Duchêne. Paris: Gallimard, 1972.

Shaftesbury, Anthony Ashley Cooper, Earl of. *Characteristics of Men, Manners, Opinions, Times*. Edited by Lawrence E. Klein. Cambridge: Cambridge University Press, 1999.

Shakespeare, William. *A Midsummer Night's Dream*. Edited by Peter Holland. Oxford: Oxford University Press, 1998.

———. *The Riverside Shakespeare*. General editor, G. Blakemore Evans. Boston: Houghton Mifflin, 1974.

———. *The Tempest*. Edited by Stephen Orgel. Oxford: Oxford University Press, 1987.

———. *The Winter's Tale*. Edited by Stephen Orgel. Oxford: Oxford University Press, 1996.

Shippey, Tom. "Creation from Philology in *The Lord of the Rings*." In *J. R. R. Tolkien: Scholar and Storyteller*. Edited by Mary Saluy and Robert T. Farrell. Ithaca: Cornell University Press, 1979.

———. *J. R. R. Tolkien: Author of the Century*. London: HarperCollins, 2001.

———. *The Road to Middle-Earth*. Rev. ed. Boston: Houghton Mifflin, 2003.

Sillars, Stuart. *Painting Shakespeare: The Artist as Critic, 1720–1820*. Cambridge: Cambridge University Press, 2006.

Smith, Hallett. *Shakespeare's Romances: A Study of Some Ways of the Imagination*. San Marino, CA: The Huntington Library, 1972.

Smith, Logan Pearsall. *Four Words: Romantic, Originality, Creative, Genius*. Oxford: Clarendon Press, 1924.

Spacks, Patricia Meyer. " 'Ev'ry Woman is at Heart a Rake.' " *Eighteenth-Century Studies* 8 (1974): 27–46.

———. *The Insistence of Horror: Aspects of the Supernatural in Eighteenth-Century Poetry*. Cambridge, MA: Harvard University Press, 1962.

Spenser, Edmund. *The Faerie Queene*. Edited by A. C. Hamilton. Text edited by Hiroshi Yamashita and Toshiyuki Suzuki. Harlow, Essex: Longman, 2001.

———. *Poetical Works*. Edited by J. C. Smith and E. de Selincourt. Oxford: Oxford University Press, 1912.

Spingarn, J. E., ed. *Critical Essays of the Seventeenth Century*. 3 vols. London: Oxford University Press, 1908.

Spurgeon, Caroline F. E. *Keats's Shakespeare: A Descriptive Study*. Oxford: Clarendon Press, 1966.

St. Clair, William. *The Reading Nation in the Romantic Period*. Cambridge: Cambridge University Press, 2004.

Stephens, Frederic George. *English Children as Painted by Sir Joshua Reynolds*. 2nd ed. London, 1884.

Stewart, Susan. *Crimes of Writing: Problems in the Containment of Representation*. New York: Oxford University Press, 1991.

Stillinger, Jack. *The Hoodwinking of Madeline and Other Essays on Keats's Poems*. Urbana: University of Illinois Press, 1971.

Swinburne, Algernon. "John Keats." Vol. 14, *The Encyclopædia Britannica*. 9th ed. Edinburgh, 1875–1889.

Thaler, Alwin. "Milton in the Theater." *Studies in Philology* 17 (1920): 269–308.

Thomas, Keith. *Religion and the Decline of Magic*. New York: Scribner's, 1971.

Tinker, Chauncey Brewster. "A Note upon the Paintings." In *L'Allegro and Il Penseroso* [by John Milton], *with the Paintings by William Blake*. New York: Heritage, 1954.

Todorov, Tzvetan. *The Fantastic: A Structural Approach to a Literary Genre*. Translated by Richard Howard. Ithaca: Cornell University Press, 1975.

Tolkien, J. R. R. *The Fellowship of the Ring*. 2nd ed. Boston: Houghton Mifflin, n.d.

———. *The Letters of J. R. R. Tolkien*. Edited by Humphrey Carpenter. London: George Allen & Unwin, 1981.

———. *Tolkien on Fairy-stories*. Edited by Verlyn Flieger and Douglas A. Anderson. London: HarperCollins, 2008.

———. *The Two Towers*. 2nd ed. Boston: Houghton Mifflin, n.d.

Traub, Valerie. *Desire and Anxiety: Circulations of Sexuality in Shakespearean Drama*. London: Routledge, 1992.

Trilling, Lionel. "The Fate of Pleasure." In *Beyond Culture: Essays on Literature and Learning*. New York: Viking, 1965.

Tuveson, Ernest Lee. *The Imagination as a Means of Grace: Locke and the Aesthetics of Romanticism*. 1960. Reprint. New York: Gordian Press, 1974.

Wall, Wendy. *Staging Domesticity: Household Work and English Identity in Early Modern Drama*. Cambridge: Cambridge University Press, 2002.

Walpole, Horace. *The Yale Edition of Horace Walpole's Correspondence*. General editor, W. S. Lewis. 48 vols. New Haven: Yale University Press, 1937–1983.

Warner, Marina. *Phantasmagoria: Spirit Visions, Metaphors, and Media into the Twenty-first Century*. Oxford: Oxford University Press, 2006.

Warner, William. *A Continuance of Albion's England*. London, 1606.

Wasserman, Earl R. "Collins' 'Ode on the Poetical Character,'" *ELH* 34 (1967): 92–115.

Watkins, Daniel. *Keats's Poetry and the Politics of the Imagination*. Rutherford, NJ: Fairleigh Dickinson University Press, 1989.

Wheeler, Richard. "Fantasy and History in *The Tempest*." In Murphy, ed.

White, R. S. *Keats as a Reader of Shakespeare*. Norman: University of Oklahoma Press, 1987.

Wickham, Glynne. "Masque and Anti-Masque in *The Tempest*," *Essays and Studies*, n.s. 28 (1975): 1–14.

Williams, Gary Jay. *Our Moonlight Revels: "A Midsummer Night's Dream" in the Theatre.* Iowa City: University of Iowa Press, 1997.

Wilson, Edmund. "Oo, Those Awful Orcs!" In *The Bit between My Teeth: A Literary Chronicle of 1950–1965.* New York: Farrar, Straus and Giroux, 1965.

Woodcock, Matthew. *Fairy in The Faerie Queene: Renaissance Elf-Fashioning and Elizabethan Myth-Making.* Aldershot, Hampshire: Ashgate, 2004.

Woodhouse, A. S. P. "Collins and the Creative Imagination: A Study in the Critical Background of His Odes (1746)." In *Studies in English by Members of University College Toronto*, edited by Malcolm W. Wallace. Toronto: University of Toronto Press, 1931.

———. "The Poetry of Collins Reconsidered." In *From Sensibility to Romanticism: Essays Presented to Frederick A. Pottle*, edited by Frederick W. Hilles and Harold Bloom. New York: Oxford University Press, 1965.

Wooton, David. "Scott, Reginald (d. 1599)." In *Oxford Dictionary of National Biography*. Oxford: Oxford University Press, 2004. Online.

Yeats, William Butler. *Uncollected Prose.* Collected and edited by John P. Frayne. New York: Columbia University Press, 1970.

Ziolkowski, Jan M. *Fairy Tales from before Fairy Tales: The Medieval Latin Past of Wonderful Lies.* Ann Arbor: University of Michigan Press, 2007.